Joy in Living is a wonderful insight into the work of the Holy Spirit in our lives, a real encouragement about the overcoming power of God in times of struggle. I wish all young couples looking ahead toward a life of ministry would be required to read this book. What shoulders to stand on! I found it worth reading and a great blessing.

—**Dr. Jay Kesler**
President Emeritus of Taylor University
Former President Youth for Christ U.S.
Upland, Indiana

Don't miss Joy Boerop's amazing account of God's incredible providence and provision. What a story of faith, family sacrifice, and lasting fruit. The Lord has used Joy and her husband, Bill, in helping thousands of churches all over the world (including ours!) to have effective world missions ministries!

—**Dr. Frank Barker**
Pastor Emeritus of Briarwood Presbyterian Church
Barbara Barker, Director of Briarwood Ballet and Ballet Exaltation
Birmingham, Alabama

Joy in Living is pure joy and a blessing to read. Joy Boerop has lived a very full and varied life. A life filled with blessings but also one filled with many challenges. Throughout the book it is evident that Joy has always been dependent on and trusted in her Lord.

As I read, it became very clear that the joy of the Lord has been her strength. What an encouragement this book has been to me and will be to you, the reader. It has truly enJOYed my heart.

—**Gigi Graham**
International Speaker, Bible Teacher
Black Mountain, North Carolina

As I traced the steps of her life's journey along with Joy Boerop in what might aptly be called a present day *Pilgrim's Progress*, I was reminded, as I followed her story that her vertical perspective kept her from horizontal panic. *Joy in Living* is a poignant, often wistful and compelling diary of dedication to a preeminent purpose, determination to finish the course set before her on a pathway of service unto the Lord Jesus Christ, and courage during crises.

The journey is told with candor, sensitivity, and unusual intimacy—a page-by-page reminder of Jeremiah 29:11 (NIV): "For I know the plans I have for you," declares the Lord, "plans to prosper you and not to harm you, plans to give you hope and a future."

Thank you, Joy, for sharing your joy in serving the King of Kings and Lord of Lords.

—**Dr. Ed Lyman**
President, The Cause
Nashville, Tennessee

Joy Boerop was born in China, worked as governess in Switzerland and Executive Secretary in Germany, studied in France and finished her formal education in America, married a Dutchman, served with YfC in Belgium, emigrated to the USA, lived in South Africa, and fractured her hip in Indonesia. She has battled cancer; raised a family; and partnered with her husband, Bill, around the world, sharing their conviction that the Christian message is one of joy and hope. They are encouraging churches to mobilize their resources to take the gospel to the unreached peoples of the world. She was well named "Joy" by a Chinese Bible woman.

—**Dr. Stuart Briscoe**
Broadcaster on "Telling the Truth"; Minister at Large Elmbrook Church,
Brookfield, Wisconsin

Joy Boerop's memoirs give us a glimpse of what happens to those MKs who grow up in another culture. Joy's parents served in China with China Inland Mission before and during the years of the Communist takeover of China.

She has lived a cosmopolitan life of ministry for the Lord all over the world. The Lord reminds her often that she wasn't called to a life of Christian service, but volunteered!

May Joy Boerop's memoirs inspire many more of us to a life of dedication, trust and joy in the Lord!!

—**Dr. Robert M. Statler**
Founder, Stephanies Ministries
A Ministry of Encouragement
Greensburg, Pennsylvania

In Joy Boerop's story we learn that trusting in God and being obedient to His direction will, through His timing, result in His provision for needs. We also learn that the simple pleasures God provides, such as the wonders of nature and the warmth of family gatherings, far extend the value of the material things that the world seeks after.

I recommend this book as an excellent "what happens next," suspense-filled account of a follower abandoned to God's calling. It will be an encouragement to all followers of Christ who are facing challenges in their personal missions and in their walk. Joy's recipe, as handed down through the generations—trust and obey!

—**John Stein**
National Bank Examiner,
US Office of the Comptroller of the Currency
Dunwoody, Georgia

The life story of Joy Boerop as a missionary child in China is fascinating. It is very different than the background of most. The eyes of the reader will be opened to many new, intriguing facts about the history of the war years in China.

May many be enriched and enlightened by Joy's journey. Read this book and be blessed!"

—**Judy and Larry Roberts**
Roberts Business Group
Hillsborough, North Carolina

Joy Boerop was born in war-torn China; went through World War II; and was separated from her parents most of her growing up years, which taught her many invaluable lessons. Her life story is filled with difficult and sad times, which included cancer, many health challenges, as well as financial hardships. You will be encouraged and uplifted as you read about the many unusual miracles of God's daily provisions. The overwhelming faithfulness of the Lord has given Joy a life of great joy and fulfillment. It is my prayer that you will be encouraged by reading *Joy in Living*.

—**Dr. Charles Stanley**
Senior Pastor, First Baptist Atlanta
Founder and President of In Touch Ministries
Atlanta, Georgia

A must read! Joy's authenticity opens the door for all to reap life's lessons from her rich spiritual heritage. Beginning in China and reaching to the ends of the earth, this is a real adventure story of whoever sows bountifully will also reap bountifully, whether serving on different continents or through faith offerings.

Precious family life insights imparted by caring parents to their children illustrate how the love of Christ transcends all generations. "...You, Oh Lord, sit enthroned forever; your renown endures through all generations" (Psalm 102:12 NIV). Thank you, Joy, for blessing us with your memoirs!

—Dr. and Mrs. Luis K. Bush
Coordinator of the AD 2000 Movement
International Facilitator for Transform World Movement
Lynchburg, Virginia

Joy in Living

Joy K. Boerop

Phil. 4:4

林喜樂

Joy in Living

Memoirs of an MK, an MW, and an MM

Joy K. Boerop

林喜樂

Pleasant Word
A Division of WinePress Group

Pleasant Word (a division of WinePress Publishing, PO Box 428, Enumclaw, WA 98022) functions only as book publisher. As such, the ultimate design, content, editorial accuracy, and views expressed or implied in this work are those of the author.

Hard Cover:
ISBN 13: 978-1-4141-1644-0
ISBN 10: 1-4141-1644-6

Soft Cover:
ISBN 13: 978-1-4141-1569-6
ISBN 10: 1-4141-1569-5

Library of Congress Catalog Card Number: 2009908025

For
My husband, Bill, my Cheri;
Our children, Gloria and Doug, Arlita and Butch;
And our grandchildren, Kristin, Lindsay, Kara, Shayna,
Chad, and Drew

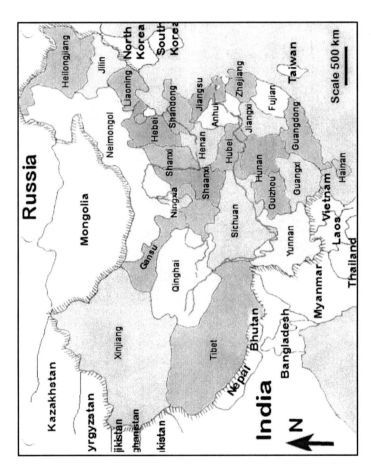

Chinese Provinces Map.

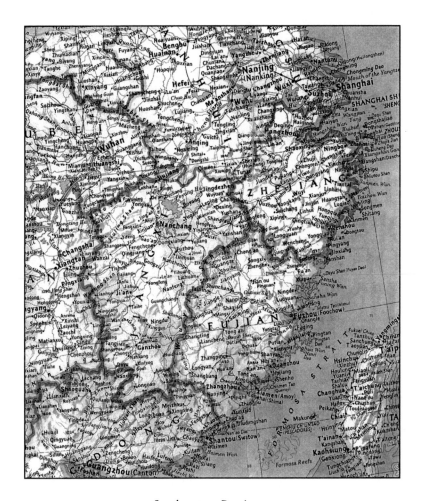

Southeastern Provinces.

Contents

Acknowledgements. xv

Introduction. xvii

1. Beginnings (1895–1935). 1

2. Facing Death (1936–1938) 13

3. Adjusting to Life in Shanghai (1938–1939). 25

4. Warm Welcomes and Sad Goodbyes (1939–1941) 33

5. Treacherous Journeys (1941) 43

6. Escapades, Adventures, and New Life
(1941–1946, in Shanghai) 51

7. Wartime in Inland China (1941–1946, in the Interior). 65

8. A Family Again (1946–1947) 73

9. Dramatic Changes (1947–1949). 81

10. Delays, Disappointments, and Departure (1949–1950) 89

11. Trials, Tribulations, and Triumphs (1950–1953). 109

12. Studying, Serving, and Singing in Paris (1954). 123

13. Delightful, Difficult, and Dark Days (1954–1955) 131

14. Ministry in France, Belgium, Holland, Sweden,
    and Denmark (1956) 141

15. Romance in Paris, Wedding Bells in Antwerp (1956–1958) . . . 149

16. Countless Tests of Faith (1958–1960) 163

17. Unbelievable Answers to Prayer (1960–1961) 171

18. New Beginnings and Many Surprises (1961–1963) 179

19. Multiple Tasks and Opportunities (1963–1966). 193

20. Finally Home (1966–1968 and beyond). 207

21. Struggles and Pitfalls in Ministry (1968 and beyond) 219

22. Joy and Sadness (1969–1970) 223

23. Discipler, Hostess, and Tentmaker (1971–1975) 235

24. The Trip of a Lifetime (1975). 249

25. Faith, Guidance, and Fulfillment (1976–1978) 255

26. Major Decisions and Events (1978–1981) 263

27. Back to My Roots (August–September 1981). 269

Conclusion. 287

Epilogue. 291

Acknowledgements

MY HEARTFELT THANKS to the many who over the years have encouraged me, even begged me, to pen my autobiography. Many have prayed for the birthing of *Joy in Living* and I will always be grateful.

The editing help from Ruth McClellan was immeasurable. Tammy Hopf, my project manager, shepherded this project carefully to fruition. My deepest thanks go to my husband, Bill, who walked beside me for over fifty years. He was there in sickness and in health, in good times and in bad, in joy and in sorrow. Bill was my greatest cheerleader in seeing this book become a reality.

Introduction

FOR MANY YEARS, the Lord has been gracious to provide me with abundant opportunities to share my testimony in different forums, such as ladies' meetings, churches, missions conferences, retreats, and home Bible studies. It is from these times of sharing from my heart about my life in China, Europe, and the United States that I have been overwhelmed with requests to write my memoirs.

As my daughters got older, married, and had children of their own, they too asked me to pen my story as a reminder of their legacy. Finally, at the Lord's insistent prompting, I have done that. My primary purpose in doing so has been to honor my Savior and to bring Him glory while encouraging His people.

I delayed writing my story due to some difficult challenges. First, I knew that I had to pen an accurate account not only of my life, but also of the lives of my loved ones and how our relationships intertwined. Second, the difficulty of being objective was a concern when so many deep feelings were at stake. I have always carefully guarded my intimate thoughts, experiences, and personal feelings. My greatest struggle involved possibly hurting someone's image or causing misunderstanding of loved ones who were led by God in highly unusual paths, difficult for most to comprehend.

It was not easy to delve into the past, remembering long-forgotten experiences in war-torn China, recounting emotions of life in Europe as a unique individual, and recalling countless miracles of God's love in a new homeland. Some memories were tough to relive and brought back tears, shame, or sorrow. The vast majority of others brought unspeakable joy as I rejoiced in God's goodness and perfect leading.

I am deeply grateful to my parents for their foresight in leaving me with written accounts of their journey. Over the years, father faithfully penned his experiences in his diaries during times when diaries were difficult to come by in the interior of China. He also sent reports to the mission, and he wrote letters. Mother's fertile correspondence to her family helped me to grasp some of her impressions and thoughts as a young, single missionary in China.

Since my parents and I did not have the conveniences of today's phones, cell phones, e-mail, or Internet, I developed the skill of regularly writing letters. This was a habit formed in early childhood. Letter writing resulted in accurate accounts of my life, even into marriage and motherhood, since my father kept almost all of my letters from the time that I was eight years old. Thus, armed with my memory, many personal materials, and my mother's and father's diligent preservations, my story has been written.

To facilitate understanding of the chronology, I have added dates to the chapter titles. This also lends insight into some of China's history in the 1930s and 40s and helps the reader to comprehend the story line.

The reader should also keep in mind that life in China during the mid-twenties until the take over and the liberation of China by the Communists in 1949, was extremely confusing. Fighting factions and parties in control changed constantly.

From the time my parents met, they were confronted with the dilemma of unrest in China. The first few years after their marriage, they had to constantly flee from the Communists (late 1920s, early 30s). Mao Zedong and his leaders had started a revolution and uprising against the National Party in Nanchang, the capital city of the province Jiangxi, where my parents were working. His famous "Long March" in the early 1930s started in the very province and areas where my parents served the Lord as missionaries.

When Japan became a threat to China by invading some of its northern territories and declaring war in 1937, the Communists, under the leadership of Mao, joined forces with Chang Kai-shek, the head of the Nationalist government, against their enemy, Japan. The Japanese were never successful in occupying all of China during World War II. They did manage, however, to gain control from Mongolia all the way down to some of the eastern and southern provinces, including some parts of Jiangxi. Once Japan was defeated in 1945, Mao Zedong slowly began to work on gaining control of China by occupying more and more of the northern provinces until 1949, when all of China was in Communist hands.

Much of my life's story happened when air travel was very unusual for most people and non-existent in the interior of China. Highways and expressways had not yet been built. A network of trains connected only larger and mostly capital cities of the various provinces. During and after World War II, I went to school in Shanghai. Shanghai was in Japanese occupied territory. At that same time, my parents were in the area where the Kuomintang, under the leadership of Generalissimo Chang Kai-shek, ruled.

Again, my fervent prayer is that the Lord Jesus will be glorified through my life's experiences as a Missionary Kid (MK), a Missionary Wife (MW), and a Missionary Mother (MM). As you come along and share my journey with me, may you be encouraged by the overwhelming faithfulness of our great Savior, who has given me a life of great joy and fulfillment even though it has been fraught with struggles and adversities.

Chapter 1

Beginnings (1895–1935)

MY EXCITEMENT REACHED a feverish pitch as the landing gear of the old plane lowered and I felt the thud of the wheels touching the runway. It had been exciting enough to visit Peking and its forbidden city, the Great Wall of China, and the Summer Palace. Now I was back "home." After thirty-one-and-a-half-years, I was finally going to see the city of Shanghai again, my hometown for twelve years.

It was August 27, 1981. I was sure the other passengers could hear the pounding of my heart. Not only had I returned to my childhood home after leaving it so many years before, but also this date was extremely significant because it was my father's birthday. Although he was in heaven, I was going to celebrate my homecoming in his honor. Almost fifty-six years ago, in 1925, he had landed in Shanghai…but first things first.

My father, Gustav Heinrich Burklin, was born in 1897 in Mannheim, Germany. He was one of eleven children. Sadly, his father, my grandfather, died in 1909 before my father's twelfth birthday. Less than four years later, my father's sorrow was multiplied when his mother also died. The traumatic experience of losing both parents by the time he was fifteen years old was expressed in a letter he wrote years later:

To lose my parents so young cast a dark shadow over my youth. Still today my eyes tear up when I think back and ask why did I have to

1

lose my parents when I was so young? Life grabbed me with rough hands. But how great that God intervened early on and drew me to Himself out of pure grace. Before my mother died I became a follower of Jesus Christ. Now my young life had meaning.

My father first heard the good news of Jesus Christ when one of his teachers took him to some youth meetings. It was not long before he accepted the Lord as his Savior. He also heard about ministry among the people of China and immediately began to sell mission literature to his friends, even though he was not always paid. He did not know then that one day he would end up in China. He wrote:

> I did not forget that I didn't always get paid, for I did not have much—just lived from hand to mouth and many days I did not get enough to eat.

Gustav joined the army during World War I and spent some time in France as a prisoner of war. During this time, he felt that God wanted him in His service. In 1920, he entered St. Chrischona Seminary in Switzerland. He was always grateful for the four years of excellent education he received under the tutelage of some wonderful, godly professors. It was during this time that he felt God's call to China. In order to fulfill this calling, he was required to spend one year in a pastorate in Germany.

Upon completion of his German pastorate, Gustav went to London, England, to learn English. There were no German/Chinese textbooks available that could help him learn the Chinese language, so he had to learn English first. By Christmas 1925 he was finally on his way to serve the Lord with the China Inland Mission or CIM (founded by Hudson Taylor).

After a rigorous journey, Gustav started Chinese language school in Anking, China, and then continued private lessons in Chinese with a teacher assigned to him on his mission station. It was extremely difficult for my German father to take and pass the required six examinations when he had been exposed to the English and Chinese languages for such a short time. The newly arrived male missionaries were given two years to complete the six exams before they could begin any kind of in-depth ministry. Ladies were required to take only two exams.

One sunny afternoon, Gustav was reading a mission paper when his eyes fell on a photo of a young lady with a number of Chinese children. As he looked closer, it was as if God touched his shoulder and said, "*Young man, this lady is to become your wife.*" He had no idea who the young lady was, where she lived, or with what mission agency she was working. To find someone in the vast land of China seemed an impossible task. Added to this difficulty were the strict rules of the China Inland Mission. A young man could not contact a young lady without the proper permission and seemingly endless paperwork that involved the superintendent of the mission, the supervisor of the area, and the senior missionary of the mission station where the young woman was working. These restrictions did not deter my father, who went to great lengths to find out the name of the young woman and get the proper permissions required to write her letters.

Lina Pfeifferling was from a small town in middle Germany. After she and Gustav corresponded for a time, he wanted to meet her. Since there were no planes or cars and very few buses in those days, Gustav began to walk on narrow paths between rice-fields and on dusty roads. The journey was long and tedious in the hot weather. For days he walked, the only white man among the many Chinese. Finally, Gustav arrived in Nancheng, the mission station where Lina worked. He wondered what Lina would really be like and if they would have anything in common besides their vocation of being missionaries. After all his effort, would their meeting be in vain? Had he really felt God's touch and the promise of a life partner?

As Gustav entered the large gates to the "Yesoo-Tang," the Jesus Hall, the senior missionary greeted him kindly and said, "Young man, I wanted to see if you really meant business, so I sent Miss Pfeifferling to the next mission station. Keep on walking." So Gustav continued his arduous journey to find Lina, a journey he was to thank God for the rest of his life.

Lina, who became my mother, was born in 1895. She was the third of five children born into a happy German farming family. In the tradition of that area, she was given four first names: Lina, Minna, Marie, and Wilhelmine. For all of the family and the various maids and field hands, hard work on the farm and in the fields was rewarded with laughter, camaraderie, and a caring spirit.

Especially close to her father, Lina was deeply homesick when she left home in her late teens to learn the art of housekeeping. It was a great relief when she finished her two years of study and could go home. To complete her training to become an accomplished housekeeper, she took sewing classes in a nearby town. Her teacher was a devout Christian who did not miss any opportunity to share the Lord Jesus with her young pupils. This was the first time Lina had heard a clear presentation of the gospel, and she accepted the Lord Jesus as her personal Savior.

It was not easy for her to be the only one in her family to follow the Lord. In her biographical sketch, Lina wrote:

> I was free to follow the calling of my Savior. Unfortunately, my parents were not believers and it was not easy to be the first in the family to step out for the Lord without compromise. A new life started for me. The Bible was a new book for me, but what comfort, strength, and joy could I glean from it!

Lina Pfeifferling attended Bible school in 1922 and 1923. Then she spent two years in nurses training. It was during that time that she felt the call of God to serve Him in China as a missionary. As required, she went to England for several months to learn English in order to be able to learn the Chinese language. It was a heart-wrenching experience for Lina to leave home and all those who were dear to her. Soon after she had become a believer, Lina had given her mother a Bible. In the Bible was this note my Grandma Pfeifferling had written:

> On November 12, 1925, our daughter Lina left us, and November 17 she went on board the ship *Coblenz* in Genoa, Italy, to immigrate to China in order to bring the gospel to the Chinese. May the Lord bless her. Who knows if we will meet again here on earth.

More than five weeks later, on Christmas Eve of 1925, Lina arrived in Shanghai. By January 1, 1926, she was in Yang Chow, in language school for missionary ladies. She was very apprehensive about learning Chinese, not really having mastered the English language yet. In one of her many letters home she wrote, "Oh, how will I be able to learn these languages, first English and then Chinese!"

Lina was blessed with many family members and friends who kept up an enormous flow of letters to her in China. She wrote back in one of her letters, describing her first impression of Chinese life:

> Yesterday afternoon I went for a walk with three other missionary ladies. One of the Chinese helpers went with us so that we could find our way back home. Oh dear ones, one cannot imagine that people live in these houses. When I think back to Europe, my wonderful home, where everything is neat and clean, the life here seems horrible. But on the other hand, it is all very interesting. I wish I had a camera to capture some of these scenes. The houses look like shacks, all in a row and open to the street. They are cooking, baking, making shoes, doing carpentry work, anything you can imagine, and all out in the open. I don't think they know what a warm living room is. They also eat on the street, holding their bowl in one hand and the chopsticks in the other. That's how they walk around on the street and eat.

Some of the conditions she experienced caused my mother great pain:

> If you take a longer walk through the streets, it makes you really sick. These narrow streets, these masses of people, the beggars and the lame, you just cannot imagine. When we came back to the language school my Swedish classmate said, "Oh, now we are in heaven."

My mother was very concerned about her family not having a personal relationship with the Lord. She was very wise in sharing her faith when she wrote, detailing her experiences while witnessing to them:

> Today is Easter where we again are reminded of the resurrection of our Savior. His resurrection is an encouragement to us. He did not only die, but He conquered death and lives. Scripture tells us that "whosoever believes on Him shall live also" and because of this message we came to China. Oh, I am so thankful for the part I may have, however small it may be, to bring this message to the Chinese.

By the end of May 1926, Lina was finished with language school and was on her way to her first mission station. In a letter to one of her brothers, she describes travel in China in 1926:

> Meals are quite an event. Using chopsticks is still very difficult, the steamed rice is not the greatest and the other dishes I am not too sure about. I still have to get used to the Chinese cleanliness....We seem to be very interesting personalities. If we are in bed, about a half a dozen Chinese are observing us through the window. When we ask them to leave, they only do so after we cover the windows, still trying to check on us through the keyhole in the door. When they see us women writing letters they are amazed, because a woman in China does not need to be educated. If we travel through a village, only one Chinese needs to spot us and soon the whole town comes out to see the foreigners. Then they check us out. They look under the hat of my coworker, then they admire the earlobes, the ears are pierced, but no earrings, yes, these foreigners are strange people. I am only sorry that I don't understand them yet. I am sure it would be fascinating to hear their comments.

Kienchangfu, later renamed Nancheng, was Lina's first mission station. In one of her letters home, she made sure her family in Germany knew that, although the name had changed, she still lived in the same city. To receive mail from home was a true lifesaver for one who in the past had been very homesick even during short separations. In many of her letters Lina expressed her longing to be able to look in on her family, the farm, and her friends. Her eldest brother was amazed that his little sister, who was always so homesick, was now a missionary in China. Truly, the Lord was doing far above anything that a farm girl from a small town in Germany could have dreamed possible.

One day, among the many letters she received, there was one addressed to Miss Lina Pfeifferling, but she did not recognize the handwriting. It had come from Changshu, a city quite a distance further north from where she was. Not knowing anyone from that town, Lina wondered who could be writing to her. It was a letter from Gustav Burklin. Many more letters followed. Then one day he requested a meeting. Under the watchful eye of the senior missionary and out in the open, Gustav

Burklin finally met the pretty lady from the Reiherbach, whom he had walked so many days to meet and whom he hoped would be his future wife. The first time my parents saw each other was under a bridge close to the river. An elder missionary stood nearby.

A steady stream of letters and several meetings culminated in Gustav asking for Lina's hand in marriage. This request was met with much concern on Lina's part. Although she was in her early thirties, she felt he first had to ask her parents for her hand in marriage. As a big smile spread across Gustav's face, he reached into his pocket and pulled out a letter from Lina's father, which gave his blessing on their union. As always, Gustav was prepared. He already had her father's permission.

It is with a grateful heart for my father's insight in preserving his correspondence that I was able to share in his and my mother's joy. Their deep love and commitment to the Lord and to each other in a faraway land shines through my father's letter to his future in-laws:

February 20, 1928, China Inland Mission, Changshu via Siberia.

My dear parents! Now after a long time I again may call someone "Father and Mother." Very young, I already lost my dear parents. Can you understand the good fortune which is mine through my relationship with Lina? Now again I know where home is. From the bottom of my heart I am thrilled with your whole-hearted acceptance.

Thank you for the greetings, but especially for the nice letter from you, dear Mother. I immediately sent them on to Lina, so she could share in my joy. Since dear Lina sent me a wonderful photo, I can visualize the farm, the sheep grazing in the field, the little bridge right by the large barn...

I never dreamed that I would get such a dear, wonderful, straightforward country girl. Now don't think that I am such a highfalutin city slicker. On the contrary, already early in life did I experience sorrow and want. My biggest joy would have been if my brothers and I would have been able to support our dear mother. We wished we could have eased her life somewhat after the untimely death of my father. But then she died and we all had to leave home.... So don't be concerned, early on I learned to do without and to be content with what I had. God lovingly looked after me and brought me through. In my service among the Chinese I am happy, and now He has brought

Lina to me as my life partner. I know you are rejoicing and thanking the Lord with us.

Together we have already experienced happy and sober times. I am aware of my responsibility, but God will help. I understand Lina's loneliness, especially during this time. How precious would be the counsel of her mother, a word of encouragement from her father. I too am missing my parents, but I can trust you completely. If you should notice that I am doing something wrong, then please tell me openly, I will be always grateful. Especially you, dear Father, I will appreciate each encouraging word.

What do I give my dear Lina? Myself, just as I am, with all my mistakes and weaknesses. She already knows about them. With all my gifts and abilities I want to serve her with humility, love, and faithfulness. I sense our happiness will be fulfilled only in our oneness through our faith. This is also the foundation upon which we can always build.

Should all fall into place, we will travel to Shanghai the end of April or beginning of May to be married there. Until then we will get some more mail, I am looking forward to that.

With hearty greetings I am your thankful son,

Gustav

The Lord confirmed what He had impressed upon my father's heart when he was reading the mission magazine that sunny afternoon so long before. He wanted Gustav and Lina to serve Him together in the land of their calling. On May 19, 1928, they were married in a double wedding ceremony with another couple in the city of Shanghai, China.

The years that followed were stormy years. The Red Army—the Communists—became stronger as they sought to gain control of China. South China became their territory, and the infamous "Long March" started in Jiangxi, the province where my parents lived and worked.

In 1934 Mao Zedong decided to flee his southern bases in Jiangxi and retreat to the North of China. This march lasted 368 days; covered 6,000 miles; and crossed 24 rivers, 18 mountain ranges (some of which were covered in snow), and eleven provinces. The long trek ended in the caves of Yenan in the province Shanxi. About 80,000 people started the march, but only 6,000 made it. There were 15 major battles and many skirmishes. A total of about 200,000 participated in what became known as the "Long March."

The first few years of my parents' married life were spent continually fleeing from the Communists, living and working in five or six different cities. In May 1929, my mother gave birth to a little boy in Changshu, Jiangxi, whom they named Fred. On one occasion after his birth, three missionary ladies from Finland and my parents were warned by the Chinese that the Communists were getting close to their town. They prepared to leave, knowing that the ruthless soldiers had not been kind to the population and especially not to foreigners. The only way to escape was by houseboat. The Scandinavian ladies hired one and my folks another. Their Chinese friends urged them to hurry, since the Communist soldiers were getting closer by the minute.

Just as they were about to leave, little Fred started to cry from hunger pangs. In their hurry, mother had not been able to give him his bottle. Since she did not have the luxury of a diaper bag, which was unheard of in those days, Lina searched their few pieces of luggage only to realize that she had forgotten the bottles and left them in the kitchen at the mission station. Fred did not sympathize with their plight. He was hungry! No amount of soothing would console him. Finally, my father decided that they would go back and get the bottles. The Chinese again warned, "The Communists are so close that if we don't leave now it may be too late."

Unable to wait any longer, the Finnish ladies left, trusting the Lord that the Burklins would be able to leave in time. When my parents arrived back at the mission compound, they received word that the Communists had changed their route. They now were on their way to the town where my parents had intended to flee and the Scandinavian missionaries were headed.

The Scandinavian missionaries, three dear servants of the Lord, were never heard from again. Several months later, some of their clothing was discovered, and it was evident that they had been brutally murdered. For Mom and Dad, it was a bittersweet realization that their lives had been spared but their fellow soldiers for the Lord had laid down their lives. Indeed, God's ways are not our ways, nor can we always understand His leading.

Keeping a step ahead of the Red Army brought my parents to Wuhu in Anhui, the province north of Jiangxi. There, in November 1930, their second son, Werner, was born. Mother had the good fortune to deliver this baby in a hospital.

In the Northwest part of the province Jiangxi, there is beautiful Lake Boyang. Close by this lake is the mountain range Lushan. It is well known for its natural beauty. Over the years, many illustrious personalities like Generalissimo Chiang Kai-shek and even Chairman Mao Zedong had sought reprieve there from the extremely hot and humid summers in the cities. Fleeing again from the Red Army in the summer of 1932, the Burklin's little family went to Guling, a quaint little town in the Lushan Mountains.

In those days, if a woman bore a son there was great rejoicing and celebrating. Eggs were boiled and dyed red and were sent around to friends and family to announce the arrival of a son. Red in China is the color of joy and happiness. The mother who bore a son did not have to immediately go back to the fields to work, but could take it easy for a few days. If a girl was born, however, she did not have this luxury.

Mother was esteemed by the Chinese ladies. She had given her husband two sons! Now she was expecting a third child. This time it was a girl. After her birth, one of the Bible women who helped with the children's and women's ministries ran to my father and cried, "Lin Muh-si, Lin Muh-si." She said, "Pastor Lin, Pastor Lin! You have a little girl. You must name her She-loh' (Xi-Le)." In Chinese, the name means "JOY." My father looked at her in amazement. A Chinese lady who got excited about a little girl being born could only have had her outlook changed by the Lord Jesus. Culturally she would never have rejoiced over the birth of a girl.

And so my name became Lin She-loh' (Lin Xi Le). The Chinese characters for She-loh' are found in Philippians 4:4, "Rejoice in the Lord alway: and again I say, rejoice" (KJV). The power of this text is especially beautiful in the Chinese Bible, where Paul exhorts, "Be full of joy in the Lord, and again I say be full of joy." To rejoice indicates that we must make an effort. The Chinese are simply encouraged to be full of joy, letting the Lord fill their hearts and lives with His joy. I have proudly carried this name and have often thought about that Chinese lady. And I do not think it is a coincidence that the midwife who helped bring me into this world was a Swiss missionary named Elma Froehlich. Froehlich in German means "Happy."

When Father went to China, each missionary was given a Chinese name. Because Chinese script does not have an alphabet, the Chinese teachers searched the list entitled "Hundred Family Names." A Chinese character was chosen that somewhat sounded like one of the syllables in the foreigner's name. Since Dad's last name was Burklin, the last syllable was chosen, with Lin meaning forest. Although there are more than one billion Chinese people, there are only about 300 to 400 family names. So anyone with the name "Lin" is related to us. This has been nice and has been a lifesaver in some precarious situations. On one of my return trips to China, a Pastor Lin greeted me with a big smile and said, "We are family because your name is also Lin." A girl, although married, keeps her father's family name.

Providentially, the Lord allowed my parents to return to Germany in 1934 at a critical time. It was their one and only furlough in twenty-five years of service in China. Mother was thrilled to introduce her husband and three children to her family. How wonderful it was to be back home in her beloved Reiherbach valley, but the Lord also allowed a shadow to be cast over this happy time. During the furlough, her dear and precious father died. For Lina, it was a great heartache. The man she had greatly respected, admired, loved, and looked up to was gone. She thanked the Lord that He had allowed her to spend this special time with her father, mother, and family. When she had left them in 1925, she had always feared that she might never see them again.

During their furlough, disturbing news came from China. In December 1934, the Communists stormed an ancient city known as the "City of the Kings" in South Anhui, the province just north of where they had served the Lord. John and Betty Stam, fellow missionaries with the China Inland Mission, lived there. Before they could flee, the Red Army had stormed into the city and held the Stams captive for 24 hours. John was able to write to his mission that he, his wife, and little baby had been in the hands of the Communists, but he praised God for the peace He had given them during this dangerous time. His one concern during that terrible time had been that God be glorified whether they lived or died.

On the morning of that fateful day, John and Betty Stam had been led through the streets of the city, stripped of their outer clothing, and painfully bound. As they were led to their deaths, the Chinese inhabitants were told by the Reds to "watch the foreign devils die." With a quick flash of the sword, they both had been beheaded. Those who had watched were amazed with what calm, strength, and commitment to God they had faced their death. Their little baby, Priscilla, was saved by Chinese Christians who hid and cared for her until she could safely be taken to another mission station.

With these reports resonating in his mind, Father had to make a decision. Should he take his family back to China and risk going through the same ordeal as John and Betty Stam? Would he be able to face death as they had? Was the Lord really all powerful to protect them? He had not spared the Stams! As my parents prayed about the steps they should take, they once again realized the promise they had made long before to serve the Lord in China, the land of their calling. They had made an unconditional commitment of their lives to the Lord. They knew that their ministry was not yet finished.

In December 1935, the Burklin family once again crossed the ocean to resume their ministry in Jiangxi, one of the southern-most provinces in China. This time they were assigned to the city of Tsungjen, currently known as Chongren. A Czech couple had served the Lord there years earlier. They'd had to leave one of their most prized possessions behind. Their little daughter had died from one of the many tropical diseases and had been buried there. This was yet another stark reminder that the cost of serving the Lord Jesus could be very high.

Chapter 2

Facing Death (1936-1938)

THE YEAR 1936 was an extremely tumultuous year. Father was assigned to build a house on the property of the orphaned mission station in Chongren. Construction began in the middle of February. While Dad was in Chongren, the family lived at the closest mission station, Linchuan, with another missionary family.

Dad's diary detailing those difficult days vividly reveals his frustrations at every turn. He had to get all the materials together, including the beams, planks, bricks, doors, windows, and roof tiles. Everything had to be cut, formed, or molded. Bricks had to be burned. The right prices had to be negotiated. Time and again, materials were stolen. The timbers that were floated down the river disappeared more than once, only to be found again days later.

Not only did Dad weather the numerous physical frustrations of the job, but also he did so while plagued with the horrible disease of malaria. Mosquitoes were everywhere and attacked viciously. Once attacked, parasites from the disease remained in one's system from that time on, causing recurrences of the long-term infection. Weakness was accompanied by high fevers, chills, and nausea. Dad described fevers so high that he was forced to lie down. His teeth chattered from chills that were so pervasive that he shook while the room temperature registered one hundred degrees. Of course, there were no air conditioners, no ice-cold drinks, no electricity, no running water, and no flushing toilets available in the interior of China in those days.

While overseeing the work of the building, Dad also continued his ministry. He was faithful to conduct Bible studies, preach, visit believers in their homes, and disciple a young man who became a helper. This young man who often traveled with Dad to several of the outposts to minister there was called the Evangelist. I am sure that in his wildest dreams my father had never believed that as a missionary he would have to be an architect, builder, subcontractor, and so much more. Fortunately, a young Swiss missionary tremendously helped my dad as he became more proficient in the language. Dad audited his language exams.

Mother was anxious to be with her husband and begin a ministry among the women. As soon as their furniture had arrived from Boyang, she persuaded Dad to let the family join him in Chongren. Above the chapel, right under the roof, was a large room that became the bedroom, living room, and study. In one of her reports, Mother describes that it was livable during the cooler months, but once the summer heat started in April, it was unbearable. Often during the night, she would sit in a large tub of cold water to find some relief. The meals were prepared in the kitchen of the evangelist who occupied several rooms next to the chapel.

To flee the heat of the mission stations, the missionaries sought reprieve in the mountains of Magushan during the summer months. In June the thermometer showed 106 degrees. On July 1, 1936, the family traveled from Chongren via Linchuan to Nancheng at the foot of the mountains. They stayed overnight in the same mission station where Mother had begun her missionary career ten years earlier. The journey to Magushan was memorable, as the men walked and Mother and I were carried in a sedan chair.

Walking the trail up the mountain was quite an event. The path was narrow, often meandering among rice fields that the Chinese planted in terraces high up onto the mountain. Hundreds of stone steps had to be climbed. Two men carried the chair, one in the front and one in the back. A second pair of men walked alongside it. Should the first set of men tire after walking such a treacherous road, the second set would move swiftly under the long bamboo poles behind the other men and, with a jerk and a pull, free the first carriers from their load. For a split second, the sedan chair was in mid-air, with no one supporting it. Many times, I was afraid that they would drop us, but they never did. After about six hours, we reached our destination.

In 1914, the mission was able to acquire a forested section of Magushan, a 1,800-foot mountain. A long, rectangular building with rooms all in a row, a kitchen, and some side rooms was built. This served the missionaries as a haven from the overpowering heat during the summer months. Fortunately, this area also had a spring that provided wonderfully clear and clean water for cooking and quenching thirst. Over the years, several of the missionaries were able to build their own small bungalows. The pine trees in the area provided the needed wood. Large sections of the bark were carefully peeled off the trees to use as roofing material.

We all loved the time in Magushan. Some of my fondest memories include Daddy going swimming with us in mountain brooks or close to a waterfall, taking us for walks and hikes, and singing as we walked along—Dad had a beautiful tenor voice. One of my favorite memories was getting up before dawn, climbing one of the high peaks, and watching the sunrise. We would then search for blueberries that grew in abundance on some of the mountain slopes. Mom made scrumptious blueberry pancakes. Other times she would prepare a picnic basket. Those peanut butter and jelly sandwiches tasted wonderful after a long walk or a good swim.

We were not familiar with lunchmeat or fresh cheese. A rare treat would be some foreign goods from the CIM headquarters in Shanghai. Since these were extremely expensive, Dad did not order them often. It was a full-time job for some of the missionaries in Shanghai to receive the orders and then supply the missionaries in the interior with their requests. The China Inland Mission was one of the largest missions in China and had missionaries stationed all over that country.

Fellowship among the missionaries during an afternoon or evening was always a highlight as it centered on discussions about how we might better serve the Chinese and about prayer. It was also a time of fun-filled activities and games. We might celebrate a birthday with cake and hot chocolate for the children and tea for the adults. Usually, a game of "Ring-Toss" was the most popular activity after supper. Instead of a volleyball, a rubber ring about twelve inches in diameter was tossed over a net.

Enjoyable times were also accompanied by preparing the Sunday services for the mountain people, visiting them in their homes, helping them with various projects, and sharing the gospel in outlying villages. There were always sick people who needed care and children's meetings to conduct. The missionaries experienced a great rapport with the local Chinese villagers.

All too soon, Dad had to return to Chongren to relieve the young Swiss missionary, who was ill. The construction of the mission house was not yet completed, and it was almost the end of July 1936—one of the worst years to build. Over and over again, Dad wrote in his diary about torrential rain or about the extreme heat with its terrible host of mosquitoes. Constant references alluded to his ongoing battle with malaria.

On Magushan, the mosquitoes were also busy. Both of my legs were covered with bites. As a four-year-old child, I could not stop scratching. It was not long before the bites became infected and I began to experience terrible pain, along with high fevers. There was no doctor in the area, and there was no hospital. The closest mission hospital and doctor were in the neighboring province of Hunan.

My mother did not know what to do for me. Her husband was miles away on the mission station, and her little girl was getting worse by the moment. Then the infection turned into blood poisoning. The missionaries gathered around and prayed, asking the Lord to intervene on my behalf. Still I worsened. On August 13, 1936, Mother sent Dad a telegram, telling him that I was violently ill. He immediately packed some things, and since there was no bus early in the morning, he left Chongren at 3:30 A.M. on his bicycle. Dad rode for four hours to reach Linchuan. From there he caught a bus and arrived in Nancheng at noon. Then came the march up the mountain, where at 6 P.M. he was reunited with his family on Magushan. He immediately sent a telegram to the mission doctor in the next province of Hunan, asking him to please come quickly.

The S.O.S. telegram reached Dr. Roehm in the Nanyo Mountains south of Changsha. He, too, along with other missionaries, had fled the summer heat in the plains. He knew the call for help was urgent. Immediately, he began the three-hour descent down the mountain to where he could catch a bus to Changsha. At the hospital there, he picked up medication, some instruments, and other necessities after learning a bit more about my illness. Then he boarded a bus to Nancheng, via Nanchang, the capital of Jiangxi. His last leg of the journey was the walk up the mountain Magushan. It took several days for the doctor to come. The trip took three bus rides to travel a total of 500 miles, and it included one mountain descent and another mountain ascent. It was a long wait for my parents, who, while anxiously trying to trust the Lord, felt totally helpless as they watched their precious little girl suffer.

In the meantime, my fever did not let up. Daddy writes that I was very patient and sweet, but when the doctor came, I got nervous and even mean. The next two weeks were filled with anxiety. On August 29, the doctor lanced one of my lymph nodes after putting me under an anesthetic. Dad wrote, "The Lord had mercy upon us, we are not worthy. May He give quick healing."

Two days later he recorded:

Our little girl is getting weaker and weaker. The high fever stays, the infection hurts terribly, she cannot sleep.

On September 4, Dad penned in his diary, "Sometimes it seems to us as if we may not keep our little girl. She persistently has a high fever." Then on Sunday, September 6, he noted, "The fever is down. Praise the Lord! She is truly getting better." Ten days later, we were on our way back to our mission station in Chongren.

Another challenge that faced my parents was the schooling of my brothers. A children's home was to be opened in Shanghai, but no house parents had been assigned. Since Dad was not able to get materials to homeschool them, there was great concern about what would happen to the education of the boys. Finally, on October 19, late at night, a telegram arrived, saying that house parents had been located and the boys were welcome. The children's home would be opened.

Mother and the boys left for Shanghai, with Daddy escorting them to the capital city, Nanchang. There they were heartily received by a British couple, the Faircloughs, also CIM missionaries. The next day Dad put Mom and the boys on a direct train to Shanghai. They arrived at the end of October 1936. After staying several days in the China Inland Mission headquarters, they moved to the new children's home. Dad went back to Linchuan, where I was staying with missionary friends. Leaving me there, he returned to Chongren to finish the house and continue to take the gospel to the Chinese people there.

Dad faced many challenges. With the delays, the rain, the unwillingness of the workers to move along swiftly, and the constant attacks of malaria accompanied with high fevers, it seemed the job would never get done. His joy came in ministering to the people and not in building. Time and again, his diaries mention his visits with the evangelist to the marketplace to hand out tracts, visit the sick, or go to the prison to tell the prisoners about Jesus. Then at other times, he would visit his few church members and encourage the unbelievers in their homes to come to the services. Conferences were held in outlying posts where travel was dangerous due to bandits and robbers being active in the area.

Danger was common to missionaries serving in China in those days. Coming by bus from Ihwang, my father heard a loud banging sound. Thinking the vehicle was having motor problems, he looked at the driver, who opened the door and ran off. A man in a tattered uniform stood next to the bus and shouted that everyone should stay seated. Immediately Daddy knew—bandits!

All of the travelers ducked down. Daddy saw one of the rascals aiming at the fleeing driver. He immediately folded his hands and called out the name of the Lord Jesus in Chinese. Thinking the gun was not working, Dad shouted to the Chinese, "Everyone get out!" Boldly, he walked up to the robber, who in the meantime had loaded his gun. He looked at my father and was so shocked that he moved back a step or two. "Buh pa," Daddy said in Chinese, which means not to be afraid.

Immediately, the robber pointed his gun at my father and shouted to his comrades, "Lai, Lai" (come, come).

Five more robbers appeared and started to take anything they could from the passengers, including watches, rings, and money, but they did not lay a hand on my father. During this time Dad paced back and forth next to the bus, debating what he should do. He knew that if he ran, the robbers would shoot him down on the spot. To try to help his fellow travelers would also be in vain, so he remained calm in the Lord. Daddy then walked over to the driver, who was terrified and by now lying on the ground near the bus. He told him not to be afraid. When one of the robbers aimed his gun at the driver, he begged for his life while giving the bandit all that he carried with him.

When another thief pointed his weapon at Dad and shouted, "Here is one more!" my father looked him straight in the eye. Although the thief shouted again, none of his accomplices dared come closer. Suddenly the bandits left with their plunder. Dad's bag lay in the ditch untouched. The fear of God had not allowed the thugs to harm him or to steal his things. Quickly, all passengers boarded the bus, and they went to the next station to report the attack. As the Chinese discussed why nothing had happened to Daddy, one of the men said, "He truly had courage… look at his huge nose." All of them had a good laugh. The Chinese think all Caucasians have large noses. Judging external features, the Chinese think a large nose indicates courage. They concluded that the robbers were so shocked to see a foreigner with such a large nose that they had left the "foreign devil" unharmed.

Back in Chongren with my parents, I was well-immersed in Chinese life. All of my little playmates were Chinese, of course. My favorite friend was Loo-deh', Ruth. She was about my age. Daddy had built a sandbox for me. We spent hours playing imaginary games. We washed clothes the Chinese way, pretending that the sand was the river. We put a large stone down, and then with a piece of wood, we beat on the imaginary clothes. We turned them over skillfully and beat them some more, just as the Chinese women did at the riverbanks close by. Then we would cook meals, putting the sand into our cupped hands. Small sticks served as our chopsticks. The different designs we drew in the sand were the various delicacies I knew from the banquets we were sometimes invited to by our Chinese friends.

On several occasions, I went with my parents to outlying stations. There was Ihwang, which was a distance of about one day's travel, and Kaoping, Leh-an, Swenfeng Guy, and others. Father usually walked while mother and I were situated on a wheelbarrow, sitting on a narrow board on either side of a large wheel with one strong man pushing. The paths were often narrow, single threads with rice fields on either side. Spokes attached to the boards protected us from the turning wheel, but many times I was sure we would land in the rice fields. Rice is planted in muddy water. From my vantage point on the wheelbarrow, all I could see was water under me. Had my strong pusher stumbled on the uneven road, we would surely have landed in the rice paddy. After a successful journey, we usually spent several days in these areas and stayed with the local Christians.

I shall never forget one particular night. Of course, we had no electricity, no running water, and no conveniences, but we had warm hospitality. The Chinese believers put us up wherever they could. This time it was in the attic. While Dad held an oil lamp, he, Mom, and I climbed a simple ladder and went through a small trap door in the ceiling to our sleeping quarters. In China, you always traveled with your bedding. A quilt-like comforter was placed in a large oilcloth. Then a large mat made from palm fibers was put around the bedding and tied with strong ropes. This was called "Poo-kai."

Soon we were settled, having spread our bedding on the floor of the attic, which also served as a storage place for rice and grain. The roof had a small window from which we could see the beautiful moonlit night. It seemed as if shining moonbeams were dancing on our resting place. It was not long before I heard scratching noises in the wall. Suddenly, a big rat danced in the moonlight, ran across my feet, and jumped onto one of the large sacks of rice. Another followed. Soon there were several frolicking around, running back and forth over our blankets and jumping on the sacks of grain, which they began eating. We did not get much sleep that night. I was glad when day broke and we moved on to the next town.

We always packed up early in the morning, long before dawn. My parents felt it was important to arrive at their next destination before sunrise or during the morning hours before the day got hot. I can still hear the roosters crowing and the dogs barking as the sky turned from gray to soft colors when we entered a village or town. Many times, I would be carried on my father's shoulders. I was proud to be much taller than anyone else was. It was a wonderful reprieve from sitting on the hard board of the wheelbarrow.

A new missionary arrived to help with the work among the women and children and still needed to learn the language. Mother encouraged the junior missionary to visit some of the ladies of the congregation. At times Mother was busy with other activities, so the junior missionary asked me to go along and show her the way. I knew who these Chinese women were and where they lived. We trudged through the streets, greeting folks everywhere. Many of them came out to see these foreigners, a five-year-old girl and a lady dressed in strange clothes. I was used to this and not at all intimidated by them.

I thought it strange that the missionary lady was amazed by the lifestyle of the Chinese. I could not understand why she was surprised that the babies and little ones did not wear diapers. Was it not practical that their pants were open at the bottom and they could just squat down and relieve themselves where they happened to be playing?

The old ladies told stories and asked questions. I was surprised that the junior missionary did not understand them and would just shake her head instead of offering a simple "yes" or "no." I thought it odd that she seemed so ignorant. I could not understand why she did not speak Chinese when everyone here did, including the children. The junior missionary also thought it peculiar that the Chinese ladies considered it polite to cover their mouth with their hand when they laughed.

One of my favorite people was Choo-Sau-sau, my "Amah." She took care of me, but also helped mother in the home. She had very small, bound feet. In my days in China, many women's feet were still bound—a sign of beauty. When a baby girl was only a few days old, her toes were turned under her foot with the big toe laying straight. Then the foot was tightly bound with bandages. It was agony for those precious babies! As a girl grew, her feet remained tiny, sometimes only four to five inches long. Her arch and ankle grew five to six inches wide. The feet had to be bound for the rest of her life. Her legs looked like broomsticks and she seemed to have no calves. In the eyes of Chinese men, the smaller the feet, the more beautiful the woman.

How my "Amah" was able to move around and do her work on such tiny feet was amazing. After her work was finished, I would often visit her in her small apartment in the compound. We would chat and talk while I watched her cook. As soon as she was finished, she would fill a bowl with steamed rice, put some black beans and hot red pepper sauce on it, and hand me some chopsticks. That was one of my favorite foods. Mother was not too excited about my meal. She knew that Choo-Sau-sau did not have much and needed to feed her own family. She was also concerned that so much hot pepper sauce was not healthy for her little girl. To this day, I still love rice with black beans and a smidgen of red pepper sauce if I can get it.

War and rumors of war were again the daily norm. After the long years of strife between the Communists with Mao Zedong as their leader and the Kuomintang with Chiang Kai-shek at the helm, the warring parties finally agreed to stand together against the Japanese who, in 1937, were already at war with the Chinese. Large sections of North China had already been occupied by the Japanese. Rail lines had been destroyed, and travel by bus or houseboat was dangerous. Enemy lines were everywhere. This greatly affected my family.

Unlike girls in China who seldom attended school, it was time for me to enter school in Shanghai. Since travel directly to Shanghai was impossible, we detoured and headed west and then south instead of going north. We started our travels at the beginning of March 1938, first spending several days on a small houseboat, then taking a train to Changsha in the neighboring province of Hunan. My brothers, who had come home for a few months, were now with us on the way back to Shanghai when we three children became ill.

My parents worried and questioned if we would be able to get well quickly and then be strong enough to make the long trip. Fortunately, we could be helped in the hospital in Changsha. The doctors and nurses worked hard to speed up our recovery. Fervent prayers were also lifted up to our heavenly Father, and He answered.

We were then faced with the dangerous train ride to Canton that we completed safely. From this southern city, we took another boat to Hong Kong and immediately were able to board the Italian ship *Conte Rosso*. Cruising up the coast along the Formosa Strait between Formosa (now Taiwan) and China, we finally arrived in Shanghai. Thanks to the Japanese, a voyage that normally would have taken eight days, took us 28 days. Not only was it a very dangerous trip, but also the expense was enormous. Jokingly, Daddy remarked, "We should send the bills to the Japanese."

Chapter 3

Adjusting to Life in Shanghai (1938-1939)

IN SHANGHAI, MOM and Dad took advantage of shopping for necessities that they could not get in the interior. Fellow missionaries also had given them long lists of things they needed. For two weeks, my parents were able to enjoy some of the normal comforts of life, like running water, electricity, and flushing toilets. Streetcars, trolleys, and city buses facilitated trips to the wonderful department stores of Wing-on and Sincere. A rickshaw was always ready to take them where they needed to go. (A rickshaw was a chair fastened between two wheels. A man would run in front, pulling the contraption by two poles that were attached to the chair.) Being invited by friends into their homes or to a tearoom was also a treat.

My parents loved the precious fellowship with other missionaries at prayer meetings that were held in the China Inland Mission headquarters. All of these servants of the Lord had come from around the world after being challenged by the mission's founder, Hudson Taylor, to answer the call to service in China. Mom and Dad were greatly encouraged to hear reports from other distant parts of China. Their spirits were refreshed as they were spiritually fed at the Shanghai Free Christian Church, receiving a much-needed break from a rigorous schedule of teaching, training, and discipling the Chinese. Several of the CIM directors had started the church to minister to the many expatriates living in Shanghai and to be a blessing to the missionaries coming through on their many travels.

Our goodbyes were extremely difficult. My parents left on Monday, April 11, 1938, to return to the mission by a different route. I will never forget the night before their departure. Mother was wearing a bright red blazer, a white blouse, and a black skirt. As she was tucking me in, she looked at me lovingly while she hugged and kissed me. Then she said, "Cuddle-mousy," (an endearing name she called me at tender, special times), "tomorrow when you wake up, we won't be here, but the Lord Jesus will be." Then she hugged me again. When I awoke the next morning, I realized that Mother was right—she and Daddy were gone. However, she was also wrong. I wanted to see Jesus, but I could not find Him.

Mom and Dad had left with heavy hearts. God had called them both individually, and they had promised to serve Him and the Chinese together. Almost ten years before, they had joined hands in marriage in this very same city, Shanghai. Now their path led them back to Chongren in the province of Jiangxi without us children.

In a letter Mom wrote to her family before leaving Shanghai, she mentioned that they would have loved to stay longer:

> How lonely it will be when we get back to the station. The other morning, as soon as our little girl opened her eyes, she begged us to stay longer, but we cannot stay away from the mission station too long. Since we will be alone this summer without the children, we are staying on the station. This trip has cost us an arm and a leg, so we won't be going to our summer retreat in the mountains. We will be able to manage in spite of the heat....Please pray for the children that they will do all right in school and that they won't be too homesick. They cannot understand why we have to be separated.

Both of my brothers had already been in Shanghai at the children's home for a year and a half. They were used to life in the big city. Things were different for me, however. I was used to a small town with no cars, streetcars, city buses, or rickshaws. Shanghai was filled with huge buildings; broad, paved streets; and large shops. It was all very strange to me. I wasn't used to all of the hustle and bustle. We had tranquility in the interior, and my playmates were all Chinese. Here in the children's home, there were seven Caucasian kids including me. It was even difficult for me to understand the local Chinese. They spoke Shanghainese—a different dialect from the one I knew. All of this intimidated me, and I became very shy. I missed Mom, Dad, and my friends and was extremely homesick. For months, I cried into my pillow at night. We had phones in Shanghai, but there were none in the interior. Phone calls were out of the question. Mail came from my parents, but the war had escalated and the front line lay between us. A letter could take two weeks, a month, or even longer to arrive.

Shanghai was a very cosmopolitan city, unlike any other on earth. Actually, there were two Shanghais—the foreign one and the indigenous one. Most folks who had come from foreign lands could not believe how unique this city was, so different from what they had imagined or expected. It had become the home of Shanghailanders, Europeans, Americans, businessmen, merchants, adventurers, White Russian immigrants, and Jewish refugees from Nazi Germany. Many had come to make their fortunes. It was a typical British colonial outpost, with clubs, the waterfront, churches, schools, and the racecourse. However, it was also Chinese—a Chinese that was very different from the rest of China.

Shanghai was one of the world's great cities. Filmmakers and novelists helped to make her famous, often embellishing and mystifying stories about her. More shops and stores around the world bear the name "Shanghai" than the name of any other city. To the Chinese, it is the city of fashion and style.

Revolutionaries were also drawn to Shanghai and found a home there. The Chinese Communist Party was birthed in this city. Some of the fiercest political conflicts in recent history played out in Shanghai. If the city could speak, it would tell tales of unparalleled splendor amidst atrocious horror. Adopted into the English language, the word "shanghaied" alludes to sinister dealings of the underworld, including inducing others to do things through force or deceit.

The city Shanghai lies south of the Yangtze Estuary where the Huangpu River breaks off from the Wusong, a tributary of the Yangtze. Since 1916, the Wusong has been popularly known as "Suzhou Creek." The Huangpu River divides the city into two parts. To the west are the residential area and the center of town. To the east are the shipyards, docks, industrial quarters, and farmlands (known as the "Pudong"). Today this is one of the fastest growing residential areas of Shanghai. Many beautiful hotels, as well as a modern airport, are there. To this day, tourists take relaxing boat rides on the Huangpu River, gliding up and down the Shanghai riverfront past the wonderful, old, British-style buildings along the Bund. These include the former Customs House with its gigantic clock tower, the Hong Kong and Shanghai Banks, the Shanghai Club of yesteryear, and the former Palace Hotel, all still in typical European styles.

To truly understand Shanghai, China, one must delve into her past. In the 19th century, in June of 1840, the Opium War began. China was ruled at that time by the Manchurians. Their rulers prohibited the importation of opium, an addictive narcotic drug made from poppy seeds. Greed overruled, however, and the British East Indian Company, as well as many others, shipped large quantities of opium from India to China. Soon over half of all of China's imports from abroad were opium from India. After fierce fighting, the Chinese lost the war. For the first time, the British flag flew over some parts of the Chinese Empire, including Shanghai, which is a harbor city. China not only signed several treaties and agreements with the British, but also signed some with the French and the United States, officially making her a "treaty port." It was not long before foreigners came in droves. Additional agreements with the Chinese dealt with land regulations. Foreigners could lease land for an unlimited time.

On the waterfront of the Huangpu River, privileged zones were formed. This gave birth to the British, American, and French concessions. Several years later, the American and the British concessions became known as the International Settlement. The Chinese still far outnumbered the foreigners in these areas, and soon these areas were extremely cosmopolitan. The White Russians came after the fall of the Czar of Russia in 1917. Then in the 1930s, throngs of Jewish people fled Germany during the persecution of Hitler's Nazi regime and settled in Shanghai.

The streets in the International Section bore English names, such as Great Western Road, Bubbling Well Road, Avenue Rock Hill, Amherst Avenue, and Edward VII (which changed to Edouard VII in the French

Concession). There, common names included Avenue Joffre, Rue Lafayette, Route Chevalier, Avenue Pétain, and many others.

Most streets in the French settlement were beautiful, tree-lined, broad boulevards. It reminded the French of their beloved Paris. Beautiful villas and stately mansions adorned the streets. The police were Frenchmen who wore the same blue uniforms, including caps and large sticks that they twirled while blowing their whistles as the police did in France. Since India was part of the British Empire in those days, many of the police force in the International Settlement were Indian and were called the Red Turban Sikhs.

A most popular area was the "Bund." The word itself is an Anglo-Indian word that means quay, embankment, or a dike built of stone and dirt. Here people strolled, enjoying a balmy evening while merchants in stalls sold their goods. It was a promenade, a business hub, and a thoroughfare. The Huangpu River boasted watercrafts of every description. There were houseboats, sampans, bamboo rafts, fishing boats, sailboats, and ocean liners. During wartime, there were even French, British, American, and Japanese warships. The Huangpu River was the official entrance to Shanghai via the enormously broad Yangtze River.

The children's home on YuYuen Road was very small and had no yard, with only a small patio in the front that was hidden behind a huge iron gate. Behind the house was a concrete alley leading to other homes. Here we could roller skate, ride scooters, and jump rope. To really be able to run around and tumble on a lawn, we went to Jessfield Park. This park was about a twenty-minute walk away. When more children joined us at the home, our foster parents, the Wehmeyers, looked for a larger building.

In 1939, we moved to a beautiful villa in the French Concession. The yard was huge, with trees, flowers, and plenty of room for a swing set, sandbox, and play area. We were all extremely thankful for this wonderful home. I was especially awed by a wide, beautiful wooden staircase that led to a landing where you could bask in the sun as it shone through a marvelous, oversized, lead-glass window.

I had never seen such an elegant home with so many surprises. What a thrill it was for my roommate and me to climb a winding staircase to our bedroom in a turret. We often imagined that we were princesses or

Rapunzel, and we dreamed that a prince would rescue us some day. The attic area with its large room and stage was another source of wonder and excitement. On rainy days, we children amused ourselves by putting on plays or reenacting fairy tales.

Besides the Wehmeyers, who had been missionaries in Zhejiang and had been asked to move to Shanghai to start the children's home, we also had a single missionary lady who helped care for us. Poor soul. She was an easy target on which to play tricks. One day, one of the boys rigged a bucket with water above her bedroom door. When she opened the door, she got completely soaked. Of course, none of us knew anything about the culprit when she questioned us. Another time, she ran out of her bedroom yelling, "There is someone in my bed! There is someone in my bed!" When the housefather tried to calm her down and went to investigate, he found a mop on her pillow and two more pillows under the blanket.

Occasionally, she did get even with us. After lights out at night, we were not allowed to talk to our roommates or even to whisper. If she heard us, and I'm sure she often listened at our doors, she would come in armed with an extremely sticky adhesive tape that she firmly fastened over our mouths. Pulling the tape off the next morning was not only painful, but also it left a mark above and below our lips that was very hard to remove. Needless to say, it was very embarrassing to face our schoolmates and teachers with those marks on our faces. Her time as a "helper" was short-lived.

During the twelve years I spent in the children's home in Shanghai, I lived with more than forty different children of six or seven different nationalities. The majority were missionary kids (MKs) like us, but others were the children of business people who lived in inland China. We were, for the most part, a very close-knit group, sticking together and looking out for each other. Of course, we had our ups and downs, including some disagreements and even some fights, but we were never bored. We were kept busy attending school, walking there together, doing homework, participating in sports, and playing together. We learned to share and not be selfish, to be considerate, to take care of the younger children, and to adjust to changes without complaining. These are things for which I will always be grateful.

At times, with fifteen to twenty children in the home, life had to be very regimented. Breakfast began at 7 A.M. with Bible reading and prayer. A bowl of "she-fan," a porridge cooked with lots of water and rice, and a peanut butter and jelly sandwich or two were the norm. Then we were off to school that began at 8 A.M. and concluded at 1 P.M. We had our main meal of the day when we got home, before we began our homework. All of us gathered around the large dining room table, and, under the supervision of our houseparents, we studied. Only after homework was completed were we allowed to play. Croquet, softball, and field hockey were among our favorites. Scripture was again read before a simple evening meal. Then we would read or play games again. Games included Shanghai Millionaire (the local version of Monopoly), Chinese Checkers, board games, Pit, and a number of other card games. Bedtime depended on the age group. One of the adults prayed with us before lights out.

We seldom were given sweets or candy, but Christmas and Easter were exceptions. At Christmas, we would get a plate filled with nuts, fruit, and candy. At Easter, we were treated to a small basket with all kinds of Easter goodies. There were sugar eggs, large and small, and some wonderful chocolate ones as well. What a delight! I can still remember the taste of those treats! I especially remember one particular Easter morning when we each went to the sunroom, where our baskets were lined up on the windowsill. Uncle Wehmeyer, as we called our foster father, read the Easter story. We sang some hymns, and then we eagerly received our baskets. Among a number of small eggs, each basket contained one large candy egg. To our absolute horror, the large egg in each and every basket had been eaten in half! We were all in shock and completely appalled that anyone could be so low! We all sat down as the adults attempted to discover the culprit. No one would admit their grievous act or accept responsibility, although we were questioned over and over again.

After the adults left, we were all in an uproar. Who would dare to do that to all of us? Did he or she not know what that meant to their brothers and sisters, who so seldom got treats? Still no one confessed. Then my brother, Fred, being the eldest of the group, spoke up:

You all know the story about Jonah disobeying the Lord. He ran away from God and boarded a ship because of his disobedience. The Lord sent a horrible storm and everyone aboard thought they were going to drown. The sailors tried to find out who caused the storm, but no one admitted to being the guilty one. Then they drew lots, and the lot fell on Jonah. So Jonah confessed and told them his story.

This is what we are going to do. We are going to pray, then we are going to cast lots, and the one who draws the short one is the guilty one.

That is exactly what we did, and the lot fell on the guilty person. One of the boys confessed that he had snuck down the stairs early in the morning and bitten into every large egg in the baskets. After we were finished with him, there was no need for the adults to discipline him! From Mrs. Wehmeyer's diary, we know that she prayed earnestly and fervently that morning that the Lord would honor our childlike faith. She had heard what Fred proposed and that we all were in agreement.

I am extremely thankful that the Word of God was presented to us several times each day. Although I became a follower of Jesus much later, we did hear the Bible stories, and they had an impact upon our lives. During our devotions at breakfast one morning, Mr. Wehmeyer asked, "Who knows when God created the world?" My brother Fred quickly raised his hand, "It was in January!"

"What makes you say that?" questioned Uncle Wehmeyer.

"Well," answered Fred, "the Bible says: 'In the beginning God created the heaven and the earth' (Genesis 1:1 KJV), and the beginning is January." That was my brother—a deep thinker!

Chapter 4

Warm Welcomes and Sad Goodbyes
(1939-1941)

WAR ALWAYS INVOLVES heartache, and we were not exempt. As the war condition became more volatile, our parents' original plans to have us home each summer during the long holidays were eventually taken out of their hands. We were separated by an insurmountable barrier—the frontline.

Shanghai was occupied by the Japanese. My parents were in the Kuomintang area under Chiang Kai-shek. Mother wrote in her report from 1939:

> To see our children, who are in Shanghai, again was a longed for wish. But would it be fulfilled? Again and again this was the question. As the time came closer, we made all of the arrangements. A letter came, the way is open, nothing stands in the way. Only one thing we were clear about. We cannot let the children come into the interior, since our mission station lies in the war zone.
>
> All the highways are torn open and travel is very, very difficult. Since our passports were lost when we turned them in to renew our visas we hoped that our mayor would issue a certificate for travel. But our efforts were in vain and we had to disband our plans. It was not easy, but instead of going to our children we went to Magushan to escape the heat, since it was by now already July. But the thought about our children did not let me go.

We had prayed so fervently and often and the Lord guided so graciously. The Lord led us to discuss the matter with our missionary family. We all prayed about it and He gave us the inner assurance to try the voyage, even without our passports. So without any further ado we left and in three days we were at the coast in Ningbo. The whole way no one asked about our papers. On the whole trip the people were helpful to do what they could. Also in Ningbo we got our exit permit without any problem. Was that not of the Lord?

Apparently, crossing the enemy line, my parents were required to get a special permit to enter Japanese territory. Mother continued:

Unexpectedly we arrived in Shanghai. Our daughter was playing in the yard when we arrived by taxi. Oh the joy, to see each other again after one-and-a-half years. She immediately recognized her Daddy and put her arms around his neck. I was amazed how she so vividly remembered everything. Both boys were not at home. What a surprise when they got back. Fred exclaimed, "Oh, Mom!!"

Seven wonderful weeks we were allowed to be with them. Oh, if there only would be no good-byes. It was not easy for the children. I have seen again what it costs them to work all of this through. They cannot understand why we cannot be in Shanghai. Fred doesn't say much, he is a courageous boy, and yet he could not quite hide his feelings. It was wonderful that they could come with us to the ship, but the crowds were so huge that unfortunately they could not come on board. There they stood with all the children from the home and the house parents, waiting until our ship started to move.

I remember this visit from my parents vividly. Whenever Mom and Dad left to do their multitude of errands and we did not go along, I stood in the yard by the large iron gate until they came back. I was only seven years old and was afraid they would leave again. Our one and only professional family photo was taken at that time. To this day, it hangs in my bedroom. In my mind, I can still see us standing at the pier in Shanghai, Mom and Dad waving "goodbye" with white handkerchiefs as the boat slowly pulled away.

A few weeks later, we received news that my parents had not really left that day. They stored their belongings in their cabin and went back on deck, where, to their surprise, they found that they were still in the harbor. The ship had lost one of its iron doors, which had to be searched for and then fished out of the river. The delay caused them to leave at 4 A.M. When I heard about what had happened, I wanted to cry. Had we stayed longer at the pier, we could have spent one more day with Mom and Dad.

In 1940, we got to go home to the interior. That stay brings back many precious memories. We were able to enjoy the lovely home Daddy had built in Chongren. To me it was a beautiful house. With limited resources Mom tried to make it a haven for all of us. She was especially thankful for the wood-burning stove she had been able to bring from Germany. Today it would be considered an antique and a rare find. A Chinese stove would have smoked up the whole kitchen. Mother, with the help of our cook, was able to prepare meals with ingredients that often had to be substituted in the recipe. Local stores did not carry foreign ingredients.

As a family we ate three meals a day. We sat at the dining room table covered with a white tablecloth, set properly with white cloth napkins. Since our yard produced a variety of flowers, Mother usually had more than one bouquet of flowers somewhere in our home. I am deeply grateful to her for bringing beauty and decorum into our lives amidst much of the filth and squalor of our surroundings outside of the mission station.

To this day, I am grateful for the modern conveniences in my current bathroom. There in the Chongren house we had no running water. We used a wooden tub and a water heater that was heated with wood once a week for baths. A stand with a large ceramic basin and pitcher with water was used for sponge baths and washing hands. The toilet was a large bucket covered by a square wooden seat with a lid. Newspapers cut neatly into squares and hung on a hook were our toilet paper. The bucket was emptied once a day by our helper.

We had no electricity, running water, air conditioning, or central heat. We had no modern-day conveniences, but it was home, and we loved it. The furnishings were spartan compared to today's elaborate interior designs, but we did not mind.

On one of the shelves on the bookcase in Daddy's office was a photo of his brother who had immigrated to the United States in 1925. Uncle

Otto and his family lived in New Jersey. Many times, I would stand in front of that photo and stare at my uncle and aunt with their two daughters. I wondered what they were like and what it would be like to live close to each other, be friends, and play together. One sacrifice made by a missionary kid is growing up without family.

The "pièce de résistance" in the living room was a pump organ Mom loved to play. Couches and easy chairs, as well as dining room and office furniture, had been shipped from Boyang, the last mission station where my parents had been before furlough.

A broad staircase daddy designed led to a large attic, which had a walkout terrace built into the roof. He was especially proud of this accomplishment.

The large yard surrounding our home had a play area, a meticulously planted vegetable garden, and a fenced side yard where Mom had her chickens and ducks. Most of our vegetables and berries came from our own garden. The eggs and meat came from our fowl and provided delicious Sunday dinners. Beef was not a commodity, since very few Chinese, if any, owned cows. Most mission stations had their own well, just as we did. The well was also used to cool watermelon, cheese, butter, canned milk, and other perishables that had to be ordered from the coast through the China Inland Mission. These items were placed in a bucket and lowered into the deep, cold water.

That summer we also went up to Magushan to escape the heat. Mother's family had sent enough funds for my parents to build a small bungalow, just as several other missionary families had done. It had been fun to live in the long house up the road with the other missionaries, but now we had our own place.

Evenings were especially fun. After dinner, most of the missionaries would gather on an open field behind our house to play "Ring-Toss." Some rainy nights they would gather on our verandah/living room or at someone else's home. By the light of an oil lamp or two, we played games. Some exercised their minds playing chess, while others discussed the news of the day. The war situation was always on people's minds. We usually ended the evening with singing and prayer.

Sunday mornings were always special. Just after daybreak, one of the missionaries would take his trumpet and situate himself on the mountainside across from our house. He played wonderful hymns and tunes to usher in the Lord's day. As soon as I woke up, I opened my shutters, put my arms across the windowsill, and searched diligently to see if I could find the musician in the densely-wooded forest. Soon my brothers joined me, and all three of us had a contest to see who could spot Uncle Victor first. Since we had no blood relatives on the mission field, we addressed all missionaries as uncle and aunt.

It was wonderful to take long walks, hike up one of the highest peaks early some mornings to see the sun rise and have a picnic breakfast, and play with the other missionary children whose families were also seeking to escape the heat in the cities. Family times were the most cherished. Daddy would take us swimming in the cool streams that were in abundance or to some waterfall. In the evenings, we would gather around as Dad read us stories.

We also had chores to do. Fetching fresh, clean water from a spring was not my favorite chore. Walking along a rocky path down to the source of the spring in the summer heat took us about twenty minutes. Walking back to the house loaded down with several pitchers or buckets full of cold water was exhausting. I am sure that by the time we got home the water was no longer ice-cold, but at least it was clean and pure. Water purity was always a concern, and trying to keep the intestines healthy was a must. A veteran missionary had built his house next to the spring. That had made us all envious. He had only to step out his front door to get a cool drink. We all got our drinking water from this spring.

It was not only the heat and mosquitoes that bothered us. We also had to be careful where we walked, since poisonous snakes were often hiding in the underbrush. Our missionary doctor treated villagers for snakebite more often than we liked. The Chinese liked to catch snakes and use the meat to enhance some of their vegetable dishes. Other parts were used for medicinal purposes.

Other creatures also lurked in the mountains. On one occasion, Mom packed a picnic and the family went to our favorite swimming hole. As the three of us played in the water while Mom read a book, we heard Dad's stern voice tell us to hurry and pack up. We did not understand, but the urgency in his voice told us to obey immediately. Quickly we grabbed our belongings as we saw what looked like a number of dogs in the distance. Daddy told us not to run but to get away as fast as we could. He explained, "That pack of animals you saw were not dogs. They are wolves." Dad then started to pray and ask the Lord to protect us, as we moved swiftly along the mountain paths.

One of our great loves was wild blueberries. We were always ready for Mom's blueberry pancakes, and certain mountainsides had lots of blueberry bushes. Armed with buckets and containers, my brothers and I gladly went looking for the luscious and delicious berries. I'm sure we ate as many as we picked.

One day while picking blueberries, we heard the shrill voice of a woman calling, "Lao-foo, lao-foo, Chiu-ming, Chiu-ming," which means, "Tiger, tiger, save life, save life!" An older woman with small, bound feet appeared at the top of the hill, screaming and crying, trying to run down the many stone steps that were built into the path. We did not hesitate but immediately turned around and started to run as fast as we could down the path. Blueberries flew right and left, but we did not care. She called after us, and we knew this was serious. Tigers did attack humans if they were hungry enough, and it had happened before in these mountains. Out of breath and shaking, we arrived home to tell our story. I have often wondered if the old lady with her small, bound feet made it safely back to her family like we did.

All too soon, the time on Magushan came to an end. The summerhouse was closed up and locked, the bags were packed, and the sedan chairs arrived. Mom and I were carried down the mountain. The boys shared a second sedan chair with the luggage, taking turns being carried and walking with Dad.

After several hours of walking, we noticed that the sedan carriers were getting restless. They started talking excitedly among themselves. Suddenly one of them shouted, "Lao-foo, Lao-foo," or "Tiger, Tiger." Others joined in. They wanted to stop and lower the chairs to the ground, but Dad knew that was not wise. How could we escape? The path down the mountain was narrow and steep, often packed with stone steps hewn into the mountainside. There was no way out. We could not hide. With the words, "Buh-pa, buh-pa," or "Don't be afraid, don't be afraid," my father marched to the front of the group and resolutely opened his oilcloth umbrella. As he held it high and started to sing a hymn, a large dog jumped across the path in front of him, followed by a growling tiger. I could clearly see both animals, and I was shaking with fear. My mother held me tight. As soon as the poor dog and his pursuer disappeared into the woods, Dad thanked the Lord that the hungry tiger chose a dog as his meal.

Once again back at the mission station in Chongren, Mom and Dad seriously thought about making our trip to Shanghai in time for the starting of school in September. The war between the Japanese and Chang Kai-shek's troops had escalated. We were in the war zone, and Shanghai was in Japanese-occupied territory. Rumors of war with all its atrocities reached us in the interior. In some areas, there was heavy fighting.

My parents wrestled with serious questions. Should we attempt the dangerous trip back to the coast? Could we make it? Did we dare trust the Lord to go before us and keep us safe? We prayed much and tried, without the help of TV, radio, or even a newspaper, to learn what we could about the front line. Mom and Dad finally decided to lean heavily upon the Lord and try to get us through to Shanghai. Once again, we had the difficult task of saying "goodbye" to Mom, since Dad was taking us.

A week or two went by, and Mom and the junior missionary lady had not heard a word from their travelers. Alone at the mission station, they were shocked to hear the voices of children—and these were not Chinese children! Then they heard my father's voice! Mother came running and could not believe that all four of us were back home again. It had been too dangerous to continue on to Shanghai with roads torn up and rail lines bombed. There simply had been no way to get through enemy lines.

Now back in Chongren, we faced a decision regarding our schooling. Our ever-ingenious father had a plan! Although he had no access to materials with which to teach us, he still wanted to try to home school us. This was in addition to his many responsibilities of sermon preparation, visitation, discipling young men, teaching the Chinese, setting up conferences, taking trips to the outlying posts, writing his monthly reports, and doing many other duties. Mom's little study at the end of the hall was set up as our classroom. I don't remember much about the lessons, but I do remember that we had an overabundance of flies in that little room. It seemed that they bothered us the most whenever father left the compound to do his ministry and we had to work hard at our assignments.

Ballpoint pens were unknown to us in those days, but we had an inkwell and penholders. The pointed pens could be detached from the holder. My brother Werner was pretty good at catching flies. Once caught, we speared them on the penholders and drowned the creatures in the inkwell. When the pens became dull, we removed them from the holder and replaced them with new ones. It did not take long before the inkwell was full of flies. We constantly needed to fill the inkwell with new ink and used an enormous number of pens. I wonder if we impressed Dad with our diligence that required so much ink and so many pens! Here my memory leaves me!

One of our favorite activities was swimming in the river. Dad took us out several times to our special spot, a sandbank upstream. There he taught the boys to swim. I played in the water, built sandcastles, and had a wonderful time. We admired our father most when he dove off a large, high concrete block at the edge where the river ran deep.

One sunny afternoon we decided to play in the sand at our sandbank. The river was running very low that day, and there were sandbanks everywhere. Father was not with us. As we turned the corner to get to the river, we were shocked to see our sandbank covered with incense sticks that were used for idol worship in the Buddhist temples! We knew that after the twelve-inch-long bamboo sticks had been dipped in incense, they had to be dried. What better place to dry them than in the sun on a sandbank? A smart merchant, who no doubt planned to sell these sticks, had planted hundreds of them right where we wanted to play.

Many times, we had seen men and women, and even children, lighting these sticks and then falling on their knees in front of wild-looking idols. Some of these scary idols had twenty-four arms or two heads with grotesque faces and distorted bodies. Some held daggers as if they were ready to kill. They had been made by men and could help no one. We knew that and felt sorry for the misled masses. After all, Mom and Dad were here to help the Chinese to see the Light and find true peace with God. So we felt we had a mission to accomplish. It did not take us long to decide what to do with these tools of idol worship.

We picked the sticks up one by one and broke them in half, until every single one was destroyed. Then we went home, feeling satisfied we had done God's work.

At an early age, I was aware that the Chinese had different beliefs than my parents. There were times at night when I would hear a ruckus and loud noises up and down the street. People would be screaming, yelling, and holding torches high up in the air while racing through the street adjacent to our property. It scared me terribly. When mother came into my bedroom to console me, I could not stop shaking and crying. She had a hard time explaining to me that these people thought they were chasing evil spirits and demons through the streets. I could not understand why they did that. Mom always prayed with me and assured me that the Lord Jesus was right there with me and that He would protect me.

According to the Chinese, a person has three souls. One soul goes into the grave, another goes to the kingdom of the dead, and the third goes into an ancestral tablet. This tablet is inscribed with the name of the deceased. It is then put in a place of honor in the home or in the hall of ancestors along with other tablets. The eldest son has the responsibility to regularly pay homage to the ancestors. To honor and respect parents and forebears was a strong tradition that was deeply rooted in Confucian ethics.

Often at night, I would hear a woman crying in the street because one of her children was sick. She would walk down to the river close by our house, calling out in a lamenting singsong. Her mourning sounds were horrible to hear as she pled with the soul of the child to return. She held the corners of her apron with one hand, while with her other hand she performed a sweeping motion as she tried to catch her child's soul and place it in the open apron. She believed this would help her child get better.

The Chinese in our area were also certain that evil spirits could only walk straight lines. During my father's twenty-five years in China, he traveled hundreds of extra miles, especially to the outlying posts, because the roads and paths were always crooked. He had to walk those continual bends and curves. Many of the homes also had a brick wall in front of the main entrance. The only way to enter was to go around the wall either on the left or on the right. Often you would see a pair of scissors, a mirror, a sieve, and other paraphernalia over the front door to ward off evil spirits. The Chinese believed that the scissors could cut them in half, the mirror would shock them when they beheld their ugly image, and they would get lost in the sieve.

Months went by. Father did his best to teach us, but he soon realized that it was almost impossible to do all of his work as well. As always, my parents sought the Lord for guidance. By faith, they claimed that Father would be successful in taking us through enemy lines, and preparations were made. I can still see us standing in a circle in our living room with Father earnestly pleading with God to help us reach our destination. Then he began to sing the doxology, and we as a family joined in:

Praise God, from whom all blessings flow,
Praise Him, all creatures here below,
Praise Him above, ye heavenly host,
Praise Father, Son, and Holy Ghost.
Amen!

It was extremely difficult to leave home again. I knew I would desperately miss Mom and Dad, our Chinese friends, and all the familiar places. We could not help but wonder when we would see each other again. We never dreamed that because of World War II, we would not see Mom and Dad again until July of 1946.

The situation in China had become extremely volatile. I did not know it at the time, but I would never again see the house my father built or the mission station. The Japanese burned the mission house to the ground and destroyed the compound. It was not until forty-six-and-a-half years later that I saw Chongren again, and I did not recognize any of it. Time changed the China I knew. The place where I spent so much of my early childhood is now only a memory.

Chapter 5

Treacherous Journeys (1941)

IT WAS APRIL 1941, and we were making a second attempt to get back to school in Shanghai. A seasoned missionary lady, who had served the Lord for many years in China as a nurse and midwife, joined Dad and the three of us children on the trip. This missionary lady was retiring and going back to her homeland.

It was remarkable that we made it through Jiangxi, our province, then on through Zhejiang. It was not an easy journey. Although the roads had been torn up and the rail lines were partially destroyed by the aggressive Japanese planes, God led us through. Before reaching Shanghai, however, there was yet another obstacle to overcome. We had to traverse a large bay in northern Zhejiang by boat. Daddy had been warned that we were in the war zone and that we had to cross over into Japanese-occupied territory. Nothing seemed to deter him. We had come this far. The Lord had protected us, and Dad was convinced He would continue to do so.

As he had done so many times before, Dad gathered us around and began to pray. It always amazed me when I heard my father talk to God. He was strong, self-disciplined, and determined; yet when he prayed, he was as simple as a child was. He talked to God as I would talk to him. I trusted my father, knowing that he would do what was best for me. That was the way it was between Daddy and God.

Sedan chairs had been hired to take us out to the boat that was waiting in the bay. The carriers and Daddy waded knee-deep through muddy and slimy waters. It was slow and laborious trying to make any headway. Soon we realized that we were not alone. Merchants, farmers, women, and children hurried along as fast as they could to reach the boat. This was possibly a last chance for all of us to cross the bay during those war-filled days. It was also extremely dangerous since the tide was coming in. At first, the waves played gently about the men's legs, but soon the water became violent and rough, with huge waves that threatened to engulf us. A strong wave almost toppled the sedan chairs, and the carriers had a difficult time keeping them steady.

We plodded slowly along, trying to control our fright. It was with deep relief and praise to God that we finally made it safely to the sampan. As we were hoisted up and lifted into the boat, I saw huge waves crashing over some of the children. Their parents were holding onto them as best they could. Then I saw a sight that greatly disturbed me. A woman who was holding a little baby in her arms tripped and fell as she fought the tidal waves. She screamed and begged the other passengers to help her and her baby, but no one did.

Another wave crashed over more people who could not hold their stand and who obviously could not swim. I was horrified as I watched the waves carry them out to sea. I will never forget the look on their faces as they desperately thrashed in the water, knowing that there was no hope. The Chinese believed that if they rescued someone, they would be responsible for that person for the rest of his or her life. Very seldom would you hear of a Chinese person helping another in a life and death situation.

Our faith and patience were tried time and again, as the boatman and his helpers did not move. Days went by, and we wondered if they knew something we didn't. Each family's food supply ran low and had to be rationed. Still we did not move. The days seemed to get longer and longer. There were fights and angry words as people irritated each other on that crowded sampan. We were soon to find out why we did not leave that area.

One evening, after endless days of waiting, we heard harsh voices outside our little nook on the boat. Daddy stepped out onto the long plank that ran alongside the sampan and found several soldiers of the Kuomintang, Chang Kai-shek's troops. He recognized them immediately. Mother had often helped wounded soldiers in their makeshift hospitals in Chongren. Many times Daddy had gone with her and preached to them, giving tracts or New Testaments to those who could read.

One of the soldiers waved a flashlight in Dad's face, "Do you have a permit from the Nationalist Army to leave our territory?"

Dad shook his head, "All I have is my passport."

Then they commanded sternly, "But that is not enough. You have to come with us immediately. Leave the children and the white lady here on the boat!"

Dad did not know what to do. We all wondered what would happen to us and if we would make it to our destination. No one had told Dad that this remote corner of the world required a travel permit, and he had conferred with many Chinese in the area. All he could do was follow the soldier's orders.

A few days passed, and no word came about where father was. Then one evening a carriage drawn by water buffalos arrived at the boat. A Chinese man jumped off the coach onto the boat and told Aunt Minnie that we had to come with him. She asked, "Where is Lin Muh-si? Did he send you to get us?" He only shrugged his shoulders and urged us to hurry before the tide came in again. All we could do was pack our bags and follow the man into the darkness.

Back in the village we learned that Dad had been sent all the way back to the capital city of the province to obtain the required permit. No one had heard from him or seen him. I was very concerned. Where was Daddy, and would I see him again? These were valid questions in those war-torn years.

Daddy also wondered what had happened to us. Had we been sent on with the Chinese in the boat, or had we been ordered back like he was? How could he find us? As we walked through the dark streets one evening with Aunt Minnie, we saw a foreigner in a dingy sidewalk restaurant. In the scant light from an oil lamp, I thought he looked like Daddy. Indeed, it was him. He had just arrived from mostly walking the long, dusty roads from the capital.

Dad had felt an urgency to pray that we were safe and that he would find us and had stopped to ask the shop owner if he had seen any foreigners in his village. And here we were! What a miracle-working God! Who had sent the coach to pick us up and bring us to this particular town? Why did Aunt Minnie choose to walk this particular street in the dark where Dad had stopped at a sidewalk restaurant to inquire about his family? Only the Lord can arrange circumstances like that.

Once again, we were on our way to Shanghai. We wondered if we would reach our goal this time. After a few days on another boat, the boatman told Dad that he could not go any further. We had crossed the enemy line, and the boatmen could not venture further into enemy territory. All of the passengers had to wait until the tide went out and then wade to shore. It was quite an undertaking for Dad to oversee the safety of three young children and one lady over sixty years of age. Travelers were willing to carry our luggage for a high price, but there was no way to hire sedan chairs or a coach.

My father jumped out of the boat and sank deep into the mud. The slimy, muddy ground reached far out into the bay. One after another, Dad took us into his arms and carried us to where we would not sink into the mud above our knees. Then he carefully led Aunt Minnie out to where she could grasp my hand, and together we sloshed and tediously shuffled through the black, slimy mess. Daddy went back to pay the boatman, who warned him to hurry because the tide would be coming in soon.

When I saw Daddy go back, I started to cry and would not walk to the shore. Aunt Minnie's insistent pleading did not help. I was sure I would lose my daddy again. Then I heard my father calling my name and telling me to keep on walking. From the stern tone of his voice, I knew I had better obey. In the distance, he had seen the white crowns of the tide rolling in, and he knew that I might not make it if I did not move toward the shore immediately. Daddy had learned that in this area the tide was especially strong and could have easily carried me out to sea.

With long, difficult strides, my father tried to catch up with us. We were trying hard to reach the shore, but it was almost impossible to make any headway since I was immersed in mud up to my knees.

Small ripples of water began to come closer, until they were lapping at our legs. We could see the shore that the boys had reached safely when Daddy caught up with us. He put me on his shoulders and supported Aunt Minnie with one arm.

The shoreline was crammed with watching Chinese. We would have greatly appreciated their help, but to them we were the yellow devils, and they were afraid of us. These people had never seen a foreigner before. Then a wonderful thing happened. A man broke away from the crowd and dared to overcome his fears as he came to our rescue. With his help, we soon reached the safety of the shore. We had eluded the dangerous tide that had mocked us with its forceful roar as it closed in on the bay. Daddy was the last one to set his foot on the shore.

In our struggle for life, fear had been put aside. Now the Chinese smiled and laughed as they welcomed us, the foreigners. Soon one of them called the mission headquarters in Shanghai. We considered it a miracle that in this small, remote corner of the world they had a post office with a telephone.

Daddy took us to a restaurant, where he ordered a large bowl of noodle soup for each of us. In China, it takes a while to cook a meal, and we were disappointed that a truck from the mission came to pick us up just before the meal was ready. Since we had not had a decent meal in days, we could almost taste the delicious noodles in the broth with vegetables. The driver could not wait. The Japanese soldiers were always on the prowl, and he did not dare risk falling into their hands.

Just before getting into the front seat with the driver, Daddy bowed his head in humble adoration toward the Lord. With a voice full of praise, he thanked his Heavenly Father for His care and safekeeping on this treacherous journey. We, the weary, hungry, dirty, and spent wanderers were glad to get to the children's home in Shanghai. With faith in God, determination, and self-discipline, Daddy had achieved what no other white man up to this point had been able to do—we had crossed the large bay close to Ningbo into enemy territory during a time of war.

Dad was anxious to get home to Mom, who was all alone on the mission station in Chongren. It was not good for a missionary lady to be alone during wartime. There were always soldiers from the Kuomintang regime around, seeking help for the wounded or looking for a handout or a free meal. In those days, to be a soldier was the lowest class in the social ranks of society. After so many years of fighting the Japanese, they were not well-equipped. They were not fed properly, and their lives were not worth much. If they were ill or wounded, they were often left behind. Mother was grateful to the Lord that in all her years in China she was never molested or treated disrespectfully. Dad was extremely anxious to get back to her.

At dawn one morning, Dad left with his few belongings, including the ever important "Poo-kai," the bedroll, and a small suitcase. A Chinese was helping him carry the load. He did not get very far out of town when he ran into a Japanese officer. "Where do you think you are going?" was the harsh question from the man in uniform.

"I have to return to Jiangxi, the province where I make my home," came Dad's answer.

When asked to show his papers and permit, father did not have any. In a very gruff voice, the officer said, "You are not going anywhere. You are staying right here, and don't dare let me catch you again." My dad's pleadings that he must return to Chongren and his wife who was alone fell on deaf ears.

Never one who was deterred easily, Daddy waited a few days and then tried again. He made good headway this time and reached the large city of Ningbo in Zhejiang, the neighboring province. Here he was received by some Chinese Christians, who took him in and gave him shelter for the night. Since Dad had a habit of always leaving very early in the morning on his trips, he did so this time also. As he and his carrier were turning a corner, Dad was shocked to encounter the same Japanese officer who had accosted him in Shanghai a few days before. The officer immediately recognized my father. He could not believe that Dad had defied his strict order and was now standing in front of him. He drew his gun, pointed it at Dad, and said, "I gave you an order not to travel. If I ever see you again, you will not live to see another day and especially not your wife." With these words, he turned around and marched off with long strides.

Now Dad was separated from his children and his wife. At that point, he wondered if he would ever see any of us again. Then he did what was second nature to him—he prayed and asked for God's guidance.

Leaving early the next morning with a small suitcase, he walked for many miles. Trains were not running, and buses were hard to find and were often broken down. Dad walked most of the way until he made it back to my mother, who was thrilled to see him. He related the many trials he had to pass through: the dangerous trip to Shanghai via the bay near Ningbo, the scary encounter with the Japanese officer, and the perilous trip back to her. They held each other close.

I did not see my parents again for a little more than five years. I had to wait that long to learn of the many challenging experiences they faced during those years we were apart.

Chapter 6

Escapades, Adventures, and New Life (1941–1946, in Shanghai)

FOR ME, LIFE in Shanghai became routine. Of utmost importance was school, of course. There were between twenty and thirty pupils in my class that consisted mostly of the children of an elite group of professionals, including the diplomatic core, businessmen, professors of some of the local universities, bankers, and office managers. The national backgrounds of those in my eclectic group of classmates were German, British, American, Russian, Chinese, Scandinavian, Swiss, Eurasian, and others. The school had been under the German system of jurisdiction and was considered one of the best schools in East Asia. Its prestige made it the school of choice for those seeking an excellent education for their children.

Some of my fondest memories of those school days are of parties to which I was invited and long afternoons spent in the homes of some of my friends. Pleasant times included such events as an Easter egg hunt at my American friend Virginia Smith's home or a delicious Chinese meal at Margaret Lou's or Anna Tsi's home. Wonderful birthday parties were held at my German girlfriend Inge Miss' home. These were residences that were beautifully decorated and surrounded by lovely yards with manicured green lawns and pretty flowers.

Since cars were scarce at that time and were used for driving the fathers to work, many of my friends had private rickshaws to take them places. Their Amahs, Chinese nannies, dressed in crisp white cotton Chinese blouses and black trousers always escorted them to special functions. The Amahs loved the parties, as it was a time for visiting and gossiping with the other children's Amahs. Since most mothers were busy with activities such as tea parties, social functions, and fund-raising activities, the Amahs were entrusted with the care of their children. As a missionary kid, I did not have a private rickshaw. I walked or took a public rickshaw if the distance was too great to walk. As I got older, I was often allowed to use Aunt Wehmeyer's bike since I did not have my own.

I remember several field trips we took into the outlying areas of Shanghai. One of the areas that was visited by the various classes was the Longhua Pagoda. A pagoda was usually an eight-sided tower that was reserved for evil spirits so that they had a place to live. The year that my class visited the Longhua Pagoda and its adjacent temple, we had fun playing in the area and having our brown-bagged sandwiches. While visiting the temple, several of my classmates took some incense sticks and, like the Chinese, stuck them in the containers in front of the idols. I knew this was an act of worship. Not wanting to be different from my classmates, I helped myself to some sticks and placed them in front of the idols as I had seen the Chinese do often in our area in the interior. It felt strange doing something that I knew was opposed to the teaching of my parents.

The third children's home we moved to was a double house. It had a large home in the front with a smaller one attached to it in the back. The house was at the end of an alley, off a long street called Great Western Road, now named Ian 'an Road. It was in the International Settlement. There were more than twenty rooms that helped house eighteen children. This was the largest number of children we had at one time during the twelve years that I called the children's hostel "home."

Every year we were required to be vaccinated for diseases such as cholera, typhus, typhoid, and smallpox. In Shanghai, I had a bout with malaria. I also contracted pneumonia every spring in my tenth, eleventh, and twelfth years. Medication was scarce during the war years, and penicillin was not yet available. The last time I had pneumonia was the worst. I was very ill and could not get better. Finally, a doctor from the mission, who was in a Japanese camp at the time, got permission to make a house call and came to see me. He told Mrs. Wehmeyer, our foster mother, that there was nothing he could do for me. We could only trust the Lord to be merciful and weather what he called "the nine-day crisis." If I lived to see the tenth day, there was a chance that I would pull through.

I will never forget the evening of the ninth day, when Aunt Wehmeyer came to my bedside. She brought my brothers, along with her eldest son and her only daughter. I had known her children since I was five years old, and they were like my brothers and sister. One by one they looked at me, hugged me, and then left. At the time, I had no idea why they had come.

Early the next morning, I vividly recall Aunt Wehmeyer running up the stairs, flinging the door to my bedroom open, and shouting, *"She lives! She is alive!"* My fever was down, and I was still breathing.

It took a long time for me to recuperate, and I remember spending many afternoons on a lawn chair under the willow tree in the yard. Many weeks of regular injections were the norm and were rather painful. Seven years later, when I was x-rayed at the Swiss border before crossing, my lungs still showed scar tissue from that experience.

Several children in the home took either piano or violin lessons. When I was eight years old, I too longed to learn how to play the piano. The Lord graciously provided me with a wonderful couple, Mr. and Mrs. Beck, who became my benefactors. They had lost two little boys, who were buried at the Bubbling Well Cemetery. For some reason, they wanted to do something special for a little girl, and they chose me. For five or six years, they paid for my piano lessons. My teacher was a kind gentleman from Romania. I remember him as being an excellent pianist who had a heavy accent. I will never forget Mr. and Mrs. Beck and their generosity to me. Thanks to their investment in a small, shy missionary kid, I learned to play the piano. Over the years, the Lord has allowed me to play for thousands of people in evangelistic crusades and churches, as well as for many other events on three different continents.

Not only did the Becks pay for my piano lessons, but also for many years they did something special on my birthday. Every year Mr. Beck would come and pick me up at the children's home. He and I rode in a special rickshaw to a wonderful tearoom, where I could choose any of the delectable pastries I wanted. I was so shy that I could not tell him what I liked, so he would choose for me. He always added a cup of hot chocolate. Then he would take me to one of the large department stores, where, with the help of one of the salesladies, I would choose a complete outfit, including dress, matching hat, socks, and shoes. Finally, Mr. Beck would take me to the toy department, where he would try to get me to tell him what I would like. Again, being so shy, I could never bring myself to tell him what I wanted. Several years I was presented with a beautiful doll that had eyes that could open and close.

One year I remember being determined to tell Mr. Beck that I wanted roller skates. Several of the children in the home had gotten skates, and I wished I had some. As determined as I was, I could not bring myself to tell Mr. Beck what I wanted. Again, I received a wonderful doll.

I will always remember feeling embarrassed as I returned to the home in my new clothes and bearing a beautiful gift because I felt sorry for the children who did not get anything new like I did. Quickly I would run to my room and change.

I don't think the Becks ever knew how much their love and concern meant to me, but I will always be grateful to them and cherish their memory. Later in life, their example made it easy for me to give and bless the lives of others as I had been blessed. It is a wonderful feeling to gladly share with those who have a need and to open my home to many, including strangers, whom the Lord places in my path.

While I was at the home in Shanghai, a young missionary lady joined the Wehmeyers to help with the enormous task of overseeing our growing-up years. Her name was Leni Wink. I knew her from the past during the summer months on Magushan in our province Jiangxi. At that time, she had been a new arrival to China and was still learning the language. During the vacation months in the mountains, she was a great asset to the missionary community.

Aunt Leni, as we called Miss Wink, could make stories and childhood fables come alive. She spent many hours with us children. I will always remember when she had us play Hansel and Gretel. One of my brothers was Hansel, and I was Gretel. The other brother had to play the birds that ate the crumbs so that Hansel and Gretel could not find their way back home. She was the witch. With a large cardboard nose and a black cape with a dark hood, she looked every bit the real scary witch. What fun it was to push her into the "oven." This was under the dining room table, where several chairs were set around it.

When Miss Wink came to help out at the children's home, I was delighted. She made it a point to take my brothers and me under her wings. We had been at the home the longest, and she knew us best. A special bond developed. The Wehmeyers, who had five children of their own, took care of us along with the help of Aunt Leni. There was order, discipline, and consequences when the rules were broken, but we also had many fun times with the adults. Chasing Uncle Wehmeyer around the house outside or around the large dining room table inside was exhilarating. Aunt Leni loved to play chess and could get upset when she lost. And many afternoons after we completed our homework, we could be found playing croquet with Aunt Leni, who always wore a large hanky tied around her neck to cool her in the summer heat.

One year all of us children went to visit some friends in the outlying area of Shanghai during the cold winter months. That morning, we found a large pit behind the house that was filled with what we thought was water. It had frozen over. We were delighted at the prospect of being able to ice skate. With our regular shoes on, we all had a few turns. Then my brother Werner dared to venture further into the middle of the frozen pit. The ice made strange noises and then started to break. Instead of panicking as my brother started to sink, we thought quickly and formed a human chain. As we stretched and reached, we all hollered out orders for Werner, who was finally pulled out of the pit. There was no way he could go home soaking wet because we knew Uncle Wehmeyer would surely notice and punish him. So we all shared the clothes we had. Someone gave him his shirt, another his socks, and someone else his jacket.

As we were sneaking into the house, being careful not to make any noise, we looked up to see Uncle Wehmeyer! He called all of us into his office and asked, "Is something wrong; why are you so quiet? Did you not have fun this afternoon?" We all assured him that everything was fine and that we did have fun. Then he said, "Is there something you want to tell me?" No one was eager to share with him what had happened.

"There is an awful odor coming from someone. In fact, it really stinks. Did one of you perhaps fall into a honey ditch? I see Werner is wearing a strange assortment of clothes," Uncle Wehmeyer said.

Early in the mornings men went through the streets and picked up the night soil from the people who had no flush toilets in their homes. They then would deliver their cargo to the sewer ponds of the farmers who used the night soil to fertilize their fields. It was precious to them. The color reminded the folks of honey, that is why the Shanghailanders called these carriers, "the men with the honey wagons."

Werner had fallen into one of these sewer pits. We had no idea that our wonderful frozen "lake" was a honey ditch! We confessed our transgression of ice-skating on the pit to Uncle Wehmeyer.

On rare occasions, we could travel by bus to the YMCA across from the "racecourse," now the "People's Park," in downtown Shanghai to swim in the Olympic-sized pool. Another girl from the children's home and I went one particular afternoon and met another school friend, Mary Koyamaya, a Japanese girl. Both of these girls were good swimmers, but I was not and had told them this. The three of us began playing in the shallow water, but it was not long before we drifted into deeper waters. My two companions were laughing and joking as they pushed me around, pulling me by my hands. They were having a good time, but I began to get scared. Once again, I warned them that I could not swim, but they just laughed.

For some reason, the lifeguard was on a break and no one was present to supervise the swimmers. The three of us were the only ones in the pool. Two girls were sitting at the far end of the pool by the diving boards, talking. Suddenly, I realized that the water was too deep. I could not stand any longer. I shouted that I could not swim and that the water was too deep. My two friends became concerned and started to try to push me to the side of the pool, but they were not strong enough. In their panic, they pushed and shoved me until I was going up and down, swallowing large amounts of water. In my nervousness, I began to call for help when I was under the water, and then I would keep my mouth tightly closed when I was above the water. I don't know how long this went on because I went unconscious. The girls by the diving board responded to my friends' desperate cries for help and came running. They were able to pull me out of the water as the lifeguard arrived.

The lifeguard put me across his knee, and a great deal of water rushed out of my mouth. It took a while before I responded to his procedures. When I came to, I found myself on a bench in the locker room. My head was throbbing, and I did not feel well. When I could finally leave, my friend from the children's home asked me again and again to please not tell anyone what had happened. On the bus ride home, I assured her that I would not tell anyone in the children's home about our scary episode. My word was my bond, and I kept that promise, even when the adults asked me if I felt unwell since my color was not good.

The years rolled on. The war still raged, and I was now a teenager. I still remember vividly the howling sirens announcing an air raid and the adults gathering us children into the hall under the staircase in case of bombs or shrapnel flying too close. The windows were cross-taped to prevent flying glass should the windows shatter. At night during an air raid, all-black window shades had to be lowered for a total blackout of the city.

In those days it was a common sight to see Japanese soldiers in the streets with the ever-present bayonets attached to their rifles. After fierce battles on many fronts in the Pacific, the Japanese Emperor finally surrendered. The war was one of the longest in modern times, beginning in 1937 and ending in August of 1945.

Thousands of allied servicemen came to Shanghai at the end of the war. They were the sailors, marines, soldiers, and airmen from Australia, England, Canada, and the United States. Honky-tonks and bars sprang up everywhere overnight. We learned about Glen Miller, Duke Wellington, and the big bands. Warships were anchored in the harbor at the Bund, flying flags from multiple nations. For the first time in my life, I met a black person. I was amazed by how white his teeth were and wondered why the inside of his hands and the soles of his feet were so much lighter than the outside.

Many of the China Inland Mission folks returned to Shanghai when Japan capitulated in August of 1945. Some had left for their homeland when the United States entered the war. Others were in Japanese camps in the Shanghai area or remained in the free Chinese territories. The mission headquarters had been occupied by the Japanese and had to be put back in order before it could once again be used as the hub for one of the largest mission organizations in China.

The Shanghai Free Christian Church, which had been started by CIM missionaries many years before, was opened again. Many of the GIs, soldiers, and sailors were Christians. They looked for fellowship and wanted to worship with believers, so they came to the church that we attended. Sunday after church, many of those young men went to the children's home. There was hardly a Sunday when we did not have half-a-dozen or more servicemen joining us for Sunday dinner. It was remarkable how Aunt Wehmeyer always made room for one more person at the table.

Soon the quality of our food improved. The GIs brought some of their food rations with them, and we saw foods we had never seen before, like huge cans of cheese, powdered milk, powdered eggs, canned fruit, vegetables, ham, meat, and our favorite—powdered ice cream. During the war years, we often had rice porridge with weevils for breakfast. Fruit was a rarity, and vegetables were scarce. Sometimes we got pork, but were appalled when we saw that the skin was still sprouting hairs. We hardly ever had chicken, and since cows were rare, we had no beef. To receive goodies from the soldiers was wonderful. We had not known what chewing gum and American candy was, but we learned quickly!

After Sunday dinner, many of the servicemen stayed for the afternoon. We had played stickball, but they taught us how to play softball. In the evening, they joined us for the evening service at church. After the church meeting, we would all meet at the home of some of the China Inland Mission secretaries who were involved with our young people's meetings, or we would go back to the children's home for light refreshments. We sang choruses to our hearts' content and heard testimonies from those who shared what the Lord had done for them. Some people dubbed it "the happy noise meeting."

Church life became interesting and fun. We attended Sunday school, church service, Sunday evening meetings, prayer meetings during the week, and young people's meetings on Friday nights. If anyone could get to heaven for having been in church, I am sure that I would be number one in line. But that is not how it works. I was religious. I knew the Bible fairly well, but I did not have a personal relationship with the Lord. Many times when I would hear a sermon about heaven and hell, I would tell the Lord that I was okay. After all, my parents were missionaries. I knew they had suffered much during their service for Him. Surely, the Lord would let me slip into heaven with them. I did not realize that God does not have grandchildren. The Bible only speaks about becoming a child of God, not a grandchild.

One day in March of 1946, a GI from North Carolina asked me to go with him to visit a sick friend. Before leaving her that afternoon, he quoted a Bible verse from the Gospel of John, where the Lord Jesus is talking to Nicodemus. Jesus said, "You should not be surprised at my saying, 'you must be born again'" (John 3:7). I don't remember anything else, but that verse would not leave my mind. In bed that evening, I kept hearing the words, "You must be born again." I knew what that meant. The Lord Jesus died for me. If I was the only sinner on this earth, He would still have died for me. I had to be born again. I had to believe in Him and ask Him to forgive my sins.

My greatest sin was not lying, cheating, disobeying, or treating the other kids badly. My greatest sin was unbelief. I knew the gospel story. I knew why God sent His only begotten Son, but I did not believe. I was just as lost as the Buddhists and the Taoists that my parents were trying to reach. That night I prayed and asked God to forgive me. I accepted Jesus Christ as my personal Savior. I will be forever grateful to Ralph Brunson from North Carolina for quoting a verse of Scripture that was not even meant for me. He obeyed the prompting of the Holy Spirit when he shared that verse. John 3:7 sealed my relationship with the Lord forever. I am only sorry that I never met Ralph again after he left Shanghai, China, in 1946. I wish I could have thanked him for helping me find my way to the Savior.

Whereas Scripture had once been boring and commonplace, it was now exciting to study the Word of God. In our youth group at the Shanghai Free Christian Church we were privileged to be visited by many men and women of God. The first city and major commercial center where people arrived, whether coming from overseas or inland China, was Shanghai. It was not only the GIs who influenced my life with their walk with God, but also others were influential in modeling godly lives. These included the leadership and missionaries of the China Inland Mission, as well as men and women from all walks of life.

Some of the people who had a profound effect upon my young life included Dawson Trotman, founder of The Navigators; Bob Pierce with Youth for Christ, who later founded World Vision and Samaritans Purse; Dave and Helen Morken with Youth for Christ, a fledgling organization at that time; Dr. Baker James Cauthen and his wife, Director of the Foreign Mission Board of the Southern Baptist Convention; Dick and Margaret Hillis with the China Inland Mission, who later founded Overseas Crusades; Roy Robertson, the first missionary of The Navigators; and Mrs. Helen Weller, who was an outstanding teacher on Daniel and Revelation and a CIM missionary.

At our young people's meetings I was challenged to live the Christian life in sincerity and truth. Bible study, personal devotions called "quiet time," and memorizing Scripture were a great part of our training. We were taught how to witness and how to lead someone to the Lord. All of these were invaluable lessons that have stayed with me throughout my life. It became a daily routine for me to have one hour of Bible study, prayer, and memorizing Scripture before breakfast. I loved learning new things and was grateful for the teaching that helped me to apply the Word of God to my life.

One day I came across the Lord's Prayer in the Gospel of John, chapter 17. I read where the Lord prayed: "Father, I want those you have given me to be with me where I am" (John 17:24). I started to wonder. It had been more than five years since I had seen my parents. What were they like? What had been their war experiences? Mail had only come sporadically, so there were many gaps in my knowledge of them and what had transpired in their lives. I wondered if I could also pray: "Father, I will that they who you have given to me shall be with me also."

I asked Aunt Leni if she thought it was appropriate for me to pray that we could see our parents. She assured me that the Bible was God's Word, written as a love letter to His children. Of course I could ask that God would open the way for us to see our parents again. So I started to pray. I also wanted to do something special for my parents. After school, on weekends, and after summer vacation, I began to work for a family, baby-sitting and entertaining their three children. It was a new experience for me at fourteen years old, but I was determined to buy something for my parents if and when I saw them again.

About three months later the Lord answered my prayers. On June 21, 1946, my brothers and I received our permit to travel into the interior. Three days later, we were on our way. During the first stretch of the trip, an older missionary from the neighboring province traveled with us. What a journey it was! My eldest brother recounted some of the experiences we had on that trip, which has helped me to describe it here for you.

Leaving Shanghai, we traveled by train just like the Chinese. Kind US Navy men offered us seats in their first-class compartment. The four-hour train ride to Hangzhou took us through towns and villages that had suffered greatly during the war. There were destroyed homes everywhere. The villagers were working to get back to a normal life by tending their rice fields, which they had plowed with buffaloes.

We spent the night in the home of one of the Chinese Christians and received a big surprise. Our friend showed us a poo-kai and told us that a number of years before, a foreign missionary had stayed with them. Because he'd had to leave suddenly very early one morning, he could not take this large bundle with him. Now our friend wanted to know what he should do with it. We were shocked when we opened the bedroll and found our father's belongings—his Bible, a shaving brush and cup with shaving soap, Dad's razor, a small mirror, and a notebook.

Our friend had kept that bedroll for five years, wondering if it would ever be returned to its rightful owner. How happy he was when he discovered that the missionary was our father. I remember the moment we opened the bedding, and I could still smell my father's scent. Here was something tangible that belonged to him. This seemed to be a confirmation that we were going to see our folks again very soon.

It was a blessing that the mission had many posts and stations all over China. No matter what the nationality of a CIM missionary, there was an immediate bond formed and a warm welcome extended to any colleague who came to their town. One lady, Miss Graeten, graciously received us and spoiled us with a delicious noon meal. After some rest, we went by rickshaw to the river and boarded a houseboat, which became our transportation for the next three days and nights. We did have to endure a terrible attack from bedbugs. The bites caused welts and were extremely itchy. We caught more than 200 of these creatures, but that certainly was not all of them.

Our journey included staying overnight with Chinese Christians, traveling by buses that on many occasions almost tipped over because of the bad roads, and sleeping on a Ping-Pong table that, (thankfully) was free of bedbugs. We were constantly watched by the Chinese who had never seen foreigners before. At one point during our travels, it was refreshing to spend the night in the home of Miss Barham, whom we knew well from our church in Shanghai. She was then serving the Lord in the interior. The last few days of the trip we traveled by ourselves, since the older missionary had to return to his mission station in Zhejiang.

Finally, after eight long, hot, trying days of traveling in remote areas, we arrived on July 2, 1946, at the bus station in Nanfeng, the city where our parents lived. No one was at the bus station, however, because Mom and Dad had not received the telegram saying that we were on the way. Fortunately, we had the help of some carriers who took our luggage to the "Yesoo-Tang," the Jesus Hall. We followed, trusting them completely.

We could not get to the mission station fast enough. Arriving at the huge gate, we knocked impatiently. It seemed like a long time before the gate was opened a little by the cook. Rather than let us in, he ran back into the house calling, "The children are here! The children are here!" The cook was extremely excited, as were Mom and Dad, of course.

It was a glorious reunion after so many years! As we sat down for a meal, everyone talked at once. It was not long before Daddy asked each one of us if we had accepted the Lord Jesus as our Savior. During those years when they could not directly influence our lives, my parents had fervently prayed for us. All three of us had found the Lord at about the same time, but we did not know that about each other. It was a thrill for me to be able to answer my father's question with this answer, "Yes, Daddy, I found the Lord Jesus a few months ago, in March of this year."

Then I had the opportunity to present my special surprise. With the money I had earned babysitting for a non-Christian family in

Shanghai, I had bought Mom some material for a dress. The ladies in the children's home had advised me well, knowing that mother had not had much of a chance to buy pretty material in the interior. The local stores did not carry anything Western, and they certainly did not have foreign ladies' clothing. Most of the time Mother dressed in simple Chinese outfits. Unfortunately, there was not enough money left for a gift for Father.

There was so much to talk about! I soon realized that I was not aware of even half of the events my parents had lived through during our years apart. Mail had been slow and many times was non-existent. The war machine had destroyed many communication routes, and much mail never reached us. What my parents experienced in the interior during World War II follows.

Chapter 7

Wartime in Inland China (1941-1946, in the Interior)

A BIBLE CONFERENCE for Chinese pastors and evangelists with missionary guest speaker Cerny had been planned on my parents' station in Chongren for the middle of October 1941. Arrival dates were always approximate due to the uncertain travel time in China in those days. Participants arrived on different dates because of unforeseen occurrences such as bridges being washed away during the rainy season, buses hardly ever running on time, or a lack of wind that forced the junks with their sails to move slowly on the river.

On October 18, 1941, Mr. Cerny and my parents were reading from Genesis 45:16–20 during their daily morning devotions. They had no idea how prophetic a challenge one particular verse would become, especially the phrase: "Never mind about your belongings" (Genesis 45:20). As it turned out, that very day they had the reality of that verse put to the test.

No sooner had they said the last "Amen," than the mission station was suddenly surrounded by soldiers. Father was taken to the police station, and Mother was ordered to prepare to leave. They were told that they had to appear at the area district office. Soldiers followed Mom's every step as she packed a few belongings. She was so nervous and frightened that she asked the soldiers to take her to the police station and send Dad home to pack. One of them had to be under surveillance at the police station.

It was not long before the soldiers began to help themselves to various items that caught their attention. They confiscated property and began emptying the house. They also demanded my parents' money.

On the long road to the area district office in another town, Mom sat on the narrow board of a wheelbarrow that was pushed by a Chinese man. Daddy walked, as he usually did. Of course, both were escorted by soldiers.

When they finally arrived at the district office, some of the officials were upset with the soldiers. They demanded to know under what authority they had taken the missionaries prisoner. No one from the central office had given the order! After much discussion, Mom and Dad were told to return to Chongren.

Back home, they were appalled at what awaited them. Mother's new bamboo floor mats in the downstairs rooms, which would be equivalent to nice rugs or carpets in the US, had been trampled and destroyed. Her new curtains had been torn down. Her neat, clean house had been devastated.

When Mother shared this experience with me, I could tell that it was still extremely painful for her to recount it, even though it had happened years before. She had worked diligently to make their home a haven with the little she had. She had done a wonderful job, even though little could be found in the local stores. The clean, neat environment of their home in the mission had been in stark contrast to the hustle and bustle of Chinese life with its crowds of people, its filth, and its beggars.

Mom had willingly given up the country where she was raised, with its beautiful valleys and forests and the peaceful stream running through the fields at the Reiherbach. Her father had provided well for his family with the warm comforts of home. Mom had tried to bring a little piece of this to her home in Chongren, but now it was all destroyed. Gradually, a few pieces of furniture and some belongings were returned. My parents tried to live life as normally as possible, but there was always the nagging question of what their future would bring.

In December 1941, when the US entered World War II, China declared war against Germany. There was concern that this would bring changes in the relationship between the Chinese and the missionaries in the interior of China. Several months of semi-normal life followed, but then things changed. On March 19, 1942, Daddy was visited by some rough soldiers. They commanded him to leave the mission station alone within two hours.

In one of his reports on my tenth birthday, he wrote:

Today our little girl celebrates her tenth birthday. I decided to do nothing, that is, I did not open my Chinese Bible, which I normally read continuously. I also did not work in the yard, but reflected about the last experiences on Magushan.

On March 19 of this year, I was chased out of the house alone. Although my most important clothes and belongings were already packed in a trunk and suitcase, I could only take a small suitcase, my poo-kai and some foodstuffs with me. They only gave two hours of warning for me to leave. Lina still cooked a good warm meal and baked a wonderful cake and then escorted me through the rice fields for more than one hour. Our future was uncertain, but not the Lord Jesus' promise: "Lo, I am with you alway" (Matthew 28:20b KJV).

My carrier and I hurried along and so we arrived in Swenfeng, one of the outstations, in the evening, where we stayed with dear Christians. They gave me more than a "cup of cold water." They all lovingly nourished my body and refreshed my soul. The Lord will reward them for it.

Next morning I continued the hot journey on to Linchuan. There I hoped to pick up my large pieces of baggage, which arrived a few days later. From there a boat took me to Nancheng. Easter Sunday, I was already on Magushan (the summer resort) where I shared the resurrection message with the folks there. Lonely and rainy weeks followed when I heard that my dear wife was on the way. With a dark future looming, she could not stand being alone on the mission station any longer. Exactly after one month's separation we met again in Nancheng (at the foot of the mountain), healthy and happy to be together again.

The air attacks became heavier and more frequent. In the previous year, on November 14, 1941, one of my parents' fellow missionaries, Jakob Wyss, a Swiss citizen, was killed. He had attended a conference in Nancheng. He was ready to leave for his home in Ningdu that morning. He had actually gotten on a bus and was waiting to go home, but he was not able to get a ticket. Mr. Wyss went back to the mission compound.

A fierce attack occurred that day. Twelve airplanes had come from the east, most likely from the island of Formosa, now called Taiwan, which was occupied by the Japanese. These fighter planes had dropped bombs along a main street. Shortly thereafter, another six airplanes had dropped bombs along one of the cross streets. More than 200 people were killed, among them missionary Wyss, who had been lying behind a small wall in the mission compound. The Lord had called him home to his eternal reward. We do not understand why God allows these terrible incidents to happen. His ways are not our ways. Jakob Wyss's dear wife continued to serve the Lord in Ningdu for five more years before she returned to Switzerland. My parents were assigned to the Wyss's mission station after their internment in Nanfeng.

After the December 7, 1941 air attack by the Japanese on Pearl Harbor, Japan was at war with the United States. Sometimes when US planes flew their missions over Japan, they did not make it back to their bases. Some of them made emergency landings in China. Sometimes they even landed in Japanese-occupied territory. One time, because of cloudy weather, two American pilots could not find the airport and were forced to land elsewhere. They were fortunate that they landed in Nancheng, where they found shelter for several days with the Catholic priests. Nancheng was still Chinese territory.

Dad and Mom spent several wonderful weeks on Magushan. Then they heard rumors that people were being expelled from their homes and that enemy troops were marching in their direction. Several of the neighboring cities fell into the hands of the Japanese. There were air raids, and more and more bombs began to be dropped. From the mountain range of Magushan, my parents could see the city Nancheng being attacked. People fled to the mountains as fires consumed the city. Then suddenly on June 12, 1942, all was quiet and still. Nancheng fell and was occupied by the Japanese. The only way to Magushan was through Nancheng; so my parents were now cut off from the world.

Father's report continued:

What will the next few days and weeks bring? Are the occupiers coming up here, do we have to flee? Fellow missionaries Brown, a Scottish couple, fled Sunday further into the mountains, but stayed only until Thursday, since bandits and robbers were roaming the area. Daily the city below and surrounding area was burning. One morning suddenly we heard: "the Japanese are coming!" I had just memorized the Scripture verse in John 14:1 with one of the Chinese men: "Let not your heart be troubled. Trust in God, trust also in me."

Everything went topsy-turvy, debilitating terror gripped every one. I went down the main path to see if it was really true. An old man was pointing in the direction where some of the soldiers had gone. So I hurried back—my passport I had already with me—and went to the Cerny's house who already had "visitors."

The soldiers ransacked everything and took what they liked. I could not make myself understood. Finally, when a superior arrived, the plunderers were commanded to leave. Then I heard a front door being forced open. It was in the summer home of another missionary family. I went to check. A soldier was already in the house. He commanded me to unlock the bedroom door. Then he proceeded to rummage through everything. A beautiful shaving kit and case he held, I just took back from him and presented it later to the rightful owner, Mr. Brown. He also took soap and other small articles. When he had filled all of his pockets, he went to the dining room, where Mr. Cerny gave him some bread and marmalade. My, did he dig in. But it was really funny when he insisted on taking a big helping of hot mustard he found. You should have seen his face. We had a hard time to suppress our amusement.

A little later the same rascal came to our house with two of his fellow soldiers. Also here they searched through the whole house and finally took my pocket watch. Fortunately he missed the large wooden box where we kept our firewood. We hid quite a sum of money and valuables in this box.

I remember Daddy telling us that he followed the Japanese soldiers from house to house. They broke doors down and took whatever they wanted. Many times Dad was able to retrieve some of the items. He assured the soldiers that they did not have much use for a camera, since they could not buy film or batteries in the interior of China. Other times he would take back a fountain pen after persuading the Japanese soldiers that fluid ink was not readily available and it was a complicated task to fill the pen with ink. He did not volunteer to show them.

I have always admired my father's courage. In situations like these, he could easily have lost his life. It would not have been unusual for one of the Japanese soldiers to get upset. Their daggers and bayonets had been used to kill many a person who crossed them. Dad, however, was convinced of the Lord's protection.

Dad continued:

Too bad we did not realize that some high ranking officers had arrived. Every time some of the soldiers tried to enter our verandah, I showed my face at the window. Finally, in the evening, we joined our fellow missionaries and found them content. But even later on we still saw soldiers lurking around our house. One of them even climbed into our attic without us having noticed it. That night we slept in our street clothes and left the oil lamp burning. We were so glad when the whole troupe with their horses finally left.

In the following days there was much fighting. Gunshots were heard, and the sound of artillery came closer and closer. Then the Chinese soldiers arrived on Magushan. After the Japanese left, many of the Kuomintang soldiers were suspicious of the population, wondering if there were spies among the mountain people. Dad helped the Chinese whenever he could and interceded for them. I remember him telling us that the husband of one of the Chinese women was captured by the soldiers. The man's wife came to father, followed by a soldier. She fell on her knees and begged Dad to intervene for the life of her husband. He told her to stand up and do what the soldiers asked of her.

Dad's report went on:

Now this same soldier pointed his gun at Brother Cerny and me and ordered us to go with him. In the carpenter shop in the village he tied us up with thick ropes. Then he led us back to our house where other soldiers joined us. They did a thorough check of our belongings. At this time the ropes were removed. I asked the three gentlemen to sit down and have some tea. Now the questioning began. Who were we, how long had we been on the mountain, how did the Japanese treat us, etc.? Even though we gave all the answers, they ordered us to go with them. They suspected us to be spies for the Japanese. And spies had to be dealt with. So both of us, Mr. Cerny and myself, had to march with them over the mountains, all the way down to the plains of the river and into the city of Nancheng. There we were able to speak with someone in authority. It was raining cats and dogs. At night we were happy to be back with our wives, whose concern for us was not minute.

Once again, God had interceded, and they let them go. I remember Dad sharing that Mr. Cerny was so exhausted from the emotional stress, the commotion, the treacherous long walk over the mountains, and the uncertainty of not knowing what would happen to them that he collapsed on the way back and could not walk back up the steep mountain path. Daddy carried the old missionary on his back.

When they finally arrived home, they found Mom and Mrs. Cerny on their knees, pleading with God to convict the soldiers to release their husbands and let them return home. As they answered the knock on the door, they were reminded of the story in Acts 12:13–14. When Peter stood at the door knocking, the maid, Rhoda, was so shocked and overjoyed that the Lord had answered their prayers that she did not open the door but ran back to the disciples in the room. Like Rhoda, Mom and Mrs. Cerny could not believe that the Lord had answered their prayers so quickly, but they did open the door for their husbands!

Daddy continued:

On the fourth of July of 1942 a long, long train of refugees wound their way down the mountain. There must have been about 100 men, women, and children carrying their belongings, even taking some cows with them, down that very steep path. Looking back, burned out walls of the village U Long Ao stared at us. It was a sad sight.

For three days we were on the road to our internment on the mission station in Nanfeng. Here we heard the sad news that the mission stations in Nancheng and our Chongren home were bombed and destroyed by the Japanese. Also that all the houses on Magushan had been completely looted and emptied, most likely the very same day we left.

The Lord was faithful to my parents and intervened in many terrible situations during those trying war years. It was not easy for them. What has been reported here was shared by them or was gleaned from their letters and reports to the mission. Mom and Dad never questioned why the Lord would lead them through deep waters. They were unmovable in their faith. I never heard an accusatory word from my parents or expression of any self-pity. They believed God and clung to Him with great fervor. The trials, sufferings, and difficulties my parents faced were, to them, only evidence of the importance of their task. They faced everything calmly, but with immovable determination.

Although World War II in Asia ended when the Japanese Emperor surrendered and signed his capitulation in August 1945, the machinery of powers in the interior of China did not work that fast. It was not until August 3, 1946, an entire year later, that my parents and other German missionaries in Jiangxi who had been interned in the Nanfeng area were finally released. We were with our parents at that time and joined them as they went to their newly assigned mission station in Ningdu.

Chapter 8

A Family Again (1946–1947)

THE LONG BUS trip in the hot summer month of August 1946, from Nanfeng to Ningdu, was unforgettable. In those days in China, luggage was piled up in the middle of the bus. Since there were always ducks, chickens, and even occasional piglets that traveled in crates or cages with their owners, additional luggage had to be put on top of the bus. Passengers sat around the luggage and the smelly cages inside the bus and fought to keep the whole load from squashing them as the driver careened around sharp and dangerous curves.

Mother had a favorite cat that she could not leave behind, so we took turns holding her precious "Mew-choo" in a cage on our laps. Precious Mew-choo did not like the ride. Her fright made her growl, scratch, and claw us as she constantly reached out of the openings in the bamboo cage. Since there were no animal tranquilizers available, we endured the long, eighty-mile trip as best we could. I've often wondered who was more relieved to see that five-and-a-half hour trip end—the cat or us Burklins?

In order to familiarize her with her new surroundings on the mission station in Ningdu, mother tied a rope around the cat's neck. It was my privilege to take her for walks. Leashes were an unknown in the interior of China. Mew-choo did get used to the new home and was very useful in keeping our home free from mice and rats.

The mission station in Ningdu was one of the largest the mission owned. The house was of brick construction and had large rooms. Wide verandahs that wrapped around the first and second floors gave welcome relief from the hot and humid weather that occurred from early spring until late fall. Opening the windows and doors for a cross breeze and sitting on the verandah was often the only way to survive the heat.

Mother was thrilled to have a huge vegetable garden, where she could grow as many vegetables as she liked. Missionaries in former years had planted several different kinds of palm trees, large cacti of different varieties, colorful flowers, and many kinds of fruit trees. On our station in the South of China, we grew wonderful exotic fruits, like quince, which made delicious preserves. There were also persimmons, oranges, *pomelo* (a type of grapefruit, only much larger), peaches, plums, dates, loquats, kumquats, and bananas. We never got to harvest bananas because our pig loved the soft trunk and always cut it down with his strong teeth. A wonderful treat before going to bed at night was fresh fruit from our own trees.

It was marvelous to be a family again after more than five years of separation, but it was also a time of adjustment. The next thirteen months were filled with adjusting to life in the interior without running water, electricity, or any of the conveniences we had in Shanghai. There were no department or modern stores, cars, trolleys, city buses, or even rickshaws. Wherever we went, we had to walk. Of course, that always entailed dealing with crowds of people, many whom had never seen a foreigner.

One day, mother asked me to go with her to the market. As we began our walk, we were soon followed by a crowd of people that consisted mainly of women and children. Their laughing, giggling, and reaching out to touch me was extremely perplexing to me. Mother explained, "You are wearing an outfit with lots of red, so these people think you are a bride going to your wedding." In those days, girls in China wore red on their wedding day. Mother had not thought to warn me.

That year, from 1946–1947, was filled with special memories. I taught my first Sunday school class in Chinese. Fortunately, I remembered what I had learned as a little girl when I spent a great deal of time playing with only Chinese children. I also recalled many of the choruses I had learned then. Mom and Dad were always ready to help with the words I needed to be able to tell Bible stories better, and it was a great blessing to do so.

We went on long hikes in the area with Dad, visited the pagoda and other sights, and swam in the river. It was always a treat to visit some of the believers and their families in their homes. Many times, they would bring out goodies and sweets that I remembered from days gone by. There was always hot tea served in the traditional teacup with no handle, but with a lid and saucer. Our Chinese friends were always amazed that I still sipped tea like they did by holding the saucer, the cup, and the lid with one hand and slurping as loudly as they did. This was proof that I enjoyed the hot drink. If they were too poor to offer tea, they always had hot water, which I also learned to like.

One memorable outing was on Mother's birthday, September 19, 1946. Mom packed sandwiches, fruit, drinks, and a birthday cake. A Chinese man carried the goodies in two baskets that he hung from a pole he put across his shoulder. We headed out to Tsui-wei-feng that was about eight miles from Ningdu. It was a woodsy, park-like area that had a huge outcropping of rock with a large split in the middle.

During the time Mao Zedong ruled that area in the early 1930s, people from the Ningdu area, especially the wealthy, fled to this mountain. The only way to climb to the top to hide was to brace yourself with both arms and feet along the narrow split in the middle of the rock and push yourself upwards. Several thousand people had climbed up in this manner and hidden from the communists. After several months, however, their food ran out. The communists encouraged the folks to climb down, promising them safe return to their homes. Reality was that, as they came down through the narrow split, they were killed, one by one, once they reached the bottom.

At the foot of this rock was a Taoist temple. Since it was a remote area, there were only a few monks on duty. We settled in a large area sheltered by a huge rock. In our cave-like atmosphere, we ate our delicious lunch. A monk served us hot tea, and Daddy shared with him some wonderful truths about the Lord while we three teenagers anxiously waited to climb the famous rock.

Climbing was extremely difficult, but we made it to the top. It was strange to walk around this vast, desolate area that contained only a few bushes and straggly trees. I wondered if they could talk, what they would tell me of the agony, fear, and terror they had witnessed many years before from people only wanting safety. Huddled together, not knowing what would become of them, those people had probably felt so relieved to receive word that they could climb down and be safe! Then they had been murdered one by one. It was a very moving experience for me to imagine the scene.

Going back to where we had eaten, I found Mother alone, sitting in a lounge chair overlooking a beautiful valley. I joined her, pulling up another chair. I was tired from the difficult climb, but I was also very disturbed. Our surroundings included the temple on the other side of the path with its horrible idols. Incense was burning in front of them and there were offerings of fruit, rice, and other sacrifices. This all reminded me of the field trip so long before when I had joined my classmates in offering incense sticks to the idols in the temple at the Longhua Pagoda.

Now that I was a believer, a follower of Jesus Christ, I knew that I had sinned. I had worshipped man-made idols. God is a holy God. Scripture teaches us that He is a jealous God in the sense of not liking us to give our worship to anyone or anything but Him. When I accepted the Lord as my Savior and asked Him to forgive my sins, I did not think of this specific transgression. Now I remembered it, and my heart was heavy. I shared the story with my mother, and she sweetly reminded me that I could go to the Lord and ask Him for forgiveness at that very moment. She did not make light of it. We both bowed our heads, and I asked the Lord to forgive me and cleanse me from that idol worship many years before. I know the Lord did, for I felt a huge load lifted from my heart.

This experience left a deep impression on me. Ever since then, I have tried to keep short accounts with the Lord when I know that I have sinned and saddened Him by my behavior. It was also a good lesson in keeping a short account with anyone I may have offended or hurt by my actions. It is not always easy to say, "I am sorry. Please forgive me," but I try to do it before too much time has passed.

Several of the ladies from the Yah-men, the local government, wanted to learn English. They came and asked my father if I could teach them. This not only gave me a wonderful opportunity to make a little money, but also it allowed me to get to know some ladies in high positions. I thoroughly enjoyed this tutoring, especially when friendships developed from it.

Since it had become difficult to get finances from the homelands, we were thankful that many fruit trees grew in our yard, especially peach trees. The property had more than two dozen peach trees of several varieties, with a long season of peaches ripening. My brothers and I took turns sitting at the back gate of our property selling these delicious fruits. This income was a great blessing in meeting our living expenses.

The Chinese were surprised that we learned to use a Chinese scale. This consisted of a metal plate that was attached at one end with strings to a long stick with marks on it. The fruit was placed on this plate. Then a weight was moved up or down the long stick to determine how much the peaches weighed. I am sure that many of the buyers came out of curiosity to see what these foreigners were all about. Many of them had never seen a Caucasian before and certainly not this close up. They were always amazed to see my blue eyes and blonde hair. Everyone else in my family has brown eyes and dark hair like the Chinese. They could not believe that I could see. The only blue eyes they had ever seen were the eyes of the blind storyteller in the city. A bluish film covered his eyes. Often I could hear them discussing my hair, wondering if it was straw because of the strange color.

Fruits and vegetables came from our garden. Chickens, ducks, rabbits, and a pig provided us with meat. Having grown up on a farm, mother knew how to smoke ham, make sausage, and slaughter fowl and rabbits. Father purchased items that had to be bought in quantity at the local market. These included such things as coal, oil for cooking, peanuts for peanut butter, sugar, and salt.

Shopping at the local market included haggling for the right price. No one accepted the original asking price of the merchant but bargained with the seller until he was content that he had negotiated the best deal possible. Dad learned some valuable lessons in his endeavors to buy at the best price. On one occasion, we had run out of cooking oil. Dad went to the market and negotiated with the merchant, finally settling on a price. He was proud of himself that he had done so well!

Dad thought he had really received a great bargain when he asked the merchant to go with him and take the big barrel to the mission station without extra charge and the man agreed. When father asked him to empty the oil into the large container outside of our kitchen, he said he had to hurry to another appointment and would come back in a few days to pick up his barrel. All was well until a few days later, when our cook went to father laughing, "Lin Muh-si, you bought a barrel full of tea! Since oil floats, we had good oil for a few days, but when it was gone, the tea appeared! No wonder the man did not want to pour out the oil into our container." She laughed heartily as she held up a glass of tea.

Sometimes I helped to make peanut butter when our cook was busy with other chores. Two large, circular stones were placed one on top of the other. A wooden handle driven into the upper stone was used for turning it. A round hole chiseled through the stone allowed peanuts to be dropped in as I slowly turned the top wheel round and round. What oozed out on the sides of the lower wheel was scraped up. This became our peanut butter. Jelly and preserves were made in Mother's kitchen from fruits from her garden.

We often had visitors come through the mission with all of the various activities going on. When studying father's diaries, it amazed me how many missionaries were constantly coming and going and how many mission stations my father had to visit in order to attend gatherings, planning meetings, Bible conferences, and other events. Since Dad had worked as a court recorder in a lawyer's office before coming to China, he was given the job of secretary. He used his shorthand and then had to decipher his scribbles and put them into legible reports and minutes. Bible conferences held in the outposts were often attended by fellow missionaries from other stations. Once again, Dad attempted to home school us and keep up with his many missionary responsibilities.

In the spring of 1947, a women's Bible conference was held in the neighboring mission station, Juikin, now called Ruijin, close to the border of Fujian. Ladies from the surrounding areas were getting together for intense Bible study, singing, and prayer. Mom invited me to go with her. The lady who had been my parents' junior missionary when I was three years old served the Lord on this station with another missionary lady. She was the one that I often had to escort and show where some of the old ladies in Chongren lived. So on April 12, we left by bus. It was a beautiful trip. For several hours, we drove through mountains covered with blooming rhododendron, camellias, and wild azaleas. Perhaps this is why I have always loved these plants.

This was the first time I had ever attended a Chinese ladies' conference. I loved the new songs we learned, which included Scripture passages sung to Chinese tunes rather than to Western melodies. To this day, I can still remember some of them, especially the two from Philippians 3:8 and Romans 14:8.

After the conference concluded, we stayed to sew clothes for Mom, especially some new dresses. One of the lady missionaries was an exceptionally skilled seamstress. I asked Mom about the material that I had bought her for a dress with the money I had earned from my first babysitting job in Shanghai. She smiled and said that I had worked so hard for it that she wanted me to have our tailor in Shanghai make me a dress.

Although our stay was to be two weeks, it turned out to be much longer than that. As I have mentioned, you could never tell if buses would run in China because so much depended upon the weather. A torrential rain began on the day we were to leave, and several of the roads were flooded. Bridges had been swept away. Every morning for one week, we went to the bus station to see if there was a bus running that day. After several hours of waiting, we would return to the mission station. Since I had a nervous stomach when I traveled, I could not eat breakfast the morning of a departure day. This time, however, since we kept coming back every day for a whole week without leaving, I learned to eat breakfast.

Finally, on May 9, 1947, we decided to take the only transportation available to us—a truck loaded with many sacks of horrible-smelling merchandise. Mom and I believed it to be dried fish. Fortunately, Mom could sit in the front next to the driver, but I had to sit in the back on the smelly bundles with several Chinese people. Trips like that have made me truly grateful throughout my life whenever I have traveled in comfort.

I will never forget May 25, 1947. Daddy baptized my two brothers and me, along with our Chinese cook and another gentleman, at the church in Ningdu. It was a very special and precious day for me. Dad gave me Philippians 4:4 as my baptismal verse: "Rejoice in the Lord alway: and again I say, rejoice" (KJV). This verse has become my life verse.

On July 17, 1947, we left for Nancheng in order to go to Magushan, our summer retreat, one more time. Since this trip took ten hours, we spent the night in Nancheng and then went up the mountain to our beloved home on Magushan the next day. The first thing I noticed was that our home had suffered from the horrors of war. Huge pieces were ripped out of several walls. The plunderers had left the place in a mess and helped themselves to whatever they liked. We made the best of it, however, and worked hard to make it clean and comfortable. And it was pleasant to celebrate my birthday with coffee and cake a few days later.

Wonderful, relaxing days followed. We swam in our favorite swimming holes, took trips to the top of the highest peaks in the area to see the sunrise, and walked along mountainsides covered with white lilies. The higher we climbed, the more lilies we found. Sometimes we counted thirteen to sixteen of these beautiful creations of God on one stem. Again, there were church services for the local villagers and visits with other missionaries who had also come to the summer resort.

All too soon, it was time for my parents to think about our return to Shanghai to continue our schooling. We left for Nancheng at the foot of the mountain on August 20, 1947. Fred, who was eighteen years old, had taken a position as a teacher in a middle school in Ningdu; so he did not go on to Shanghai with Werner and me. On August 21, after eleven hours of travel, we arrived in Nanchang, the capital of Jiangxi. Due to a shortage of funds, Dad could not continue with us, but he put us on a train that took us directly to Shanghai.

And so on August 23, 1947, we said "goodbye" again. It was not easy for any of us. Although I had to do it often, saying "goodbye" never got easier. This could clearly be seen in Dad's diary entry for that day, "Children to children's home...with tears."

Chapter 9

Dramatic Changes (1947–1949)

IN SHANGHAI, I settled back into the daily routine that included school, fun times with classmates and children from the children's home, and attendance at the Shanghai Free Christian Church. While in the interior, I had missed the "Ambassadors for Christ" youth meetings on Friday nights and the other services at my church. Since my salvation, church had become an exciting place. Through its services and wonderful people, I became grounded and rooted in the Word of God. It was a joy to go to church, and I could not wait for the doors to open.

In high school, I was challenged by one of my biology teachers about evolution. When I had exhausted my attempts at defending creationism, I was grateful that I could go to my good friend and sponsor of the young people's group at church, Anna Swarr, and get new ammunition. There were many times when Anna would come home from the office to find me waiting at her door. Although I am sure she was tired from a long day's work, she always welcomed me. We would lay on her bed eating popcorn while I pumped her for answers to my numerous questions. Anna shared many Christian principles and biblical truths with me. I am extremely grateful for the wonderful example this special friend was to me.

We had responsibilities in the youth group, including those associated with its elected officers. I was elected by my peers to be the official pianist, and I played for several different church functions. When elections came around for a second time, I prayed along with the others that God would lead us to the right people to fill the various positions. I was chosen as pianist again, a decision which brought me to tears.

One of the missionary ladies noticed my crying and took me aside to discover why. At first, I hedged. I was so shy that I did not want to tell her why I was so unhappy to be the pianist for another year. Every time I went to the piano, I was sure everyone was looking at me and noticing how awkward I was. I thought they would find something wrong with my appearance.

The missionary lady, who was perhaps six to eight years older than I, was very kind. Because of her evident concern, I told her what was bothering me. She asked me if I had prayed that God would lead the youth group as they voted. I assured her that I had. Then she stunned me. She looked straight into my eyes and said, "You believed that God would lead us to the right person to become pianist until you found out you were elected. You are really more concerned about yourself than playing for the Lord. You think the people watching you play the piano will listen for every mistake you make. You are so wrapped up in yourself that you cannot think about playing for the Lord and pleasing Him. Perhaps this year He wants you to change and to play only for Him."

I was so shocked that I did not know what to say, but I knew she was right. To this day, I think of that dear servant of the Lord; although, I don't even remember her name. Every time I have something to do in ministry, whether it is teaching, singing, playing the piano, or something else, I ask myself this question: "Am I concerned about *my* performance, *my* involvement, even *my* service for the Lord, or am I doing it all for Christ?" That was a difficult lesson learned many years ago, but one that has been invaluable in my walk with the Lord.

On May 1, 1948, Daddy came to Shanghai for a six-week stay in order to have major dental work and to see an ophthalmologist. It was a thrill for him to visit with friends and get spiritually fed at several of the local churches. He also was able to do some much-needed shopping for things he and my mother could not get in the interior. On June 16, he left to join Mom in Ningdu.

Late in the summer of that year, I had to have an appendectomy. It was performed by Dr. Adolph, one of the missionary doctors of the CIM. The hospital was on the fifth floor of the CIM headquarters. I remember the excitement at that time regarding a new development that allowed surgeries to be done with local anesthesia. I could watch my surgery being performed in mirrors set up in the operating room. I opted not to do that!

An exciting time for us included moving the children's home to the main building of the China Inland Mission headquarters. Newly-arriving missionary ladies were no longer able to go to Yangzhou to the language school where Mother had gone when she first came to China many years before. Mao Zedong and his communist troops were making great strides in conquering China, and situations north of Shanghai became too volatile. So Mr. Wehmeyer offered the mission the big house with its large yard and additional apartments in the back. In exchange, they provided adequate housing for the children's home in the headquarters of the mission. The men who could not go to language school in Anqing, where Father had gone, were housed in the Lutheran Center close to the CIM compound in Shanghai.

Being housed at headquarters made life a little less complicated for me. After school, secretarial and business classes, and homework were done, I could easily walk to the administration building to see my friend Anna Swarr. Most afternoons I joined the staff, the directors, and the administrators of the mission for a game of volleyball. Office hours were over at 5 o'clock, and it was a tradition that volleyball was a wonderful way to relax and get in a good hour of exercise. To this day, volleyball is still played at the headquarters of the mission in Singapore, which is now called Overseas Missionary Fellowship.

Our apartment was on the same floor as the apartments of several of the CIM directors, so I got to know them well. The general director, Bishop Frank Houghton, and his wife, Dorothy, lived only a few doors down from us. They were very kind to me. The Bishop, as we called him, spent special time with me and became my mentor. It was not unusual for Mrs. Houghton to invite me for a cup of tea. I have always been amazed that the general director of one of the largest missions in China would take time to befriend an MK, a missionary kid. The Bishop and his wife had no children of their own, but they certainly had a great impact on the lives of many young people in extraordinary ways.

I will never forget the afternoon when I tasted my first hamburger. The Bishop and his wife had invited me and a special friend of mine to a country club for an afternoon of swimming and then dinner. After a great time of swimming, we went to the beautiful dining room, which offered superb service. The only item on the menu that intrigued me was a "hamburger." I had never heard of it and did not know what it was. Mrs. Houghton explained but then encouraged me to try one of the delicious steaks. Curiosity got the better of me, and I ordered the hamburger. It was great to have my first hamburger as a teenager.

The year 1949 brought dramatic changes, not only for me personally, but also for the land of my birth. In January, my oldest brother, Fred, came back to Shanghai from the interior, where he had taught at an orphanage in Kanhsien, presently known as Ganzhou, in South Jiangxi. He and Werner were leaving China.

They sailed out of Shanghai for Europe on March 4, on a small ship called the SS *Rena*. Several other missionaries were also aboard that ship, including Gladys Aylward, who was nicknamed "The Little Woman." The Lord used Gladys Aylward mightily in China, and she became well known for leading orphans over rough mountain terrain to freedom in order to escape the Japanese. Her story became a best seller and was immortalized in the movie *The Inn of the Sixth Happiness* with Ingrid Bergman. The eldest son of the Wehmeyers, who was like a brother to me, also sailed on the SS *Rena*. To lose my dear brothers was a great blow to me.

A few weeks later, Aunt Leni informed me that she was returning to Germany for a long-overdue furlough. She had been in China for more than thirteen years without having gone home. There was only one problem. No one was available to take over her position in the children's home. By this time, there were eight or nine boys and girls under eleven years of age, and there would be no one to give them special attention if she left.

Aunt Leni asked me if I would consider stepping into her shoes and assisting our foster mother, Mrs. Wehmeyer, especially in looking after the little ones. I had always loved children and had a great deal of experience babysitting for many of the mission directors' children, as well as for the babies of some of the newly-arriving missionary couples. So with fear and trembling, I accepted. To this day, I am still amazed that she trusted me and had the confidence that I could do her job while I was still in my late teens.

My duties included helping the little ones get dressed in the morning, assisting them with their homework in the afternoon, and helping them with baths in the evening. I would then tuck them in bed at night and pray with each one before they went to sleep. This was one of the most precious times I experienced with the young children as they shared some of their thoughts and concerns. Then we would pray for their concerns.

Many times I had to dry the tears of little ones who were homesick and missed their parents. One of the ten-year-old boys said to me one evening as I hugged him goodnight, "I am so glad that you are here. I can tell you know when I am sad and miss my mom and dad. You have been here a long time, and you know what it's like to be homesick. You understand." This was perhaps why the Lord allowed me to be there for those children. I also helped Aunt Wehmeyer get breakfast ready and have the children ready to leave for school on time. I would then jump on a bike and pedal off to school and business classes.

In April and May, we heard that the Communists were getting closer. Thousands of refugees poured into the city from the outskirts, as well as from the outlying areas. Paper money was devalued. I remember our foster father, Mr. Wehmeyer, going to the bank with a suitcase and returning with millions in paper notes. The large Chinese silver dollars were the only currency of value, and they were soon outlawed by the Communists.

On May 27, 1949, the Communists entered Shanghai. There was heavy fighting in some areas of the city that lasted about three days. In other sections, Chang Kai-Shek's troops left quietly. Not many people ventured out into the streets. The first change I noticed was the different colored uniforms of the soldiers. Red Army guards were everywhere, especially in front of large buildings. Shanghai was "liberated."

I will never forget the red drums. Every person in school, from kindergarten to the university level, was given a bright red drum, which he or she was required to beat continuously for hours. Then the students would be herded into large auditoriums, where they would be lectured on Marxism and the virtues of Communism. We lived near a middle school and were greatly disturbed by the constant beating of the drums. Those constant beats certainly must have contributed to the mind control of the students.

After the drumming and the lectures, all students, from the little ones to graduate students, were required to march down the streets in parade fashion. They waved bright red banners with slogans as they sang, "so-la, so-la, do-la, do…" Each student walked four steps forward and one step backward. No traffic was allowed to pass, and pedestrians were not permitted to break through the lines. To get to an appointment on time or to make it home for dinner became an exasperating experience. You never knew which streets were cordoned off and how long the marches would take.

It was not long before mass arrests and executions took place. No one knows how many Chinese committed suicide due to fear of arrest. I was horrified to see open trucks, with people in white dunce caps with their hands and feet bound, driving through the streets. Their crimes were posted in large Chinese characters on the sides of the trucks. If they had been caught dealing with silver dollars, which by now was a crime, a huge replica of a silver dollar was placed on both sides of the truck. Others had to wear large sandwich boards around their necks that stated their crime. Many of them were taken to an execution site, which was often an open-air area. Crowds of people gathered, and shouts of, "sah', sah', sah'," or "kill, kill, kill," could be heard for miles around.

Many changes were also occurring in the interior. In the middle of September 1948, a young Swiss missionary couple came to join Mom and Dad on their station. Their installation service took place on Mom's birthday, September 19, 1948. The folks were happy to get some reinforcements and immediately went to work to help the new couple with the Chinese language, taking their exams, and getting accustomed to life in Ningdu, Jiangxi. As usual, the days were filled with ministry.

Life in the interior became very difficult. Finances were meager, and money did not always arrive at the various mission stations. Dad noted in his diary over and over again that they were selling fruit from the mission compound as we had all done earlier. Dad generously shared with the Catholic priest, a gentleman from Europe, who was often short of money as well.

The many soldiers who came to the mission station were a reminder of how things were being stirred up politically in China. This presented a wonderful opportunity to witness and minister to them. On August 14, 1949, military personnel came to warn my parents and encouraged them to leave. Two weeks later, there was much fighting and commotion, which was followed on August 29 with an eerie quiet. Ningdu had been "liberated." The next few weeks were marked by skirmishes and gunshots in the middle of the night. Communist soldiers, some with horses, were all over town.

The Communists came to the mission station and invited Dad and the junior missionary, Mr. Wyss, to attend sessions on Communism, Marx, and Lenin. There was no escaping the requirements to listen to young men in their late teens or early twenties who tried to convince them of the virtues of Communism. Young people lecturing older folks would never have been permitted in "old" China. Changes became very evident. It was a frequent occurrence for them to come and order Dad and Mr. Wyss to sit down in the church and listen to their doctrine. At other times my father was interrogated regarding his purpose in the interior and badgered with many other questions. They also wanted to know if he had a radio to communicate with the outside world. Times were very difficult and uncertain.

In spite of these circumstances, the ministry of Bible study, preaching, teaching, prayer meetings, visitation, and all the other varied ministries continued. Church meetings were often held by the evangelist, Mr. Liu, or some elder of the church. Dad was thrilled at their progress and deeply thankful that his faithful discipling was bearing fruit.

Knowing the mission station was in good hands with Mr. and Mrs. Wyss, Mom and Dad felt it was time for a furlough. It had been almost fourteen years since they had visited their homeland. They made application at the police station for a travel permit, and it was granted five days later. The days of coming and going as you pleased were over. Everything and everyone became regulated. Life in China had indeed changed.

It did not take my parents long to pack. Their greatest concern was soldiers thoroughly inspecting every piece of their luggage. Everything had to be listed, down to the smallest items (like shoelaces). Every suitcase and bag was opened and searched at the main gate of the mission compound. If the folks missed listing something and it was found in one of the bags, the soldiers confiscated it. Mom and Dad watched nervously as the soldiers went through everything. It seemed like an eternity before they were finished. The Red Army did not make it easy for anyone to leave.

As was typical of Dad, he prayed and then they sang a hymn there in the open, surrounded by believers and the Communist soldiers. On October 19, 1949, they left Ningdu, their beloved mission station where the Lord had given them one of the most fruitful ministries in the twenty-five years they served Him in China.

Although they could not count many converts that were a result of their labor, they had made many friends among the Chinese in their three years there. They had discipled some wonderful believers, including a Chinese lady named Shae-Tai-Tai. She trusted the Lord as her Savior because of my parents' faithful visitation work and became one of Mom's closest friends. Mom and Dad often spoke of their years in Ningdu with much joy as they remembered its blessings and prayed for the many dear ones they left behind.

Chapter 10

Delays, Disappointments, and Departure (1949–1950)

ON OCTOBER 28, 1949, nine days after Mom and Dad left Ningdu, they arrived in Shanghai. Mr. Wehmeyer and I met them at the train station to welcome them to the big city. I still remember how surprised I was. The unrest, the uncertainty of the new regime, and the takeover by the Communists had taken their toll. My parents had aged tremendously since I had been with them in the interior two years earlier.

The application for an exit visa from China started in earnest. Various authorities' offices had to be visited repeatedly. In order for my parents to be able to return to the land of their birth, requests for an entrance visa had to be made to Germany's occupying forces. Since Germany lost World War II, the country was occupied by the Russians, the British, the Americans, and the French. Thousands of refugees coming from the East and Russian-occupied territories flooded into the American, British, and French sections of Germany. These occupying nations were not eager to receive additional refugees from China. My mother's family in Germany lived in the French Zone. France, as well as other countries, still had a consulate in Shanghai, so Dad spent days on end at their office.

There were also multiple trips to the police headquarters for exit visas. A mountain of paperwork was required, along with physical examinations, x-rays, and immunizations. Our names had to appear in both the English and Chinese local papers for four weeks once we were considered for possible exit visas. Anyone who had a grievance against us, no matter how fabricated, could go to the police and stop the whole procedure. We knew some foreigners had been ordered before the people's court. Just like in biblical times, it took only two witnesses to come up with trumped-up accusations. The penalties were executed swiftly. A few of the China Inland Mission missionaries lost their lives because of these courts. Anxious weeks turned into months.

Mom and Dad also had to have certain certifications from the authorities in Ningdu, which took a great deal of time. On December 15, I received my exit visa. Since my parents did not receive theirs at this time, mine had to be extended. Finally, on January 16, 1950, my extended visa was granted. My name was printed in the English and Chinese newspapers on January 12 and 13 respectively and appeared for one month. Eventually Mom's and Dad's names also appeared in the papers. We were fortunate that no one had grievances against us.

More disappointments followed. Rumors flew that various ships were leaving China. This gave us hope. The SS *Canton* left from Hong Kong on December 23, 1949, and there was talk that another ship was to come to Shanghai on December 28 and pick up passengers. We were not among them. Again, there was hope that perhaps in March 1950 we could leave. Dad spent weeks going back and forth from the French to the British consulate. Then he tried the American consulate, thinking that perhaps leaving for the US might be a possibility. Dad had a brother and a sister with families in New Jersey, and Mother had relatives in Idaho and in Salamanca in the Buffalo area. We wondered if this was God's plan for us.

At the end of January, Dad went to the American President Line, a shipping company that was still in existence. There was a possibility that the SS *Gordon* or the SS *Wilson* would come to Shanghai on March 21. News came, however, that SS *Gordon* went to Yokohama instead of Shanghai on March 22. My parents' hopes were shattered. In Dad's special way, he noted in his diary, "We wait." It spoke volumes. Chiang Kai-Shek had decided to blockade the Shanghai harbor, and no ships of any size could come or go. There was the possibility that we could board ships outside the harbor with landing crafts, but then that was also ruled out.

When the Communists conquered China, Chiang Kai-Shek had fled with his leadership and troops to the island of Formosa, now called Taiwan. In the fall of 1949, his air force began continuous assault attacks on Shanghai. When the air raid sirens warned us several times per week, we had to take shelter. Bombs fell in various parts of the city. On January 26, 1950, the Bund was bombed again, and the area where the oil tanks were stored burned for days. The main power station was hit on February 6, and we were without power for a number of days. When the power was finally restored, electricity was rationed. We were once again in a war zone.

My parents had come to Shanghai at the end of October 1949 with the intention of leaving China. It was now March 1950, and we were still in Shanghai. The weeks and months took a toll on my parents, especially on my father. We were now declared "DPs," or Displaced Persons. The situation looked hopeless. The directors of the China Inland Mission did their best to help, but without a passage out and the proper papers, there was not much they could do. Finally, there was a glimmer of hope. Someone found out that there was a possibility of leaving via Tientsin in the North, and on March 26, the decision was made to attempt to leave by that route. Then we wondered if the authorities would agree to our leaving.

On March 31, Dad wrote in his diary, "First red, then yellow, then green light, we leave via Tientsin with Bishop Houghton" (the General Director). On the morning of April 1, 1950, Dad went with some friends to get our exit permits, took our luggage that had been packed and repacked for many weeks, and went to the train station. At 7 P.M., we were on the train to Tientsin, now called Tianjin. In our hopelessness, suddenly God had stepped in, and permission was granted to leave the very same day! The Lord had done what only He can do. We stood by in awe and gave Him glory. After our long months of waiting and running from office to office seeking out the French, the British, and the American consulates, along with various Chinese authorities, with no results, we were leaving Shanghai! I wondered what the Lord's purpose could have been in trying my parents' patience.

The Wehmeyers and some special friends of mine came to the train station to bid us farewell. All throughout my young life, April seemed to be the month that included many changes and challenging events. Twelve years before, I had arrived in Shanghai as a shy five-year-old. Then in April 1941, we had made the dangerous trip back to Shanghai, crossing the Ningbo Bay. Even after all the waiting and stress, to say "goodbye" to this city, my native land of China, and my many friends was very difficult.

It was April 1, 1950, April Fool's Day, but what was happening was no joke. We were leaving and did not know what the future would hold. I wondered where we would end up. I felt as if my heart were being ripped out of my chest. Fortunately, my good friend and mentor Bishop Houghton and his wife were leaving with us.

Before leaving Shanghai, the Houghtons gave me a beautiful turquoise brooch imbedded in sterling silver. They also had one of their Chinese helpers make a pair of silk shoes for me that were embroidered with an intricate flower and bird design. To this day, I cherish these gifts. This same lady also embroidered the Bible verse from Joshua with Chinese characters on two silk scrolls for me: "Do not be terrified; do not be discouraged, for the Lord your God will be with you wherever you go" (Joshua 1:9b). These scrolls, another meaningful gift from the Houghtons, are still hanging in the foyer of our home.

After several days on the train, we arrived in Tianjin late at night. A Scandinavian missionary came to meet us. He made arrangements for our little party and our luggage to be transported by several rickshaws to the mission station. We were quite a caravan, and the locals watched us with much glee. I was in the last rickshaw that was loaded down with a number of suitcases. It was raining, and the lights from the shops on both sides of the street cast an eery glow over the wet cobblestones. Suddenly my rickshaw coolie swerved to the right and ran towards a narrow alley as several people on the street were excitedly talking to him. He answered in a dialect I did not understand while he laughed and ran.

I was truly afraid. As he was turning into the alley, the Swedish missionary, who was in the rickshaw in front of me, turned around to see what was causing the commotion. Quickly he jumped out of his rickshaw and ran towards my coolie, yelling at him and gesticulating with his arms. The missionary's actions caused the coolie to turn my rickshaw around and join the group again. I do not know the circumstances of that event, but I do know the coolie had ill intentions. I am thankful that the Lord protected me and spared me from harm. I could easily have disappeared and never have been heard from again, as has been the case many times with other people in various parts of the world.

Once again, we were required to visit the police station and make arrangements with a travel service before we finally had our tickets. We were not going to Japan and on to the United States as we had thought. It was ironic that we were getting on a freighter that was leaving for Hong Kong. Six months earlier Mom and Dad had left their mission station in the South and traveled about 1,300 miles to North China. Now they were headed a little further south than Ningdu, where they came from. God must have a sense of humor.

In order to be able to leave the country, all of our luggage had to be rechecked to make sure that everything was included on the famous content lists. After dealing with the authorities for months, Dad was emotionally drained. It was difficult for him to handle additional testy situations, so I took over. Daddy sat on a chair close by, and I watched carefully as the Communist soldiers went through our belongings. Since the bags had been packed and repacked so many times in the last months, there were a few things that were not on the list. The soldiers readily helped themselves to these.

We were not allowed to take anything out of the country that would shed a bad light on China. Even our photo albums were carefully inspected. This took much time. Some of the snapshots greatly intrigued the soldiers, who were not much older than I was. When they found out that I spoke Chinese, they asked a lot of questions. By the time they finished, our belongings were scattered everywhere. I tried my best to pack everything up again but could not close some of the suitcases. It became quite comical. I asked one of the guys to sit with me on the suitcase and help me close it as I tried to squeeze the contents between the lid and the bottom part of the suitcase. He gladly obliged. I'm sure it was a memorable sight to see a Communist soldier and a missionary kid struggling with over-stuffed suitcases!

We breathed a sigh of relief as we finally boarded the freighter. More than 400 of us squeezed into a space that normally carried forty passengers. The majority of the passengers were persecuted Jews from

Russia and Germany. They hoped to reach their promised land, the newly established country of Israel. On May 15, 1948, the British had left what was at that time called Palestine, and it had officially become the nation of Israel. It became a haven in which many persecuted Jews found refuge. I was astounded at what they hoped to safely take to the Middle East. Huge pieces of luggage and boxes of every size and description had been loaded into the cavernous belly of the ship. There were even pianos that made high-pitched sighs, moans, and groans as they landed on top of the cargo, most likely never playing a tune again.

People were everywhere aboard the freighter. Since there were not enough cabins for the large number of passengers, many spread out in the stairwells, the various decks, the lounge, and even the hallways. We had to be careful not to step on people. Fortunately, my family was assigned to three different cabins, with a few more people than there were beds in each. My lot was to share a cabin with several Catholic nuns. I got a real surprise when my roommates, who wore habits, took their wimple off before going to bed at night. I never knew that some nuns were required to shave their heads as a part of their vow.

On Easter Sunday evening, April 9, we passed my hometown of Shanghai. As I stood at the railing and watched the city lights flicker in the distance, I was flooded with emotions. Would I ever see this city again? How would this beloved place change under the rule of the Communists? What would happen to the many friends I had to leave behind? No one saw my tears.

My good friend and mentor, Anna Swarr, had given me a wonderful surprise before I left. She had written several Scripture verses, poems, and loving words of encouragement on a number of cards and stuck them in individual envelopes. I was to open them on the ship, one a day. These cards lasted for several weeks on that voyage. I don't remember the verses and poems, but I do remember what a comfort and shower of love they were to me. She must have known how lonely and lost I would feel, and how frightened I would be of the future. God in His tender mercies used her to give me hope.

The sea was very rough the rest of the voyage. There was enough food only because many of the passengers were too sick to eat. Most of us fed the fish if we were able to make it to the railing in time. With seasickness and the number of people squeezed into a small space, conditions were extremely unhygienic. Tables and chairs from the dining room that were fastened to chains slid from one side of the room to the other, causing dangerous situations. Huge waves that crashed over the sides of the ship soaked folks who made their quarters on deck. The East China Sea is known to be very rough, and we learned the truth of that first-hand.

Finally, Hong Kong came into sight. What a welcome sight it was! A week of this kind of travel was enough. Once in town, we swayed from side to side until we could regain our balance.

Yet again, we had to go to the police station for more papers to be approved. Hong Kong was still a British crown colony, and we had to deal with British personnel. By now, my parents were trying to get to England, so we had to get an entrance visa. There was hope because the mission headquarters was in London. I helped Dad deal with the authorities. Once again, it looked hopeless, especially when a very zealous young man asked him, "Why don't you and your family go back to where you came from?" To which my father emphatically responded, "Go back to Red China? I don't think so!" We were DPs with no permission to stay and no place to go. The Lord overruled, however, and with the help of some of the CIM directors, we were able to board the SS *Carthage* of the Thomas Cook Shipping Company. We were finally headed for Europe!

For a little over four weeks, we sailed on a sea that was as smooth as glass. It was very relaxing, and there was much entertainment provided. There were shows, dance bands, and a wonderful string quartet that played in the evenings. We also enjoyed the swimming pool, deck quoits, library, movies, and many games and competitions arranged by the activities' director. I was even awarded first prize by the captain of the ship for the ladies' ping-pong competition. Travel on ocean liners in those days was the forerunner of the popular cruise ship industry of today.

There were stops at many fascinating and exotic places. Unforgettable stops included: the Botanical Garden and the Raffles Hotel in Singapore; the Snake Temple in Penang, Malaysia, where poisonous snakes were revered and crawled everywhere; the stores selling famous tea in Colombo, Ceylon, now called Sri Lanka; and the pushy shopkeepers in India, with ladies in beautifully-colored saris. Also memorable were: Aden in Yemen; the Red Sea with a view of Mt. Sinai; the Suez Canal, which was still in British territory and being guarded by British soldiers; and Port Said in Egypt. It was fun watching local boys and men who had rowed out towards the ocean liner jump off their boats and dive for coins passengers threw over the side of the ship. It was amazing how many coins they could gather in their mouths. The Mediterranean Sea was a little turbulent as we neared the Rock of Gibraltar.

We finally made it to Tilbury in England. We lined up with the other passengers to disembark. One of the harbor authorities took one look at our papers and then barked at us, "You are Displaced Persons! Wait until everyone has left the ship. Then we will deal with you." I could see the hurt, disappointment, and even anger on my parents' faces at being treated like third-class citizens, but they said nothing. After all the trials, hardships, and want they had gone through in their twenty-five years of ministry in China, including World War II and the Communist take-over, it saddened me deeply to see them given such a terrible welcome to Europe, the continent from which they had originally come. So we waited. There were some heated discussions about whether or not we should be allowed to leave the ship. Then Mr. Keeble, one of the mission's directors who had traveled with us on the SS *Carthage*, took matters in hand. He stated that we would be in the care of the China Inland Mission and that the authorities had nothing to be concerned about.

My father remarked in his diary that we were received with loving-kindness in the headquarters of the mission. He also stated that there was a wonderful, strengthening spirit of prayer there. Several days after our arrival, we once again had to see the authorities and start over with securing the correct paperwork. I was shocked when I saw the devastation of some of the inner city of London. Hitler's powerful flying rockets V-I and V-II had certainly left their destructive and killing mark in the last days of the war.

While there, we visited several museums, attended chapel at Westminster Abbey, and heard the famous preacher Reverend Dr. Martin Lloyd Jones at St. Paul's Cathedral. We also saw an open-air play at Covent Garden; listened to some of the soapbox speakers at Hyde Park Corner; and saw Buckingham Palace, where Princess Margaret, the Queen's sister, came by in her chauffeured car. My parents attended a conference at Swanwick while I visited and stayed with some of my friends from the children's home who lived outside of London. After several weeks of dealing with the authorities in England, we finally got our entry visa and could leave for Germany.

We crossed the English Channel by boat and went through Holland by train before we entered the land of my parents' births. I thought the marks of war were bad in London, but I was not prepared for what I saw on this long train ride to middle Germany, my mother's home territory. Town after town and city after city lay in ruins. There was so much destruction that it was difficult to believe that people had once lived in those places.

When we stopped in Northern Germany and met with some of the mission leaders, they told us, "You should have seen it five years ago, right after the end of the war. It is great how much of the rubble has been cleared and how much rebuilding has started." I was bewildered, confused, and absolutely shocked. When we heard about some of the cruelties of which Hitler and the Nazi regime were capable, we shuddered. This land that was once so beautiful and well known for its people of integrity, uprightness, and virtue seemed soiled. We had no idea of the depth of the atrocities that had occurred while we were in China. I clearly remember feeling so horrified and appalled that I wanted to travel right through Germany and end up in Switzerland.

A coolie pulling a rickshaw, a former mode of transportation

Using a pole and baskets is a common Chinese way of carrying loads.

An unusual way of transporting people was the wheelbarrow.

Sedan chairs were used mainly by the upper class. Mother and I were carried in sedan chairs to our summer home in the mountains.

Chinese scissors with embroidered case

Chinese teacup: to drink tea, hold saucer, cup, and lid in one hand

Two embroidered Chinese ladies' shoes for bound feet

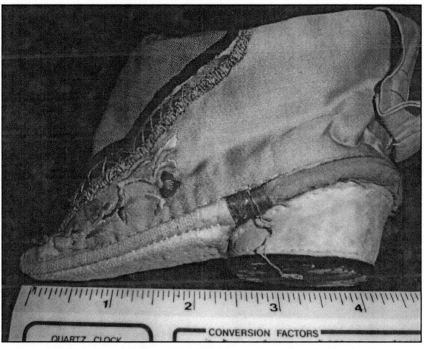

The actual size of a grown Chinese woman's shoe during the
times when little baby girls' feet were still bound

I was scared when the photographer hid under a black cloth behind his "View Camera" on a tripod, saying: "watch the birdie." Suddenly a puff of white smoke with a "pop" came out, but no birdie.

Proud dad with his trio

Mom with her "three" in Chongren

The mission house dad built in Chongren

My little Chinese friends

Travel by bus in inland China

Traveling in sedan chairs up steep mountain paths

Mom and Dad with the evangelist and his wife

Air raid on Shanghai during Sino-Japanese war

First and only professional family photo, taken during my parents'
surprise visit to Shanghai. It still hangs in my bedroom.

Children at the home in Great Western Road. Author is fifth from the left.

The "Gang" from Great Western Road in 1949

Chapter 11

Trials, Tribulations, and Triumphs (1950–1953)

REST AND RETIREMENT were not in my father's nature. Since his heart's desire was to continue to serve the Lord on the front lines, he considered re-enlisting for the mission field. Since China was closed, he thought about Japan. Only ten days after we arrived at the farm of my mother's family, Dad noted in his diary that he had discussed Japan with the mission leaders. It was one of the fields the China Inland Mission opened in the Orient after China closed. The mission leaders considered it too difficult for my parents to learn another language and to adjust to yet another culture at their ages and with their physical conditions compromised. Japanese is an even more difficult language to learn than Chinese. God knew the reason they were turned down.

We helped with chores and tried to make ourselves useful on the farm. Daddy often went on the road to preach and attend mission fests and meetings, but when he was at the Reiherbach, he labored with the rest of us. I will never forget the tremendous work that accompanied the potato harvest! I walked along the many rows, picking up potatoes until my back was breaking and my fingers were bleeding. A special plow pulled by a horse led by my cousin dug up these vegetables. I greatly envied her job of just walking along beside the horse.

I never had done such work before. After a few weeks of this torture, I determined never to do it again. One of our China friends who came

109

109

over one day to visit was roped into working in the fields. He declared, "This is a job for someone who killed his father and mother!" He, like me, was not used to this kind of hard work. This was my initiation into German farm life.

Physical exams were an ordeal for all of us. We were tested, probed, and thoroughly checked inside and out by a host of doctors at the Tropical Institute in Tuebingen. Both of my brothers joined us. They and Father were released after several days, but Mother and I had to stay for more checkups. Finally, the doctors deemed me healthy enough to leave, but Mother had many health challenges. She had not been well for some time and was often ill in bed with a fever in China before we left. The doctors were puzzled. Not wanting to keep Mom, they discharged her.

We left and went to visit one of Father's brothers near the city of his birth, Mannheim. Mannheim had been almost completely destroyed by severe air raids. The city fathers had built strong air shelters in bunkers all over town. For this reason, many of the citizens were spared, but there was not enough housing for everyone.

My uncle had a large three-story home, but the roof and top floor had been razed by bombs. Therefore, he and his family of four lived in three rooms on the second floor. By city ordinance, they had to share the rest of the rooms and the first floor with several other families. Their hope to rebuild the top floor had to wait until better days. This gracious family took us in, even with their crowded conditions. It was strange to live with people who were family and yet not know them.

When Mother became very ill, I had to admit her to a hospital in Mannheim. Fortunately, my uncle was able to give me some advice, but other than that, I was on my own to deal with all that a hospitalization entailed. It was not easy for an eighteen-year-old in a foreign country. I visited Mom faithfully as long as I could, but it soon became apparent that it was time for me to move on, because my uncle's family needed their space.

Looking back, I often wonder what Mother must have thought and felt. She was in a strange place, in the hospital, and the doctors did not give her much hope for survival. She was alone, without her immediate family. My father's siblings and half-siblings who lived in the area promised to look after her as best they could. Even they did not live close by and had to walk a distance to catch a streetcar to get to the hospital. In those days cars were a luxury, and not many people had one. This was especially true so soon after the war. Phones were also not common. The only way we could let Mom know we cared was by mail.

In October, my father got a position as an itinerant pastor in South Germany. It entailed preaching to church groups in about thirteen different cities, villages, and hamlets in the Black Forest. Dad was grateful to get a job so quickly. Many refugees were looking for work, even those in the ministry. He went ahead to get things organized. Werner, who was employed by one of Mother's brothers, stayed in Kassel. Fred and I left the farm in the Reiherbach. A trucking company carried our belongings to our new destination in the Black Forest. Grandma Pfeifferling gave us several pieces of her furniture, including an antique sofa, an oak dining room table, a hutch, some chairs, and a few other items.

On our way south, we passed through Mannheim, so we made a quick call at the hospital to see Mother. We could tell she was not doing well, and we were not sure whether or not we would ever see her alive again. It must have been unbelievably difficult for her to see us leave, but she said nothing. Had it not been for the grace of God, I'm sure she would have been overwhelmed by feelings of abandonment. Mother was a deathly-ill stranger in the country she had left so long ago. She really did not belong anywhere or know anything about this country anymore. I can't even imagine the incredible loneliness she must have felt.

Leni Wink, our assistant from the children's home in Shanghai, came to help us get settled in our new home. I was thrilled. Dad was thrown into the ministry immediately, and with so many outposts to visit, he was on the road constantly. Leni stayed for several weeks, but after that, it was my lot to keep house for Father and Fred.

I knew very little about housekeeping. In China, we had house help. Although we older kids had some household chores, I had never had to cook all the meals or do the cleaning, laundry, and ironing as I did now. It was an enormous task for me. All I knew about cooking was how to boil water. There were no washing machines, dryers, dishwashers, microwaves, vacuum cleaners, or other modern conveniences in those days. Most chores had to be done by hand—even the laundry.

Fortunately, a lady from town came to help me with that task. I toiled from early morning until late at night.

Grocery shopping was another adjustment. There were no supermarkets in those days, only "mom and pop" stores. There was a small store across the street from our home, but I was terrified to go get our groceries. To deal with a Caucasian storekeeper in any store was very intimidating for me, as I mainly was used to dealing with Chinese shopkeepers. Many times, I would go across the street to the store but forget what I needed to buy because I was so shy and felt so ill at ease. I would not make a list of what we needed because I thought people would make fun of me for not being able to remember how many pounds of flour, sugar, or whatever else I needed to buy. The baker, the butcher, and the hardware store owner were all white. What misery this was for me!

The weather was extremely cold, with endless months of snow and ice. There was no bathroom in the apartment, only a cubicle with a toilet. Our bath water was heated in a huge cauldron in the basement, and we took baths in a tub made from zinc that was next to it. Each bedroom contained a basin and a pitcher with water for sponge baths. Most mornings the water in the pitcher was frozen. There was no central heat. Our only source of heat came from a large, tiled, square wood-burning stove in the living room. Even the locals joked that three quarters of the year it was winter and the other quarter it was cold.

With all our difficulties, adjusting to life in St. Georgen was not easy. Since St. Georgen was close to Switzerland, the dialect people spoke was much like the Swiss-German dialect. It was hard to understand. Not knowing the local language immediately marked me as a foreigner. Soon I realized that even the thought pattern of the people was different from mine. In those days, the average German person had not traveled much, so his outlook on life was very provincial. St. Georgen was a small town in a rather remote area of the Black Forest. I had come from Shanghai, a cosmopolitan city with about eleven million people.

It is no wonder that I was very homesick for China. I missed my friends, especially those from our youth group, Ambassadors for Christ. Our church meetings, youth activities, and Sunday school in China had been alive and vibrant. Here in Germany, church life was cold and rigid, filled with tradition. Alone at night in my room, I shed many, many tears.

Finally, news from the hospital in Mannheim came that one of Mother's doctors had discovered the cause of her illness. He was extremely proud of the fact that he was able to discover the tropical disease that afflicted her when the doctors at the Tropical Institute, with all their probing, their microscopic research, their knowledge, and their medical specialties had missed the slowly-killing disease. New and aggressive treatments finally made it possible for Mother to join us after almost six months on her deathbed in a Mannheim hospital.

For the first time in four years, we were together as a family to celebrate Christ's birth, the Christmas of 1950. The last time we had been together at Christmas was in 1946 on the mission station in Ningdu, Jiangxi. My brother Werner came from Kassel. Fred, a student at the time, was also with us. So it was that we gathered as a family around the Christmas tree and thanked the Lord for His watchful eye over all of us in the past, very tumultuous, life-changing year. At that point, I wondered what the future would hold.

As Mother slowly convalesced, Dad traveled all over the southern region of the Black Forest, preaching in meeting places, churches, and homes. He rode his bike over the mountains, walked to the closer villages and hamlets, and took the train to the more distant cities. It was amazing that he was able to keep up with a heavy schedule of ministry in thirteen towns and villages. No matter what kind of weather, which almost always included snow, he was on the road serving His Lord. I continued to keep house until Mother was well enough to take over.

When considering my future, my parents felt it would be best for me to perfect my knowledge of French. I had studied French at high school in Shanghai, but in order for me to use it in the business world, especially as a secretary, my knowledge was inadequate. I do not remember how it was decided that this would be the line of work I would pursue. Since Dad had attended seminary in Switzerland many years before, he still had some contacts there. Switzerland is a country where French, German, Italian, and Romanish are the official languages. So it was decided that I would go to Pully, near Lausanne, the French part of Switzerland.

With the help of a Christian agency, I was hired as governess for a family with two children. I was told that there was a cleaning lady who came to the home, someone who did the laundry and ironing, and a gardener who took care of the large garden. In the evenings, I would be able to attend French lessons free of charge. The school was part of the company where the master of the house was one of the vice presidents.

My first impression of Switzerland was that it was a beautiful country, but I noticed that the Swiss border officials were not too friendly towards foreigners. When we crossed the border from Germany into Switzerland by train, all the passengers who were going to live in Switzerland for an extended period of time were required to get off the train. I was led to an office at the train station, where a doctor examined me and took an x-ray. I had to answer numerous questions about China, as well as other questions, such as what I was planning to do in his country.

After he checked my x-ray, the doctor asked if I had ever had TB. This surprised me. He told me that the x-ray showed deep scarring on my lungs. When I told him that I'd had pneumonia several years in a row, with the most severe case being when I was twelve, he was satisfied. I received a green light to enter Switzerland. One of the train officials laughed at me when I mispronounced the name of the town, Pully, where I was to reside. I learned quickly to be very correct when speaking French in Switzerland.

A long time before, I had learned that life is full of surprises. Switzerland, especially Pully, was no exception. With all of the commotion at the border, my train was very late arriving in Lausanne. It was a challenge to figure out how to use the public phone at the train station, but I got it done and was able to convey to my new employers that I had arrived. Soon I was picked up by car.

The house where I was to work was a three-story building with a basement. White stone stairs in half circles ran from top to bottom. The entrance and hall to the kitchen had marble floors. A large living room and dining room could be closed off with pocket sliding doors for entertaining large crowds. Both of these rooms had beautiful, shiny parquet floors covered with thick Persian carpets. A sunroom off of the dining room led to the terraced yard, where there were several fruit trees. Beside the kitchen were a powder room and a separate pantry with a refrigerator, which was a novelty in those days.

The second floor included three bedrooms for the family of four. These rooms also had beautiful parquet floors. A bathroom rounded out this level. The third floor included a large room with a sink and a toilet. Next to it was a small room, which was to be my quarters. When I arrived, it was occupied by the family's visiting grandma. I would later learn that she would use that room whenever she visited and I would sleep in Monsieur's home study during those times. The house was on Lac Léman, or Lake Geneva, and French doors opened to a balcony that overlooked that beautiful lake.

The first day I was told what my duties would be. I was to start preparing breakfast at 6:30 A.M. After breakfast, the dishes had to be washed at 7 A.M. and the beds made. Cleaning was then in order. Once a week, one floor at a time, the rooms had to be vacuumed and the parquet floors checked for spots. With steel wool under my foot, I had to move back and forth until the spot was removed. Then, and only then, were the floors to be waxed and polished. Polishing the floors included attaching a brush to my foot and moving my leg back and forth in the same direction as the parquet had been laid. I moved carefully around the edges of the carpets. Several times a week the white staircase had to be scrubbed, as well as the bathroom and toilets.

My duties continued with laundry and ironing, which took another two days. Fortunately, the lady of the house had a centrifuge, a spin dryer, but the laundry still had to be washed by hand and then hung up in the backyard. If there was a lull in the afternoon, I had to mend socks and clothes. When the children, a boy and a girl, came home from school, I supervised their homework. If time permitted before helping with dinner, I played games with them.

I received quite a shock my first day when I learned what the lady of the house meant by "nous," which, in French, means "we." She told me that "we" would clean the vegetables and prepare them for dinner. After telling me this, she and her mother left to go shopping while I began to do one of the many chores that were assigned to me.

When the lady of the house returned after her shopping spree, I heard her call out in surprise, "Mais rien est fait!" This meant, "But nothing has been done!" I rushed after her, knowing by the tone of her voice that she was upset. She looked at me and said, "You have not cleaned the vegetables! You did not cut them up and cook them for dinner!"

In utter disbelief I answered, "I placed them on the counter, and I thought you said *we* were going to clean them and prepare and cook them for dinner—you and I." From then on, I knew that if she said "we," she meant *me!*

The days were long and did not end until the dishes were done at night. Sometimes this was quite late when there were dinner guests. From 6:30 in the morning until about 8 P.M. was a long day. I often wondered what had happened to the cleaning lady, the laundry woman, and the gardener. Monsieur loved working in his large vegetable and berry garden, but at times, I had to help with weeding. When I asked about the promise of the other workers, I was told there was a mix-up. They always just had a girl wanting to learn French.

Monday nights I was able to enroll in the Migro French classes. After several months of not feeling that I was learning much, a Swiss girl who worked for a family two doors from us joined me in private classes with a marvelous private tutor. This girl and I became wonderful friends.

Many days I was so exhausted that I would lay down on the thick Persian carpets in the middle of my dancing with the brush attached to my foot, trying to polish the parquet floors, and cry. Of course, the lady of the house would be gone attending her luncheons with friends, shopping, or on one of her many social pursuits. In my tears, I would think of my friends. Some of them were still in China, but others had to flee to various parts of the world. I would think: *If they could see me now, toiling like this, they would have a difficult time believing it.* Even our Chinese helpers were never required to work as hard as I was working. They each had one task to perform, whether that was cooking, cleaning, or gardening, but I was expected to do it all! I still wonder how I managed to survive that year and a half in Switzerland.

There were some better days. I had one day a week that I was not required to work and half-a-day on Sundays. My friend and I joined a group of girls who often met at the home of a Christian lady in the area. She opened her home to us and other girls for Bible study, fellowship, and fun times.

A few times when my work was done in the afternoon, I would take the two children swimming in the lake. We merely had to go through the back gate to the small beach on Lake Geneva. There I learned to swim. I was able to lose my fear of the water that had haunted me because of my near-drowning accident in Shanghai. I have loved the water ever since.

Putting the children to bed at night was also a privilege. I could pray with them and answer some of their questions about the Lord and spiritual things. I had done this very thing hundreds of times in the children's home in Shanghai. The little boy was especially curious. He was going to a private Catholic school and did not always understand what the nuns were trying to teach him in class. Since the parents were not Christians, they did not pray and talk about the Lord in their home. On Sundays, they allowed me to go to church in the little town, but I don't think the pastor had a personal relationship with Jesus. His messages left me empty.

A great blessing was Leni Wink's visit when she and her employer were vacationing in Switzerland. Another special visit came from my mentor and friend Bishop Houghton and his wife (the General Director of the China Inland Mission and his first lady). They were in Lausanne on mission business and made it a point to invite me to have dinner with them at a nice restaurant. We had stayed in touch since we parted ways in Tianjin many months before. I will never forget their kindness as they encouraged me and expressed concern about my life and walk with the Lord. We had a wonderful time of fellowship and prayer. My heart sang all the way back to Pully as I walked the empty streets late at night. There were no more buses running at that hour from Lausanne to Pully, but I didn't care. My spirit had been refreshed, and I felt strengthened.

When I was in St. Georgen, Mother and I had conducted a young women's Bible study. The ladies from that study, accompanied by my mother, wanted to take a trip together and decided to come see me in Switzerland. I made arrangements for all of them to stay in a small hotel in the area. My employers gave me a few days off so I could join them and show them some of the sights of the area. Mother and I roomed together.

For some time the Lord had been dealing with me about my lack of love and respect for my parents, especially for my mother. Ever since my parents had come from the interior to Shanghai in 1949, we had grown apart. I was no longer the little girl of fourteen or fifteen they had last seen. I was mature enough to be asked to take Leni Wink's place to assist our housemother, Mrs. Wehmeyer. I also had to assume much of the responsibility of dealing with the authorities in order to leave China. Mother's hospital stay also had put a strain on all of us. In addition, I had not agreed with certain requests that Dad had made and was actually glad that he was gone a great deal of the time. I was a committed Christian, but my relationship with my parents did not reflect a close walk with the Lord. My rebellious, indifferent attitude and my disrespect saddened them. I could have rationalized and made excuses, but in my heart, I knew that I had not honored them as I should.

The first night of my mother's visit to Lausanne, we talked as we lay in bed. In fact, we talked until early in the morning. I apologized and told Mom what was on my heart. I wanted to make things right and asked for her forgiveness, which she graciously gave. It was as if a stone had been lifted off my heart. With much joy and a renewed love for one another, we joined the ladies for a trip to the zoo. I will always remember that night. I had wasted many unhappy months. Later I also had a chance to apologize to my father and ask his forgiveness. From that time on until the Lord took Mom and Dad home, I had a wonderful relationship and friendship with them.

After my year as "governess" and much more ended, I stayed on for a few more weeks. I signed up for a Christian youth camp in the Swiss Alps in the summer of 1952. The family I had worked for left for the summer to spend time with relatives in another part of Switzerland. Since they were gone for several weeks, they let me stay in their home while I watered the vegetable garden in exchange for free housing. To earn some extra income, I worked for a dairy farmer who had a store in town that sold dairy products. He was the first to sell yogurt mixed with fresh fruit.

This area of Switzerland was well known for its international boarding schools for children of the rich and famous. Many sheiks, royals, and millionaires from around the world sent their children, many of them girls, to these schools. It was fun to wait on their tables and sell them yogurt. They giggled as they told exciting tales about famous people, and it was amusing to listen to them.

Finally, the days of the youth camp arrived, and I enjoyed wonderful Bible studies, good fellowship, and lots of outdoor activities. It was at that camp that I saw my first glacier. It was exciting to cross fields of ice and form a chain by holding hands with your friends so no one would fall into any of the deep gullies. What a rush of energy it was to jump over a deep crevice and hope you would not slip. Other times we would climb up a mountain. My fellow campers were already resting at the top by the time I made it and greeted me with loud and cheerful yells, "Here comes China! Here comes China!" I carry precious memories from those days.

When I returned to St. Georgen, where my parents were still serving the Lord faithfully, I looked for a job. With the Lord's help, I was hired by an Austrian who was an engineer, an inventor, and the founder of a small and up-and-coming factory close to our home. He had married a local girl, who stood with him through the early lean and difficult days. They had three sons and two daughters. The three sons were deeply involved with the company and helped make it a great success, especially in its later years when it became one of the largest factories and firms in St. Georgen.

The father and founder of the company held several patents for small motors that were used in record players and other motorized, small mechanical devices. This company manufactured and sent motors all over Germany. After World War II, record players were in great demand. I was secretary to the gentleman who was second in command and head of the sales department. As the market expanded across Europe and overseas, we became the import/export department.

As time went by, I became quite proficient at my job, using the shorthand and typewriting skills I had learned in Shanghai. Being an executive secretary and assistant to the vice president of the company was rewarding, and my boss and I had a good relationship. As the company grew and the American market opened up, it became my task to answer the mail and translate the correspondence from English into German and vice versa. Since I was the only one who knew English, I was also asked to translate some of the patents from German into English. That was an enormous task, especially since I did not know or understand all of the technical jargon in either language, but I did it. Many days I could be seen going home with precious patents tucked under my arm that were worked on at the dining room table in the evenings.

My relationship with my parents was wonderful. In the mornings, Mom would often stand at the kitchen window waving goodbye as I walked to my place of employment. Since we were given an hour and a half for lunch, I went home for the main meal of the day. After I had worked a half-day on Saturday, I cleaned the kitchen for Mother in the afternoon and baked a cake for the traditional Sunday afternoon "Kaffeetrinken," or coffee time. Then, weather permitting, I would meet some of my tennis partners for a game of tennis, since I had joined the tennis club as soon as I found employment. Shanghai had given me a head start with tennis, and I loved it.

Sundays were a day of worship, and we attended church. Since returning from Switzerland, I had volunteered to help teach Sunday school, which was only for children, in the main city church. Several fellowships of believers had been started all over Germany by church members of the main line churches who felt a lack of true commitment to the teaching and preaching of the Word of God. These gatherings met on Sunday afternoons or on weeknight evenings.

One fellowship of believers met on Sunday afternoons in the meeting hall on the first floor of the house where we lived. Dad was the pastor and preached—if he was not on the road. I played the pump organ for the hymn singing and helped with a small choir for special occasions. It was my privilege to set the table for Kaffeetrinken in our apartment. We used Mother's special Chinese tea set, and I got the coffee and cake ready just before the meeting was over. This provided a good time of fellowship for a visiting preacher if Dad was absent. If Dad was home, it was a great time to be together before he had to leave for his next assignment.

Along with Kaffeetrinken, another German tradition included taking a Sunday afternoon walk after coffee. We enjoyed doing this, and since St. Georgen was a small Black Forest town, it was one way of meeting friends or acquaintances. Exchanging pleasantries on the street often resulted in meeting new folks.

Many years before this time, when I was a teenager, I had told the Lord that I would never become a missionary. Every time the appeal was given in our church in Shanghai to follow the Lord no matter what that might entail, I would respond with, "Lord, I'll do anything you ask me to do, but I will never be a missionary. Lord, you better write it down. I will never, never, never become a missionary. I will try to make a lot of money and support your work and your missionaries, but don't ask me to be one. I know too much about missionary life. I know about the hardships, the deprivations, and the sacrifices, and that life is not for me." I meant it, on both counts. Now that I was making good money, I supported ministries and missionaries I knew and believed in.

The Bible says in Isaiah that God's ways are not our ways: "For my thoughts are not your thoughts, neither are your ways my ways declares the Lord. As the heavens are higher than the earth, so are my ways higher than your ways and my thoughts than your thoughts" (Isaiah 55:8–9). Werner was working with Youth for Christ, and he arranged a youth conference in Northern Germany. He invited me to come and join him and the hundreds of other young people. Since I was able to take a few days off work, I went.

One evening of that conference changed the rest of my life. One of the speakers mentioned Isaiah 6 in his message. Contrary to Jeremiah, who was called of God, he said that Isaiah was simply asked by the Lord: "Whom shall I send? And who will go for us?" (Isaiah 6:8b). Then the evangelist asked a question that became a life-changing challenge for me. He said, "Young people, tonight I am not going to ask God to call you, but I am going to ask how many of you will stand to your feet and volunteer for service to the Lord. I am asking for *volunteers*!" I could not stand to stay seated but jumped up and said with Isaiah: "Here am I, send me" (Isaiah 6:8 c)! In my desire to give myself totally to the Lord, I had forgotten what I had told Him adamantly many years before about never being a missionary.

I wanted to talk to my boss after I returned from the Youth for Christ meetings, but before I had a chance, he called me into his office. He told me that the leadership of the company had evaluated my work and had decided that I deserved a substantial raise. How like Satan to tempt a missionary kid who had never known much of earthly comforts with a large increase in salary. I thought about what I could do with substantially more money. I could support even more missionaries and even help my parents more financially.

Deep in my heart, I knew what I had to do. I had made a promise to God, and I had to keep it. I answered, "Thank you, sir. I really do appreciate it, but I have to leave and cannot accept your offer."

He was shocked that anyone could turn down such an enormous increase in salary. Then he asked, "Are you going to the competition. Have they offered you more?" When I told him that I was not leaving because of any other offers but that I was going to serve the Lord and train for missionary service, he almost fell out of his chair. It is no wonder that he could not comprehend the ways of God.

My boss asked me to stay on to train another lady to take my place, which I gladly did. I had been working very hard and needed some rest. The Lord provided that in His wonderful, unique way.

Twice during the summer months, I had either cycled or walked on Sunday afternoons to a home in a hamlet not too far from St. Georgen. I held Sunday school for the children in that area. During most of the year there was so much snow that I skied through the forests and then down the mountain. This was quite an achievement for a "Chinese" who had never seen much snow in her life.

After I had decided to leave the company, it was again time for another visit to my little Sunday school class in the valley. We, in the higher area of St. Georgen, still had a lot of snow; but in the lower regions, it was different. As I came down the mountain on my skis, I did not realize that some of the snow had melted. Plowed dirt in the fields below was showing through a thin covering of snow that caused me to fall hard. When I picked myself up, my left arm hurt terribly. Picking up my skis and my satchel with my Bible lessons, I trudged on to the house where the children eagerly awaited my arrival. The long trip home with skis on my shoulder, satchel around my neck, and a throbbing left arm seemed to take forever.

When I had x-rays taken, they showed that the large bone in my swollen left arm was fractured in two places. My arm was placed in a cast, and I was excused from work with pay. For three weeks, I was able to relax and get rest before I left for Paris, France, and Bible school.

Chapter 12

Studying, Serving, and Singing in Paris (1954)

ROBERT EVANS, A chaplain in the US Navy during World War II, started a Bible Institute in a villa in Chatou, France, which grew into a mission known as Greater Europe Mission. Werner heard about the European Bible Institute (EBI) from his good friend Bob Hopkins, who was a missionary with the Navigators in Germany. In January 1953, Werner became a student at EBI, and a year later Fred and I joined him. Fred had committed his life to full-time Christian work and had been a student of theology in Heidelberg, Germany, but had become very disillusioned with the erroneous teachings of some of the professors there. A young man from Berlin and a nurse from Holland also started school with us.

The Institute was divided into the English and the French sections, with classes taught in both languages. Only chapel and choir were combined. Students came from all over Europe, the US, the Middle East, and even from Cyprus and Asia. I chose the English department but was quickly asked to help with one of the Thursday afternoon "Club de Jeudi" Bible clubs for children. Judging from my application forms, the Director of Christian Service must have trusted my French to be good enough to help in this outreach. We took advantage of French schools being closed on Thursday afternoons and had a number of these clubs in the area.

On weekends, most of us were assigned to specific ministries in the surrounding churches and meeting places. Both of my brothers and I were asked to help on two different American military bases. We were happy to be together again as we had been during our growing-up years. It was not long before we became known as the "Burklin Trio." We sang in French and English services, as well as at the European Command at Camp des Loges. On Sunday mornings, we were picked up by a car sent by the army chaplain and then brought back to the school after the two services. Besides providing the special music, we had the opportunity to give testimonies and do some personal counseling. I played the organ and piano in the respective places. It was also my privilege to play the piano for the daily chapel service at the Institute. Once again, I was thankful for my benefactors, Mr. and Mrs. Beck, who invested in my life while I was in Shanghai.

Our theme song and the most requested song that we sang as the "Burklin Trio" was "What Shall I Give Thee, Master?" written by Homer W. Grimes:

What shall I give Thee, Master? Thou who didst die for me.
    Shall I give less of what I possess, Or shall I give all to Thee?

What shall I give Thee, Master? Thou hast redeemed my soul;
    My gift is small but it is my all—surrendered to Thy control.

What shall I give Thee, Master? Giver of gifts divine!
    I will not hold time, talents or gold—For everything shall be Thine.

Chorus:
Jesus, my Lord and Savior; Thou hast giv'n all for me;
Thou didst leave Thy home above To die on Calvary.
What shall I give Thee, Master? Thou hast giv'n all for me;
Not just a part or half of my heart, I will give all to Thee.

Since my parents could not pay my tuition for the three years I spent at EBI in Chatou near Paris, I had to trust the Lord for provision. I worked hard doing a great deal of babysitting for the children of the members of the faculty. I not only took care of little ones when their parents went out of town, but also cleaned house for locals and US Army families; taught German to a little Greek boy; and painted flannel backgrounds in oil and sold them to pastors, churches, and children's ministries for their work among children. These backgrounds were used for visual Bible lessons and storytimes. They became quite popular for children's workers.

It was also my privilege to work for the Navigators, Dawson Trotman's ministry, and for Child Evangelism in their French offices in Paris. The shorthand I learned in Shanghai as a teenager came in handy. I was able to adjust the "chicken scratches," as I called them, to any language I knew. This enabled me to take dictation and write letters in French. The Lord blessed me with a gift of languages, and over the years, I used this shorthand in English, French, German, and Dutch. During my second semester at EBI, Jeanette Evans, wife of Dr. Bob Evans, the founder of the school and mission, asked me to work for her and Bob as secretary in exchange for half the cost of tuition and board. I was deeply grateful to the Lord for opening doors of employment for me, as well as for providing special anonymous monetary gifts.

There were special blessings along the way. Billy Graham and his team came to England in the spring of 1954 for his first European Crusade that was held at the Harringay Arena in London. Bob and Jeanette Evans were classmates of Billy and Ruth Graham at Wheaton College in Illinois. They became lifelong friends. The Lord used the Evanses and their connections in Europe to open many doors for Billy and his ministry. Billy and the Billy Graham Association invited the entire student body, both the French and the English Departments, to come to England during Easter break and help with counseling and singing in the huge choir. The Billy Graham Association paid half of the cost. The crusade gave us students hands-on experience and knowledge in organizing mass evangelism, as well as in soul-winning, counseling, and follow-up of new babes in Christ.

It was wonderful to be able to leave early for London and the crusade so that I could spend several days visiting with some friends from Shanghai days. These included Mr. and Mrs. Koll, missionaries who had been with the Plymouth Brethren Group in China, and their son and daughter. Ruth, their daughter, had been one of my best friends at the children's home. It also was a thrill to spend Sunday night with Reverend and Mrs. Weller, one of the directors of the China Inland Mission. Mrs. Weller was one of our favorite in-depth Bible teachers at our Ambassadors for Christ youth meetings in our Shanghai church. We had not seen each other in four years.

A special treat was visiting with Bishop and Mrs. Houghton. They invited my brothers and me for high tea and were genuinely interested in what was happening in our lives. I never ceased to be amazed that the General Director of one of the largest missions of that era had time for us.

The crusade was tremendous, and its impact reached multiple thousands. I sang in the choir and counseled with those who came forward to accept Christ at the end of the service. The attendance every night was about 11,000, with 400 to 500 people accepting Christ as their personal Savior after responding to a simple, but powerful gospel message.

The first night of the crusade, Billy and Ruth Graham were riding in a taxi the eight-mile distance from their hotel to the crusade when they heard a radio announcer say that only about 2,000 people were in the arena. The British press had not been excited about a young, handsome American coming to their country preaching the gospel message, and the Grahams wondered what the newspapers would say the next day. They turned their hearts to the Lord and prayed that He would draw people to Himself.

When the Grahams arrived at the arena, it was full! People had poured out of subways from all over town. The naysayers were silenced as people were radically and eternally changed by the power of God. Little did those of us helping at that crusade realize how God would use this young man in years to come. Today, Billy Graham has his name indelibly etched in the history books as having preached to more people around the globe than any other evangelist who has ever lived.

We students from EBI were assigned to stay in the homes of Christians from the area. The home of two single, working girls was my destination. To get there, I had to travel by subway. The crusade was so popular that the transportation department of the British underground extended train hours well past midnight. It was always very late when

I finally was able to leave the arena. It was a great thrill each evening as I entered the bowels of London's subway to hear thousands of voices singing, "This is my story. This is my song," or "Just as I am without one plea." Some echoed the words of Billy Graham's soloist, George Beverly Shea, "I'd rather have Jesus." That crusade was truly a once-in-a-lifetime experience that I will always cherish.

I will never forget Billy Graham's words to those of us who were in a small gathering of Christian workers and Bible school students. He pleaded with us, "Please do not forget to pray for me. Pray that I may keep humble and that the Lord will continue to use me." The Lord certainly answered our prayers. Having met Dr. Graham and his wife several times over the years, I must say that they have been faithful, humble servants of the Lord. It is no wonder that God has used them in such a mighty way. Although Ruth Graham has gone on to be with the Lord, our prayer is that Billy Graham will be strengthened and encouraged as he continues to live for God.

Since I had been invited to Ruth Koll's wedding on Saturday, April 24, I was permitted to remain in London while our EBI group went back to Chatou. It was not a customary wedding, but one in the tradition of the Plymouth Brethren. After the civil wedding at the courthouse, which was the only legal marriage accepted in many European countries in those days, a prayer service was held in the assembly hall, where only men could pray for the couple. The reception followed the service. Traditional British refreshments included the wedding cake, which was a special fruitcake that was given to each guest in a tiny little box to take home.

Not being familiar with the strict Brethren rules, I was unprepared to appear in the service with a hat. After scrambling around at the home of the bride to be, Mrs. Koll was kind enough to solve the dilemma by telling her son, Godfrey, to let me wear one of his hats. The only one that fit was a beret!

Back at EBI, life was very regulated. Schedules had to be kept promptly. When leaving the premises, we were required to get special permission from the respective dean. Upon leaving and returning, we had to sign a book kept in the entrance foyer. No dating was allowed with a fellow student. If a couple fell in love, one of them, usually the girl, was required to leave, even if she was soon to finish her three-year course. And it did happen!

The European Bible Institute was definitely not for students who had just finished high school, although we did have a few students in their late teens. Most of the students had been in various professions in their home countries. There were teachers, nurses, secretaries, Christian workers, and businessmen, among others. Many of them were the same age as the professors. Some of them were even older. Our desires to be trained for the ministry allowed us to submit to the extraordinary rules and regimented life.

Since the school was divided into the French and English sections, with about fifteen to twenty European and Middle Eastern countries represented, only English or French was allowed to be spoken on the premises. In order to improve my French, I tried to spend time with students from the French section as much as I could. It was fun to find out where they were from and what their lives had been like. It was especially interesting to talk to the Middle Eastern students from countries like Cyprus, Lebanon, Syria, or Armenia.

Besides the Thursday afternoon Bible club for kids, I was also asked to help by playing the piano or the pump organ at several of the local church gatherings and special meetings. Sometimes I was privileged to give my testimony or to sing. It was always a blessing to minister with my fellow students from the French section.

The professors worked diligently to instill a love for the Word of God in each of us. They faithfully taught us scriptural truths that we, in turn, might faithfully teach others. Whether it was Christian Education, Doctrine, Old or New Testament Bible, Homiletics, Music, Systematic Theology, Church History, or any of the many other subjects, the professors were always well prepared. Most had been trained at some of the best colleges and universities in the United States.

To liven things up a bit, we sometimes had "funspirations," which included socials with student entertainment, picnics on special holidays, or volleyball after lunch. We always enjoyed being invited to a professor's home. When entertainment was sparse, we girls came up with some new, although sometimes strange, ideas for having fun.

Brigitte, one of the girls in the English section, had become a special friend. She had formerly been from East Germany, where she had studied in a university near Berlin and become a teacher. Under the influence of a godly mother, she had become a Christian. Realizing that as a believer she could no longer continue her profession under the Communist regime, she left and went to England. There she perfected her English and worked for an organization called National Children's Home and Orphanages. After about a year and a half, she decided to study to become a foreign correspondent and needed to learn French. She got a job as an "au-pair" with a family in Chatou.

One afternoon on the commuter train from Paris, Brigittte met a missionary who told her about the "L'Institute Biblique Européen," the European Bible Institute in Chatou. She invited Brigitte to the Sunday afternoon meeting at the school, and Brigitte went. It was not long before she realized that the Lord wanted her to be trained at that school for full-time Christian work. She was one semester ahead of me. We became fast friends, and we have remained so until this day. To get us out of the routine of student life, she and I at times had some wonderful ideas.

We girls from the English department decided to spruce up our attire a bit. In those days, none of the girls wore pants or jeans but only dresses or skirts. Large shoulder pads were in vogue, so we thought it would be interesting to wear our dresses inside out with the large shoulder pads riding on our shoulders in plain view. The seams and hems of our clothes showing on the outside also gave an interesting dimension to our fashion.

At first it had been difficult to get the French girls to join us. They were more spiritual than we! Fortunately, I knew most of them well and convinced them to join in the fun. Early in the morning, we each made our grand entrance into the dining room for breakfast by limping down the grand and beautiful curved staircase with a low-heeled shoe on one foot and a high-heeled shoe on the other, dressed in our finery. The looks on the faces of the male students and faculty who were present were priceless. Later in the day, the wife of the director asked me if it was a European custom to dress so strangely on that particular day, which happened to be a European holiday!

At the end of the school year, Brigitte and I thought it might be nice if one of us could date a fellow student. We did not want any of the professors to get upset, so we decided to wait until final exams had been taken and the school year had officially ended. We selected a young Dutch teacher, also a Bible Institute student, who was not particularly handsome but was a nice guy. Brigitte took things in hand and made all the arrangements, telling our Dutch friend to meet me at the train station in the afternoon of the last day of school for our infamous "date."

The last day of school arrived. While students were busy preparing to leave for the summer, Brigitte ran into our room shouting, "You have to go to the train station!" She was determined that we complete our wild plans regarding our "first date." It was the end of the school year, and no one, not even the dean, could send us packing at this point. Our spirit of adventure just had to have an outlet!

I went to meet our friend at the station. He was there, nervously waiting for me. In those days, Europeans did not know the custom of dating. They met young people of the opposite sex in group outings or activities. Since the poor Dutch fellow had no idea what was expected of him, he had inquired of my brother Werner. Since Werner had come from China and had been to the United States, our Dutch friend assumed that he was far more experienced in such matters and could wisely counsel him.

My "date" suggested we take a walk. We went to the next small town, found a little park with a huge rock in the middle, and sat on the rock. He pulled out a brown bag with some cookies in it. Werner had advised him to have something to eat, but since he was a poor student, he could not afford a meal. Cookies were the next best solution. We munched on the cookies, talked some, and the date ended. I know our Dutch friend was relieved.

Chapter 13

Delightful, Difficult, and Dark Days (1954-1955)

IN THE SPRING of 1954, I was asked by Youth for Christ Germany to spend the summer helping with their tent campaigns in various cities throughout Germany. I was needed on a team to lead the children's ministry in the afternoons and to play the piano and be the soloist in the evening meetings.

At my first destination, I was surprised to find a quartet from the United States that was made up of four male students from Taylor University in Upland, Indiana. They would be singing, leading the meetings, helping with the children, and sometimes teaching in the afternoon Bible study. I was to be their interpreter in addition to my other responsibilities.

The next three months were very busy as I traveled from town to town. Our custom was to spend three weeks in one place, unless we were asked by the locals to leave. Youth for Christ, or "Jugend für Christus," was not known in Germany at that time, and many folks from the State Church considered us part of a false sect. Bible churches or independent groups were considered heretical since they were not part of the "true" church that they considered to be the officially accepted State Church. We were not deterred.

After arriving in a city, we would seek approval from the city fathers and then put up a large tent that would hold 250 to 300 people. Next, we would drive through the streets with loud speakers and invite folks to come to the evening services. The children were invited to afternoon meetings. We also handed out invitations, put up posters, and prayed a lot. We also drew many people to the meetings through the showing of Moody Bible Institute's scientific films.

Our team consisted of an evangelist; a mature, full-time Christian leader; the tent master, who was required to keep an eye on the tent day and night; the Taylor quartet; and me. Every morning from nine until noon, the Taylor men and I went from house to house throughout the city and invited folks to come to the meetings. We would share the gospel with them if they were interested in hearing what we had to say. The afternoons included a Bible study for the local people at the tent and a children's meeting. After a quick evening meal, we gathered for the crusade at 7:30 P.M. In spare moments, we prepared, practiced, and got things ready for the various meetings. I seldom got to bed before midnight, as I counseled and led women to Christ after the services. It was wonderful to see a number of people over the summer accept Jesus as their Lord and Savior or rededicate their lives to Him.

With our victories, we also met with much criticism. In those days, the German Christians were very concerned that they not be perceived as being worldly. They were very pious in their demeanor. Subdued clothing was the norm. They wore no bright, airy colors, but chose black, gray, brown, and sometimes, dark blue. The women's hair was long and pulled back into a tight bun that was fastened with pins at the nape of the neck.

Many times, I would receive anonymous letters criticizing my dress—the pink blouse or red dress with large black flowers I wore; my inch-high heeled shoes; or worst of all, the shoulder-length, curly hair I sported. Unfortunately, the criticism came mostly in anonymous letters left where I would find them on a bench in the tent or on the piano. It would have been great to talk to some of the authors of those notes. I would have pointed out the many colorful bouquets the children brought to decorate the length of the podium in the tent. God made the beautiful and fragrant roses, sunflowers, daisies, carnations, and wild flowers of every description with their incredible and varied colors. Surely, He would not be upset about us believers wearing neat, tasteful, and colorful clothes.

Wanting to do what was right and not be a stumbling block to anyone, I was extremely sensitive to the situation. I prayed and asked the Lord what I should do, since I had come from a Bible School in Paris where Christians wore bright colors and girls styled their hair short and often with perms. I told the Lord I would be willing to put my hair up in a bun. That presented a problem, since it would need to grow four to five inches longer in just a few days if I were to do that. The Lord graciously answered my prayers and solved my dilemma.

After one of the evening meetings, a local girl came to me and wanted to discuss her concerns about being a Christian and eternal security. I was able to show her from Scripture that if she had received Jesus as her Savior, she was indeed a believer: "Verily, verily, I say unto you, He that heareth my word, and believeth on him that sent me, hath everlasting life, and shall not come into condemnation; but is passed from death unto life" (John 5:24 KJV). Then I showed her the verses: "My sheep hear my voice, and I know them, and they follow me. And I give them eternal life; and they shall never perish, neither shall any man pluck them out of my hand. My Father, which gave them to me, is greater than all; and no man is able to pluck them out of my Father's hand. I and the Father are one" (John 10:27–30 KJV).

I assured this girl that if she had confessed her sins and accepted Jesus as her Lord and Savior, she had received eternal life. She was safe in the hands of the Lord. No one could snatch her out of the hand of Jesus, whose hand was covered by the Father's. Together we read: "And this is the testimony: God has given us eternal life, and this life is in his Son. He who has the Son has life; he who does not have the Son of God does not have life" (1 John 5:11–12). These verses gave this precious girl the assurance that she was indeed saved and had eternal life.

Together this girl and I rejoiced and thanked the Lord for her newfound assurance. Then she looked at me and said, "You know, you are the first person I have met who seems to be happy to be a Christian. All the other folks I know who say they belong to the Lord seem to be such sourpusses. They don't seem to enjoy life, but you do. You even have short hair and wear colorful clothes. I am so glad I met you." I could have hugged her when she said that, but I remembered that you shook hands instead of hugging in Germany at that time. All the way back to my quarters that night, I felt like singing. The Lord had graciously spoken to my heart and comforted me. After that night, I no longer worried about criticism.

My resolve to disregard criticism was tested one evening. Just before the evangelist spoke, I sang a song to prepare people's hearts for the message. As soon as I took my seat after singing, a young man marched from the back of the tent and came right up onto the platform. He came over to where I was sitting, whispered in my ear, and then walked back through the tent and left. It was evident that he had been drinking beer and smoking cigarettes. I was dumbfounded but kept my emotions under control.

After the service the evangelist came to me and teased me, "Well, what did that fellow want? Did he ask you for a date, or did he like your solo so much that he had to tell you in front of everybody?"

Quickly, I repeated what the young man had whispered in my ear, "Young lady, if I were you I would not dress in such worldly clothes, and even worse, have short hair. And then sing for the Lord?" This greatly angered the evangelist, who looked for the fellow because he wanted to confront him about what he had said, but he was gone.

The young man who had criticized me did not come to the services again until the last night of the three-week crusade. I spotted him right away and told the evangelist that my "admirer" was in the audience. As soon as the evangelist said his last "amen," he quickly went to where the young man was sitting. After some serious conversation, my friend brought the young man to me. He demanded that the young man not only apologize to me but also that he ask my forgiveness.

The summer passed much too quickly, and I knew I would miss our wonderful team. Each of them was special. The tent master, as we called him, was a gypsy who had found the Lord some time before. The evangelist had served the Lord for many years and was a wonderful speaker. The four Taylor University men had tried hard to adjust and had fit in well. We had served the Lord well together for three months, working closely and complementing each other.

The leader of the quartet had served the Lord in Germany on another Taylor University team the previous summer. So working in Germany for the summer was not new to him. In fact, he felt the Lord's calling on his life to serve Him with Youth for Christ Germany when his last year at Taylor was completed. He was an admirable young man and was very committed and dependable. Always ready to do any task at hand, he was a great encouragement to his three fellow students, who were not used to German ways. I saw things in him that I greatly liked. We had wonderful talks and prayer times together, especially when his group helped with the children's meetings of which I was in charge.

Working and traveling together so closely the entire summer allowed our group to get to know each other well. As we weathered obstacles together, our hearts were knit as a team. The leader of the quartet and I grew very close, and by the end of the summer, we had fallen in love. It was a tremendously sad day when we had to part after serving the Lord together for three months. His senior year at college lay ahead of him. He was looking forward to returning to Germany after his graduation and after he had raised the necessary funds for his mission work. When we said our goodbyes at the train station in Heidelberg, Germany, he asked me if I would wait for him so that we could be reunited and work for the Lord together. I promised him I would.

After my summer ministry, I went to my parents' home in the Black Forest for a short time of much-needed rest. In October 1954, I returned to Chatou, France, to begin the second semester of my freshman year at the European Bible Institute. Once again, it was a year filled with opportunities to serve the Lord. I studied hard and worked at any available job to earn my tuition and funds for room and board.

My letters to my parents at that time are proof that I was very much in love. I greatly looked forward to the day that I would marry the man I knew to be completely committed to the Lord and His work. Correspondence with his mother was a real blessing, for she too was a follower of the Lord Jesus. She was looking forward to coming to Germany for the "big event" when the time came.

The beginning of June 1955, Billy Graham and his team came to Paris for a crusade at a large arena called the "Velodrome d'Hiver." The EBI student body was once again asked to help with counseling and with singing in the choir. What a thrill it was to be going to my second Graham Crusade. I had fond memories of the crusade in London the previous year and of the many young girls and women I had been privileged to counsel. The Paris Crusade was equally blessed. After the crusade, I corresponded with a particular girl for two years to nurture and disciple her, since she had accepted Christ as her Savior at the crusade.

One of our fellow students from Holland arranged for my friend Brigitte and me to vacation with two ladies in his hometown. One of them had been a missionary to India and the other had been a teacher, but she was now retired. Youth for Christ Germany asked me once again to help with the children's ministry during the summer. I wanted to get a few projects ready for the ministry, so I gladly accepted the Dutch ladies' invitation. Brigitte and I were looking forward to some rest, relaxation, and fun times.

Not wasting any time after the last day of classes, we got up at 4 A.M. the next morning and took the train to downtown Paris. We had investigated and found out that the cheapest way to the Netherlands was to join one of the truck drivers who came to "Les Halles," or "the halls." This was the area in Paris where farmers and fishermen brought the fruits of their labors to sell. They arrived before dawn. Buyers for local restaurants, as well as truckers from other European countries, came to buy fresh vegetables, fruits, fish, and meat. The truckers then drove their precious cargo to their country of origin.

It was exciting to see the hustle and bustle of the market and to hear the bartering of buyers and sellers. In the midst of all this, we tried to find a truck driver who was willing to take us all the way to the northern part of Holland. Since neither of us spoke Dutch, this was not an easy task. We finally found a fellow who was willing to take us as far as Rotterdam. In those days, hitchhiking was a normal way of travel, even for girls. Since there were two of us, we felt especially safe.

Our truck driver was a nice, decent fellow. By the time we reached Rotterdam, he insisted that we come to his home for coffee. He assured us that his mother would be glad to serve us. She was a kind lady, and we enjoyed our coffee. Brigitte and I laughed when the Dutchman insisted we let him show us some new suits of which he was very proud. Perhaps he wanted to show us that he had some nice clothes besides the work clothes he wore when he drove his truck.

From Rotterdam, we were blessed to be able to get another lift to our destination of Hasselt, which was further north. There we were welcomed with open arms into the home of the two elderly Dutch ladies.

We were so exhausted that we slept more than twelve hours that first night. The two sisters did not know what to think about that. They must have wondered if we were sick or perhaps did not like their hospitality that we would stay in our room all day. After a gentle knock at the door, we found a tray with two cups of tea outside our door. When we finally presented ourselves, we assured them that we were extremely tired and needed the rest after our hectic college schedule. They understood and let us sleep as long as we pleased, which was unusual for Dutch folks as I learned years later.

Our elderly friends must have wondered how to entertain two young ladies from the Institute in Paris. The village they lived in was very small, and there was not much to do. So, we went on a tour of Holland. We hitchhiked all around the country, visiting the cathedral in Utrecht and the Zuiderzee, which was being transformed into wonderful fertile land. The ladies told us that when they were young they sailed in boats on the very spots where cows now grazed. Well-known was the saying, "God created heaven and earth, but the Dutch made Holland!"

One day we hitchhiked all the way across Holland to Amsterdam, where we went sightseeing, visited several museums, and went shopping. At that time, Holland was still a country where everything was much cheaper than other European countries. We really liked the big department stores and purchased so much that we had to buy a suitcase to get it all back to the dear ladies' house. They were quite startled when they saw us carrying that heavy suitcase through the front door. We must have amused them; they probably wondered what we might do next! Most Dutch people are very frugal, almost to the point of being stingy. They would not have spent that much money buying so many things at once.

Since our fellow student had made all the arrangements for our stay in his hometown, we thought it would be courteous to visit his mother, even though he was not in town at the time. We arrived at his house midmorning. A matron of rather large stature opened the door and welcomed us in. Although she did not speak English, or we Dutch, she motioned for us to sit in the living room.

Soon our hostess appeared with two cups of coffee and an open tin of cookies, which she placed on the table before us. Then she left, and Brigitte and I enjoyed our coffee and cookies. Dutch cookies are delicious, and we ate one after another until they were all gone. After a while, the lady of the house came back into the living room. She looked at the empty tin, and we knew immediately that she was very upset, as she began to speak faster and faster. Of course, we could not understand a word she was saying, but we knew she was getting more and more angry. We excused ourselves and left as quickly as we could!

When we returned to the home of our elderly hostesses, we told them about our wonderful visit. They explained that in The Netherlands you only take one cookie with one cup of coffee or tea. To take more is considered very impolite. Since it was a small village, it soon became known that the two of us were rude and had no manners. It was a lesson in cultural differences.

The ladies were very kind to us, and even invited us at times to go along with them to visit their friends. Perhaps they wanted to give us some further insight into Dutch life and customs. One time they asked us to come along with them to some of their special friends that lived a half-hour distance away by bus. We had a wonderful afternoon with tea being served in a lovely garden with beautiful flowers and shrubs of all kinds. The evening meal was a typical Dutch meal, consisting of many different kinds of delicious breads, cheeses, sausages, and chocolate and sweet sprinkles of all sorts.

We enjoyed ourselves so much that we did not notice the lateness of the hour. When we stopped to consider leaving, we realized that the last bus of the day had already left. The ladies cheerfully suggested that we four hitchhike. Brigitte and I had done it so often all over Holland that we felt it would be no problem. The four of us dutifully stood at the curb of the street with our thumbs stretched out. There were not many cars that evening, and the ones that did come along drove right past us.

After quite some time with no success, one of the ladies said, "Why don't we old ladies hide behind these bushes. You young ones hold out your thumbs. Perhaps that will work." With that, they quickly disappeared. Sure enough, it did not take long and a car stopped with a young male driver. We explained our dilemma to him, and he answered in good English that he would be glad to take us where we needed to go. Quickly the ladies came out from their hiding place and ran to the car. The expression on the young man's face was priceless. We made it home safely that night; and the ladies, I am sure, have never forgotten their first hitchhiking experience.

The two weeks in Holland passed all too quickly. My first assignment in July with Youth for Christ Germany was a one-week crusade with my brother Werner being the evangelist. It was great to fellowship and to serve the Lord together.

The next crusade was in North Germany. My parents sent a package for my birthday with goodies and a birthday cake, which I shared with the team. My sweetheart and his mother also sent me some special presents. Since his graduation from college, he had been diligently trying to raise support for his ministry as a missionary. The leaders of Youth for Christ International in Wheaton, Illinois, urged him to leave for Germany as soon as he was able to raise the necessary funds.

Things seemed to be going along fine, and then I received a letter that would change the direction and plans I had made for my future. It was shocking to me because my birthday, with all its nice gifts, had been just a week before. The letter was from the man I loved with my whole heart and thought I would marry. I opened it and read words that told me he was breaking off our relationship. That news was received while I was on a bus going to our next meeting. Overwhelmed and devastated, I wondered how I could possibly play the piano or sing of God's goodness when my heart was breaking. I could not shed any tears, for I had to witness and counsel women and girls that evening who needed the Savior.

In a letter to my parents telling them about the breakup I wrote:

Perhaps you can imagine how I feel and yet I have to be cheerful and happy in my work. I can only say one thing. The last two weeks were terribly dark days for me and yet, I could feel Jesus' presence. I want to take everything out of His hand. He has the best in mind for me. Scripture tells us that we are to be transformed into the image of Christ. Oh, if only that happens then a lot has been won. That through this experience I might be purified and refined. I may have to pass through this valley so that in my ministry I might be able to help other girls who are experiencing the same disappointment....Many evenings I lie awake at night for a long time. The hand of the Master seems to want to crush me and I tell Him some times that it hurts very badly.

But I want to remember that a loving hand holds the chisel in order to make something useful out of me. It hurts, yes, it hurts very much, but I want to hold still so that the potter can transform me....I cannot understand God's way, and don't need to, because I know He has a plan for me. But pray for me more than ever before that Satan might not be the victor.

I closed the letter by pleading with my parents not to be upset with or mad at the young man, "The important thing is that he is happy and will walk in God's way."

Less than eight months later, he was married—to someone else. My prayer over the years continued to be for his happiness. About twenty-five years later, the Lord allowed me to ask him face to face in our living room in Stone Mountain, Georgia, if he was happy. He answered that he was, and I thanked the Lord for that.

The summer ministry continued with tent crusades in various German cities until the end of September 1955. Before going back to Paris to continue my education at the European Bible Institute, I spent a week with my parents in the Black Forest. That summer had taken its toll, so I was grateful for a few days of rest and relaxation.

Back at school, I found it difficult to get back into my past familiar routine. It required a great deal of effort to meet my friends and fellow students after such a traumatic summer. My turmoil can be seen in a letter I penned to my parents:

Fortunately, people don't notice much on the outside how I really feel, but please pray, pray, pray. . .somehow I am scared of the future. Please don't misunderstand me. I know His rod and staff, they comfort me. But for some reason I am afraid of myself. Perhaps I should not mention all this, it sounds so despondent, so un-Christ-like....And yet, I am grateful for everything and want to gladly take all out of His hand. For in the dark valley we can see the light, Jesus Christ, more clearly.

Fred immigrated to the United States that fall, bringing an end to the Burklin trio. Werner and I became a duet. We continued to serve the Lord through singing until he finished his studies at the end of January 1956.

Chapter 14

Ministry in France, Belgium, Holland, Sweden, and Denmark (1956)

ONE OF MY professors at the European Bible Institute asked me to join a French team to minister in Southern France during the Easter holidays, and I gladly accepted. The following days were filled with long hours of practicing duets, quartets, and solos. From March 28 through April 11, 1956, we ministered in Dijon, Lyon, Vienne, Grenoble, Mulhouse, and St. Louis, which is close to Basel, Switzerland.

During that time we conducted seventeen services and meetings, along with numerous open-air gatherings. A full schedule also included visiting and handing out tracts. Seven of us students made up the team, with the others representing Italy, Spain, France, Poland, and the United States. It was a wonderful experience to work together and really get to know one another. This bonding also taught us how to exercise patience, understanding, and grace.

A highlight of that ministry opportunity included the team visiting my parents for a delicious Chinese meal of Mother's special noodles. This was possible since my parents' home in the southern part of the Black Forest was not too far from our last meeting place. It was highly entertaining to see my teammates trying to eat noodles with chopsticks. Mom was a good sport, pretending she did not own any silverware. Everyone was greatly relieved when Dad finally demonstrated the way to eat Chinese noodles by raising the bowl to his mouth and loudly slurping the contents!

Since my time at EBI was nearing an end, with only eight to nine months of course work left, I seriously started to pray about working with Child Evangelism Fellowship. This American organization had ministries all over the world that took the Gospel message to children and saw many of them saved. Since I had already worked in the office of Child Evangelism France, I met with the director. He told me I had to apply to and attend the CEF institute in California in order to be accepted by the mission. Dutifully, he gave me the application forms, which I filled out. After several weeks, I was accepted. My desire had always been to go back to the Orient, which I considered my part of the world. My brother Fred had a professor at Grace College and Seminary in Indiana who offered to be my sponsor. Fred had not even mentioned my need for one in order to be able to obtain my visa to enter the United States.

The EBI professor who led our Easter tour through Southern France also asked me to join another team he was getting together for the summer of 1956. This group would minister in Belgium and Holland. I had plans to go to Sweden that summer for three months as a volunteer to work with the Navigators, a ministry that was being greatly used to follow up with new believers after large crusades. They were Billy Graham's choice for follow-up resulting from his crusades. Dawson Trotman, founder of the Navigators, started the ministry among sailors and GIs after World War II. It was greatly used in assisting many young men to come to Christ and become strong Christians through Bible study and Scripture memorization. After several letters back and forth with Sweden, I told my professor that I would join the team for six weeks and then serve the Lord in Sweden.

One day my friend Brigitte asked me, "Have you noticed the young Dutchman with the beautiful blue eyes?"

I replied, "No, where is he?"

She laughed, "He is being picked up every Sunday morning with the car the American chaplain from Camp des Loges, the European Command, is sending to the school. And you are riding in it with him!"

It was true that every Sunday morning I was driven to the chapel along with several other students for our Christian service assignments. This Dutchman and the other students were in charge of the Sunday school, which was held in the theater of the base. My assignment was to play the organ or the piano, to sing solos, and to help with the ladies' ministry in the chapel. I had not noticed the young man of whom Brigitte spoke. Since my previous break up, I was in no mood to notice any young man, even a good-looking one with pretty blue eyes. Her enthusiasm did make me curious, however.

I soon learned that the Dutchman also had been asked to go on the summer tour. In fact, our professor had asked him to be its leader and organize the meetings in Belgium and Holland. He already had been a missionary in Belgium and had served the Lord with Christian Literature Crusade and Youth for Christ before coming to the Institute in the fall of 1955. He had contacts and was well-qualified to do the preparatory work with our professor.

The school year ended in the middle of June. The last weeks and months were filled with studies; hard work; and practicing duets, quartets, and solos for the tour. I also worked as many jobs as I could. One of the little boys I babysat for quite often was the son of one of the American soldier families I met at the chapel. When I tucked him in at night, I prayed with him. He always insisted that we both kneel at his bed. Imagine my surprise one evening when he followed my prayer with this petition, "God, please make me grow up real fast and keep Joy the way she is now so I can marry her." He was about eight years old then, and I think the Lord smiled at his request!

Right after graduation on June 16, 1956, our team left for Belgium. It consisted of my Dutch friend Rie, who had begun attending EBI when I had, five semesters before; two Dutch young men, Gerrit and Bill; our professor; and me. Bill was the Dutchman with the beautiful blue eyes.

After three services and some open-air meetings in Belgium, we ministered in the western part of Holland. The Child Evangelism workers in Holland did the children's work, which gave me another opportunity to get to know a little more about this work. Our professor preached, and Bill served as his interpreter. Rie and I sang duets. I was also asked to sing solos in the Dutch language. Since I did not know the language, it was extremely important for me to be able to communicate the message of the songs. Therefore, I worked diligently to make sure that I pronounced the words the best I possibly could.

When in Antwerp, Belgium, the team stayed in the home of Mr. and Mrs. Boerop, Bill's parents. They were Dutch missionaries with the Worldwide Evangelization Crusade and worked specifically with the Literature Crusade branch of the mission. They served the Lord through a local bookstore and through open-air meetings held in different cities at their markets.

The ministry in Belgium was very different from the one in Holland. In The Netherlands, the people were more open to the Gospel. Although we did not have multitudes attending our meetings, there were a number who accepted the Lord as their Savior. In Belgium, however, although we handed out about 9,000 invitations and tracts; drove through the streets with loudspeakers, inviting folks to come to the meetings; and many times went from house to house to share the gospel, we were often not well received. We also held open-air meetings.

In the four services we conducted in the Antwerp area, only about ten visitors came. We also met in small churches led by pastors who served faithfully in spite of their discouraging ministries. We sang solos, duets, and quartets. We also preached and gave testimonies with almost no results. When people heard us through loudspeakers we put on the outside of a building, they would sometimes stop or even hang out of windows to listen, but no one dared come to the services. When a priest or nun walked by, which happened unpredictably often, the folks quickly disappeared or closed their windows.

I wrote to my parents on July 14, 1956:

> I never imagined how fanatical the people in Northern Belgium are and how resistant to the true Gospel. It is far worse than in France or South Belgium where French is spoken. And yet, God's servants are faithfully serving Him, even if they see little or no results…The fear of the priests and the church is unbelievable.

I went on to describe some of the false and idolatrous teachings that were preached in local cathedrals and through radio messages. Having seen the idol worship in China, I exclaimed that I would never have thought this possible in Europe:

Shall I then really go to Asia when a heathen country is so close by? The last evening in Antwerp our professor spoke about giving a 100% yes to God. And the Lord spoke to me. I told him: "I'll go where you want me to serve you, even if it is Belgium where the ministry is so difficult." The people in that country don't hear the Gospel. Please pray with me for this country. You should have an opportunity to be there to really know what I mean. I am so thankful for this experience. Now we can pray much better for our brothers and sisters.

Our tour continued through the small country of Holland, and we traveled to all of its provinces except two. The meetings were blessed. We had terrific fellowship, and our professor saw to it that we had some time to relax. One afternoon Bill invited me to go on a bike-riding date. Since we were not under the laws, rules, and regulations of EBI during the summer, we could do that. Riding bicycles was the usual transportation in Holland in those days. We saw the beautiful little town with its many canals, which was typical of Holland.

One of the interesting highlights that summer was the wedding of two of our former fellow students. It was an all-day affair, with the civic ceremony at the courthouse in the morning, then the traditional coffee break mid-morning. A light lunch followed, then the church wedding and a tea break. In the evening, there was a sit-down dinner. Our team was privileged to entertain with music. This was our last act of service together as a team that summer of 1956.

On August 3, I left the team and went by train to Hamburg on my way to work for the Navigators in Sweden. There I had a short visit with two friends of mine, a sister and brother who had been with me in the children's home in Shanghai ten years earlier. After two days of fun, relaxation, and getting reacquainted with my friends, I resumed my travels to Sweden—or so I thought.

My friend took me to the train station in Hamburg. I boarded the train, put my belongings in an empty compartment, and went back into the corridor to say "goodbye" to my friend. At that moment, a young man stepped into the same compartment. Immediately, I remembered my purse and went back to retrieve it. In so doing, I passed the same young man as he came out of my compartment. I was horrified to find that my purse was no longer on the seat where I had left it. Quickly I looked around, but it was nowhere to be found.

My friend ran alongside the train to look for the thief, for he too had seen the young man. It did not take long for the police to arrive. My purse contained my passport, all my French residency papers, since I was still a student in France, and my return ticket. Without these papers, I could not travel. Quickly, I tossed my suitcase to my friend through the window. By this time, the train had already started to move, and the policeman had to help me jump out of the rolling train.

Although it was a very complicated process to get a new passport, the Lord knew I had work to do in Sweden. Within a week, I had my new passport, one with preferred issuance. Since my money was gone, I had to borrow some from my friends' parents.

My father sent some funds to Hamburg, which did not reach me. In a letter to my dad for his birthday, I expressed my thanks for his amazing generosity:

> Too bad I cannot be with you to give you a special kiss and tell you in person that I love you. So I have to write it. You cannot imagine how very thankful I am for all and everything that you and dear Mother have done for me and that is not little. It is a great joy how you both are constantly sacrificing for us. But you also let the will of the Lord rule your and our lives. Again these last days you proved once more how willing you are to give up your own needs.
>
> I am so glad that I did not receive the money you sent while I was still in Hamburg. That way I am sure it was returned to you and you can buy your coat. But again, many thanks.

The headquarters of the Navigators in Sweden was in the city of Oerebro. My help was immediately needed in the office, and I was able to help with the evangelistic crusade that was held nightly. The Swedish people were amazingly kind and friendly. They made it easy to feel at home.

My six weeks in Sweden flew by. The Lord opened many doors to minister. At that time, women were well received in most churches and Christian endeavors. In one week alone, I spoke in twelve meetings with about 4,000 people in attendance. In those days, all government schools had devotions in the morning, and I was asked to speak at several of the schools. One of the local Christian workers interpreted for me.

Each time I spoke, my helper and I would ask the Lord to bless the meeting. We would do this before we even entered the building. Then afterwards we were certain to thank the Lord for the opportunity to impact precious young lives. One Saturday, young people from all of the churches in the area got together for a service where I challenged them to commit their lives to Christian work. How thrilled I was when seven answered the invitation and stood, indicating that they were willing to serve the Lord.

It was my privilege to meet the Child Evangelism workers in Sweden. Their headquarters was in Stockholm, the capital. I had a wonderful weekend with them, getting to know their work and ministry. It was also thrilling to spend a few days in Copenhagen, Denmark, with the Child Evangelism worker there. She was a dear Danish lady who was completely committed to winning children to the Lord Jesus Christ.

Chapter 15

Romance in Paris, Wedding Bells in Antwerp (1956–1958)

ON MY WAY back to the European Bible Institute for my last semester, I stopped in Belgium. Bill Boerop, my summer tour team member, had made arrangements for some meetings in the Antwerp area at the end of September 1956. He invited those of the team who were able to join him for the outreach before going back to Paris. While in Sweden, I had received a few letters from him. One letter in particular asked me to come a few days before the meetings so that he could show me a few sights in Holland. I liked seeing new places, so I accepted his invitation.

Coming from Copenhagen, Denmark, I was to change trains in Brussels, Belgium, on my way to Antwerp. Since travel by railroad in Europe is very popular and reasonably priced, trains are extremely long. When I got off the train in Brussels to catch my connection, I was shocked and surprised to see Bill Boerop standing at the bottom of the stairs of my railroad car. He was smiling broadly, as he handed me a large, beautiful bouquet of flowers. I was astonished and wondered how he could have known in which railcar I was traveling. How could he have known I was debarking from that long international train right at the spot where he stood? Actually, he did not know and could easily have missed me.

He led me proudly to his dad's car, and we drove to his home in Antwerp. This caused me some concern. I reasoned that if this young man had any ideas about a romantic relationship, I had better let him know a few things. So I proceeded to tell him that I had planned to go overseas to the mission field. Shortly after finishing EBI, I would be leaving for the United States, since I had been accepted at the Child Evangelism Institute in Michigan. One of my brother's professors in the States would be my sponsor. I continued telling Bill a few other details, making sure to add that I would, of course, be following the Lord's leading. He just listened quietly.

Bill was a good host, and we had a great time visiting several attractions in The Netherlands, including the Peace Palace and the Queen's Residence in Den Hague. Madouradam, a miniature of a typical Dutch village, was very interesting. In Holland, there were beautiful flowers everywhere, huge windmills, and herring stands on the streets. Bill loved pickled herring! I found that these were Bill's favorite. The rest of the time was spent conducting meetings in Belgium with fellow students.

It was a blessing to have Bill's dad and a family friend they called Uncle Joe drive our team back to school in Paris. Two Volkswagens carried us students to EBI for the beginning of my last semester. The next few weeks and months were unsettling days for me. Studies went well. Because of the many meetings and the exposure I had in Sweden, I did not have to work as much in my last semester. Christians gave generously, and the Lord blessed financially. I should have been carefree, but instead I was restless. A burden regarding the great need in Belgium rose in my heart. I began to question if I was really supposed to go to the States and be trained at the Child Evangelism Institute and then go on to the Orient.

As time went by, I had opportunities to speak to Bill Boerop on several occasions. We talked while we did yard work with some of the other students. It was good to get to know him better. The six weeks of summer ministry in Belgium and Holland, with all of its challenges, frustrations, disappointments, satisfactions, and joys, had given me some insight into this handsome young man.

I tossed and turned in my bunk bed at night. Poor Rie, the young lady who had started EBI with me, was now my only roommate. Many nights she was kept awake because of my restlessness. Was the Lord trying to tell me something? Why had Bill invited me to come to Antwerp before the other team members arrived to show me Holland, the land of his birth? How did he come to stand at the very place where I descended the steps of that long train in Brussels?

Many other questions interrupted my sleep. Why was the Lord burdening my heart for Belgium? Were we to serve Him together in that country? I knew Bill was planning to serve the Lord with Youth for Christ International in Belgium once he finished his studies. I was sure Bill liked me, but I wondered if he loved me. I continually asked the Lord to guide me as my feelings for him grew deeper. I had been hurt once before. I wanted to be absolutely sure about my feelings this time.

To make matters even worse than they were in my confused state, something happened that could have resulted in my expulsion just two months before I was to graduate from EBI. A number of us students had been studying in the large living room. One by one, each student had left, until Bill and I were the only two remaining in the room. Suddenly Bill got up, came to where I was sitting, grabbed me, and gave me a big kiss! Then he ran out of the room. At that precise moment, I looked up to see the dean of men walking by the large French doors in front of the living room. Only thin voile curtains covered the doors. I think my heart skipped a few beats until I realized he had not seen us.

Now I knew for sure that Bill had feelings for me. I agonized, wondering if it was the Lord's will for us to walk together for the rest of our lives. Again, many sleepless nights followed. I had to be sure.

Christmas vacation was approaching. I had decided not to spend it with my parents, since I was going to see them only a few weeks after Christmas when I graduated. Instead, some of the professors had talked to me about babysitting their children while they went away for ministry. For some reason, that did not materialize.

Bill approached me and said that his father had invited me to come to their home in Antwerp for Christmas. "That is a very unusual invitation," Bill said. "My father never invites anyone to our home. That is always my mother's doing, but this time he asked if you wanted to come." Bill was quite surprised at his father's request.

Since Bill and I were both earnestly praying about our future, it appealed to me to spend time with him outside of our rigid school structure. It would be good to pray together and ask the Lord if He meant for our lives to be joined in service for Him. I wanted to really get to know Bill, and so I agreed to go home with him.

As vacation time approached, I had two definite requests. First knowing how unpredictable feelings of being in love can be, I wanted to seek wise counsel from mature Christians. In October of my last semester, Mr. David Barnes had become EBI's new director. He had been at the school for a number of years and was my music professor. I knew him best, however, because I had worked for his family for one semester and babysat his three children on many occasions. I felt he knew me better than many of the other professors. I told Bill that before our relationship could go any further I wanted to know what Mr. Barnes thought about us getting serious. We knew that being this candid could have devastating consequences, due to the school's strict rules. Mr. Barnes had the authority to expel one of us, but I knew him to be a godly man who would counsel Bill and me wisely. We were also in the Lord's hands.

So Bill made an appointment with the director. Mr. Barnes gave him his blessing and challenged him to remain friends even if we did not marry. Then Mr. Barnes warned him to be discreet about our relationship.

My second request was that Bill would gain his parents' blessing on our relationship. His folks had gotten to know me during the summer months, when we were working in their territory with the EBI team.

On December 21, we boarded the train in Paris for Antwerp and made it to Bill's home in time for supper. After the traditional cup of coffee at 9:30 P.M., I wished everyone a good night and went upstairs to bed. I could not sleep, as I was convinced that Bill was downstairs talking to his parents and asking for their advice. Suddenly, there was a knock on my door. Bill asked me to come out of the room. I hurriedly put on my robe and stepped out onto the landing with curlers in my hair!

Bill's parents must have approved of our relationship. Right there, on the staircase of that old house in that small bedroom community in the city of Antwerp, Belgium, he asked me to marry him. My answer to him was a quotation from Ruth: "Where you go I will go, and where you stay I will stay. Your people will be my people and your God my God" (Ruth 1:16). The Lord had given me perfect peace about becoming Bill's wife. I believe that knowing God's will for our lives is a process.

We had searched the Scriptures to be confident that our walk and our relationship were in accordance with God's Word. Then we had sought the counsel of mature believers. Finally, our Heavenly Father had sealed our uncertainties with His perfect peace.

The next days went by quickly. We had time to pray together, discuss our future, discover some of the sights in the area, and make several trips to Holland. We also looked at engagement rings. It was a good time of getting better acquainted, and we were deeply grateful. We also had some ministry opportunities before we returned to Paris. Those times were certainly a foretaste of what my life with Bill Boerop would be like. His heart for ministering is so ingrained in everything he does. There has hardly ever been a place that we have gone where ministry was not a foremost consideration.

We arrived back at school several days later than the other students did. Being late at night, the lights-out signal had already been given. As I quietly tiptoed up the stairs to my room on the top floor, Mr. Barnes appeared. His apartment was on the opposite side of my room. He leaned over the banister and whispered with his hands cupped over his mouth, "And…are you engaged?" When I answered in the affirmative, he smiled broadly and said, "Praise the Lord," as he disappeared into his apartment.

Since Bill and I had arrived together several days after the rest of the students, rumors had begun to fly around our very small school. I could not risk being seen with Bill, so we had to scheme about how we would manage our last four weeks of school. Bill's mother had entrusted a huge tin of cookies to me. They were Bill's favorites. She knew that they would be gone in a matter of days if Bill kept them in his room, because he and his five roommates would devour them. So she asked me to hand them over to her son a few at a time.

Rie was kind enough to deliver cookies to Bill every few days. Of course, this gave them the opportunity to talk. This went on for a while, until the student body was quite sure that something was going on between Rie and Bill. Nobody knew that Rie not only gave Bill cookies, but also she was our note carrier. Passing notes was the only way Bill and I dared communicate with each other. Rie played her role well. Bill and I did not allow ourselves to be seen talking together or even sitting next to each other in class or chapel.

The last day of exams finally arrived. On the announcement bulletin board a notice was attached that read, "All students watch this spot for a very special announcement immediately after the last exams. Don't miss it!" We all wondered what this could be about. Was it a list of new student assignments for the next month? Someone complained, "I hope I don't get kitchen duty again!" Another wondered if he had to clean the toilets in the men's bathroom. Clearly, not too many were eager to find out what the work program for the next few weeks would be. It didn't concern me. I didn't care. I had final exams to take.

When the bell rang, indicating that time was up for the last exam, everyone dashed over to the bulletin board. Students started to holler, laugh, and clap, causing quite a commotion. When I got close enough to see what all the excitement was about, I could not believe my eyes. In the middle of the board was a huge red heart with a large picture of Bill and me with the words, "Yes, we are engaged!" Under our names was the official stamp of the L'Institute Biblique Européen, the European Bible Institute, and the word, "APPROVED."

Everyone talked at once, exclaiming that they had no idea, or that they thought it was Bill and Rie who were in love. They were amazed that we were able to keep it a secret from the entire student body except for a few of Bill's and my closest friends. Bill and I did not know that one of the professors had put the announcement together on behalf of the faculty. It was a total surprise for us when we saw it on the bulletin board.

The dean of women told me that our professors had watched us very carefully since the director had shared with them about our situation after Bill talked to him. She said, "We as a faculty were very proud of how you and Bill conducted yourselves these last few weeks. You were an example of propriety." It was very rewarding to hear that, especially since it was her husband who had come by the living room that fateful day, November 20, when Bill gave me my first kiss. To this day, we celebrate the anniversary of that first kiss.

We could now be seen together, but that did not last long. My time at EBI came to an end. I had to say "goodbye" to my friends. As difficult as that was, nothing could compare with having to say "goodbye" to my fiancé, Bill. The next time I would see him would be at my parents' home, where we would meet during his Easter vacation. He had received permission from them to marry me, but he had not met them. He was anxious to do so. Child Evangelism Germany had asked me to come help them. Since I was still sorting out where I was to serve the Lord until we would marry a year and a half later, I had accepted. Bill still had three more semesters of school before he would graduate in June of 1958.

In need of a vacation, I had asked my parents to join me for a couple of weeks at a retreat center. It was located at a town in the Black Forest, close to where they lived. Their schedules, however, did not allow them to meet me there. So I asked my roommate and summer team member, Rie, to join me. She gladly accepted and was happy to have some time to reflect, relax, and get some rest. She had been accepted by a foreign mission board with a ministry in Dutch New Guinea, now called West Papua. Rie would study a semester at a Tropical Institute in Antwerp, Belgium, and then begin deputation to raise her financial support for ministry as a nurse in that far-away land.

Rie and I only had been at the retreat center for a few days when my father surprised us. He wondered if Rie would like to join him on his tour of ministry. It would be an excellent way for her to start deputation. He had no idea what financial help she would get, but he assured her that the folks to whom he ministered were praying folks. Dad trusted the Lord that some of her financial needs would be met.

Rie went with my dad, and it was wonderful to see how the Lord used this time to provide for her so that she could enroll at the Tropical Institute in Belgium. The folks in the Black Forest were blessed by her sharing and gained new insight into the worldwide needs for the gospel. My dad's missionary heart was still beating loudly. He was not selfish with his territory, but gladly shared it with a young lady who was called by God to reach a primitive, stone-age people with the good news of the Lord Jesus Christ.

Days of rest flew by quickly for me. It was wonderful to attend some of the Bible studies held at the center; to take long walks in the beautiful forests nearby; and to relax, read, and study God's Word. It was good preparation for the months of ministry that lay ahead of me.

My new headquarters for the next four to five months was Frankfurt, Germany. The first obstacle I had to deal with was the multitude of papers I was required to fill out at the police station and various offices. I could not believe how demanding, and even rude and impolite, the officials often were. This was a culture shock for me. The police and officials in France warmed to pleasantries or a kind word and treated people politely. In Frankfurt, however, they seemed to always shout and treat people with disrespect. This was especially true for me, since I was not familiar with their procedures. They could not understand how someone who had a German passport and spoke the language but had lived somewhere else most of her life did not know the German rules and regulations.

Fortunately, the folks at the Child Evangelism headquarters in Frankfurt were very helpful and received me with open arms. It was not long before I was on the road, traveling all over Germany holding crusades and meetings for children. In those days, very few folks had cars. Christian workers certainly did not have them, so I had to travel by train.

The trains were old-fashioned and had engines that were fueled with coal and wood. Soot flew everywhere and often landed on the passengers. I often arrived at my destination very dirty. Besides my suitcase, I had to travel with a board and easel, as well as another large bag that was filled with materials for the children's meetings. It was a lot to carry, and there was no provision made for me to pay a porter to help me. Arriving at a strange place, it was often a challenge to find the address where I was to be.

No matter what the hardships, it was a thrill and a blessing to share with children for two to three weeks at a time and tell them about a loving God who was reaching out to them. There were several who found the Lord Jesus as their personal Savior. Many years later, I met a young lady at one of the German Bible schools. When she saw me, she came over and thanked me for having come to her hometown when she was a little girl. She was one of the little ones who had accepted the Lord as her Savior.

I was also thrilled when Child Evangelism asked me to hold teacher-training classes. We invited Sunday school workers and adults who were interested in reaching children for the Lord Jesus. The classes were usually held in the evenings in a local hall to give the attendees a chance to get there after a day of work. Many of these people had never led anyone to the Lord Jesus Christ, but they were burdened for children. We taught them teaching skills and showed them how specifically to meet the needs of children. Emphasizing the importance Jesus placed upon children, we shared how He included them in His invitation: "Let the little children come to me, and do not hinder them" (Luke 18:16).

Easter vacation finally arrived for Bill, and we met at my parents' home in St. Georgen. Daddy was still working as an itinerant pastor in the area. He and Mom were delighted to meet Bill. He had to pass one test, however, if he wanted to marry me. He had to prove to my parents that he would fit in well with this family from China. Mother cooked her special dish, Chinese noodles, and Bill had to eat it with chopsticks. My sweetheart was a great sport and readily received my parents' approval.

Bill proceeded to show my folks how young men in Holland ask for the hand of a young lady. He first found a florist and then asked my father if he had a top hat. After he invited my parents to be seated in the living room, he entered, wearing the top hat and holding a beautiful bouquet of flowers. He presented my mother with the flowers, then knelt in front of my parents, took off the top hat, and formally asked if he could marry me. Although Mom and Dad had already given their permission in writing, they thought it was very special that Bill did it the Dutch way.

We had two wonderful weeks in the Black Forest. Bill presented me with a beautiful engagement ring, one we had looked at when we visited Holland at Christmas time. It was a 20-karat gold ring with three small, sparkling diamonds set in a unique antique 19th-Century setting. We took long walks or day trips, explored the little hamlets and villages in the area, prayed together, read the Word, spent time with Mom and Dad, and dreamed about our future of serving the Lord together in Belgium.

All too soon, it was time to say "goodbye" again. I had disliked goodbyes since my childhood. Bill had to leave for EBI. I had to go back to Frankfurt to continue my work with the children, and Mom and Dad had to serve the Lord in the Black Forest.

Bill concluded his second year at EBI in June 1957. Since there were no graduation ceremonies in January, I attended my graduation in June of that year. I was asked to give the farewell speech on behalf of the graduating students.

Youth for Christ Holland had invited Bill and me to spend the summer working with them in The Netherlands, and we happily obliged. For more than three months, we ministered throughout Holland in tent meetings, church gatherings, and children's services. Counseling was always a part of that ministry, and it was a privilege to lead people to Christ. I sang solos in Dutch and gave testimonies. Bill translated for me, and I learned a little of the Dutch language as the months went by. Between campaigns, we were able to go to Bill's home in Antwerp. It was easy to get from Holland to Belgium in just a few hours.

Since Mr. Boerop had limited knowledge of the English language, I was able to help him with some of his correspondence with his mission office in England. Out of this experience came the invitation from the Boerops to move in with them in Antwerp to help Bill's father in the office in the mornings and to spend time learning the Dutch/Flemish language in the afternoons.

Belgium has three official languages. French is spoken in the South. Flemish, a cousin of the Dutch language, is used in the North. German is spoken in the East, close to the German border. In the fall of 1957, I moved to Belgium and began to study the language seriously. In order to help my future husband with the youth ministry, I had to be able to communicate in, as well as read and write in the language.

The next nine months were spent working in the office, studying the language in the afternoons and evenings, and visiting with my parents in Germany. Bill joined me on several occasions during his breaks at the European Bible School. We also went apartment hunting in some of the suburbs of the city of Antwerp, and I prepared for our wedding. We planned to get married right after Bill's graduation from EBI in June 1958.

Our hearts were deeply grateful as we witnessed the Lord's provision time and again. I had been looking for several months for an apartment to rent, and Bill joined the search after his midterm exams. We found nothing suitable, however, and then it was time for Bill to return to EBI. I finally found a small place with two rooms, a galley kitchen, and a bathroom with toilet only. It also had a balcony that overlooked rooftops in the back. There was no heat, no air conditioning, and no hot water heater, which was quite common for Belgium in those days. I felt we could trust the Lord to provide the finances for this small apartment.

When Bill came to Belgium for ministry meetings, he was able to see the apartment and give his approval. It was the middle of May, and we only had enough money to pay the security deposit. We trusted the Lord that by the time we had to lease it on June 15, we would also have the funds for the rent.

Shortly after Bill arrived back in Paris, I received a letter from him that was very exciting. One of the colonels at the American army base where Bill taught Sunday school had asked him how the house hunting went. When Bill shared with him that we had found a small apartment, he said, "Bill, my wife and I felt that we should do something for you. We told the Lord that if you found something suitable we would pay the rent for the first six months."

It was also amazing how the Lord provided many of the things we needed. Bill's parents gave us several pieces of furniture. Although old and worn, we transformed them. I covered a couch and then took a hutch apart and was able to make a buffet and bookshelves out of it. I happily hammered, sawed, glued, and sewed in my role of carpenter, upholsterer, and furniture designer. Later on, Bill made furniture from orange crates that came from Spain. He always laughed, saying we had Spanish-style furniture. I painted or sewed material to cover them.

We soon found that it was not simple to get married in Europe. Not only did we need a marriage license and blood tests, but also we had to have our names posted for several months in the places of our residence in the past few years, as well as in the town where we wanted to marry. For Bill it was in two places only: in Chatou and in Wilrijk near Antwerp, where he had lived with his parents. For me it was Chatou,

Frankfurt, and Friedrichstal, a small town in Southern Germany where my parents had moved.

On June 14, 1958, Bill graduated from the European Bible Institute. Immediately after his last exam, my sweetheart came back to Antwerp to pick me up so I could be present for his big day. We were blessed that Bill's dad let him use his car.

Since in Belgium, as in many European countries, only the ceremony at the city hall counted as the official marriage, we dutifully followed the law of the land. On Friday, June 20, 1958, at ten o'clock in the morning, Bill and I went to the town hall with two of our Belgian friends as witnesses, as well as his parents and his sister. In those days, a minister could bless a union, but he did not have the authority to make it legal. Although we had the necessary legal marriage at the town hall, Bill and I did not consider ourselves united as husband and wife until Saturday, June 21, 1958, when we had a ceremony witnessed before God and those present.

Sharing our ceremony were both sets of parents and a host of friends and family. Daddy led me down the aisle, and Werner married us. We were deeply moved to have friends come from great distances to share our special day. I was overwhelmed that even one of my childhood friends from the children's home in Shanghai was able to attend. She had come from Brazil. The day was wondrous, blessed, and memorable.

Bill had a wonderful surprise for me. The last year at school, he had worked hard, not only to pay for tuition, room, and board, but also to have a little extra for our marriage. I could not believe it when a taxi pulled up in front of the hall and took us to the outskirts of Antwerp. We were driven up a beautiful, long, tree-flanked lane to a castle, the "Kasteel van Brasschaat." Bill told me that I was his princess and deserved to stay in a real-live castle. This one had been turned into a hotel with a wonderful restaurant. We dined on delicious roasted chicken in a majestic dining room, which overlooked the breathtaking grounds in the back of the castle.

After a wonderful breakfast the next morning, we walked down the long lane and sat on a bench there. My husband pulled out his wallet and several envelopes containing money we had received as wedding gifts. We had to decide where to go on our honeymoon. Spain was an inexpensive vacationland and our first choice, but our money would not allow that. In fact, it was not enough to get us to the French border! Being the smart husband I married, Bill, who was very good in math, decided that Holland was the cheapest and closest place to go.

Bill had been in the southeastern part of Holland in the province of Limburg, but I had not. It is a pretty, hilly part of The Netherlands with wonderful forests. So we took a bus to the train station, boarded a train, and ended up in Valkenburg, a new place for both of us. We found a cute little "pension," and for one week enjoyed one another and the Lord's goodness in bringing us together.

Time and again during that week, we prayed together and committed ourselves to the Lord for the task that lay ahead. Our calling was to reach the young people of Belgium, mostly in the northern part of Flanders.

After our honeymoon, we settled in our little apartment in Deurne-Zuid, a suburb of Antwerp. Just one week later, we left for ministry. Youth for Christ Holland asked us to come help them with a crusade in Northern Holland.

Chapter 16

Countless Tests of Faith (1958-1960)

COMING BACK TO our little place, we immediately set a precedent for the rest of our years together as husband and wife. In ten days, we had twenty-three different visitors. We dedicated our lives and our home to be a blessing to people. They were sometimes welcomed with a home-cooked meal and always made to feel at ease as we listened to their problems and concerns. The major theme of our wedding ceremony had been to be a blessing and to minister to all those with whom we came in contact. The Lord took us up on that challenge immediately, reminding us that we were stewards of what He had entrusted to us physically, financially, and especially, spiritually.

The next weeks, months, and years were filled with much hard work and many disappointments and financial needs and concerns. No matter what our circumstances, we lived with the assurance that the Lord was with us and that He would not leave us or forsake us. Youth for Christ International is a faith ministry, and it was understood that all workers had to trust the Lord for their personal and ministry financial support. When we started our ministry in Belgium, the only promise of regular monthly support was from a church in Ohio. It was for $5.00 per month. The rent for our apartment was $20.00.

My first year at Bible college in Paris, I had come across Dr. Oswald J. Smith's book *Passion for Souls*. Dr. Smith pastored The People's

Church in Toronto, Canada, one of the most mission-involved churches in the world. The church supported more than 400 missionaries. In his book, Dr. Smith described how he learned to trust the Lord for $10.00 a month. He called this his "faith promise" for world missions. His pastor's salary was only $50.00 per month. The Lord always provided the necessary funds for Dr. Smith's faith promise, and he was able to increase the amount each year.

When I read that book, the Holy Spirit impressed upon my heart that I should trust Him for $10.00 per month as my faith promise. If the Lord could do it for Oswald J. Smith, He surely could do it for me! Although I had to work hard to meet my EBI expenses, the Lord provided the extra $10.00 month after month for my faith promise. It was unbelievable that at the end of the nine-month school period, the Lord gave me back every dollar I had given to Him in faith. He even doubled the amount, and I had $180.00 left over. The Lord Jesus already knew about my need and provided for it (my volunteer work with Youth for Christ Germany for the three summer months' ministry was without income).

My second year of college, I doubled my faith promise. Again, the Lord provided. At the end of that school year, I had twice as much money left over as what I had given. My third and last year, I could not wait to make my faith promise. This time it was for $30.00 a month for missions. With hard work and some unexpected gifts from family, friends, and anonymous donors, I was able to return to the Lord what I had promised Him in faith. At the end of that school year, I again had money left over, but the Lord knew I did not need a triple return. He allowed me to minister in Sweden that summer, and the believers there were extremely generous.

Bill too had learned the principle of a faith promise. As the president of the Student Foreign Mission Fellowship at EBI, he had taught the student body the faith promise concept. It was a thrill to see the students collectively trust the Lord for their faith promise to support world missions and then increase their goal year after year.

When we got married, we both knew the blessings of giving and were compelled to continue to support God's workers in various endeavors. In looking back at my diary of those first years, it amazes me to see how the Lord gave us what we had promised Him by faith to give. This happened month after month. At the beginning of every year, we asked the Lord what amount of money He wanted to channel through us to missions in the coming months and whom we should support. Often we were tempted to use the funds for our daily living or to pay some of the expenses of the ministry. It was not easy when funds ran out and there was not even one penny left in our wallets. This was a common occurrence for us.

Almost one year after we married, I wrote, "Countless, countless times the Lord saw fit to test us and then glorified His own name by not letting His children be put to shame." We had to write and print prayer cards and letters. We visited churches and friends in England, Holland, and Germany to raise prayer and financial support. Bill faithfully visited pastors of local churches—these were mostly men from The Netherlands who were ministering to Dutch folks living in Belgium. Bill asked if they would help us reach Flemish young people. Most of them were not keen on reaching the unreached, and Bill's pleas fell on deaf ears.

Belgium was a very fanatical Roman Catholic country in those days. Most people had no idea who Protestants were and wondered if they believed in God and if they knew how to pray. They asked, "Why do the Protestants not believe that Mary is Christ's co-redeemer and the mediator between God and man?" The church threatened people with "committing sin unto death" if anyone dared attend a service or meeting of the heretical Protestants. They never had heard of a personal relationship with Jesus Christ and God our Heavenly Father through the death on the cross of the Lord Jesus. Although we had personally handed out more than 9,000 invitations, put posters up all over the area, and rented a hall for a rally, the hall was empty.

Then we tried open-air meetings. In order to get permission to hold open-air gatherings, Bill had to apply at the various police offices of the specific towns where we desired to minister. Most of the time, he was turned down. The Catholic priests had no problem getting permission to hold their processions that carried statues of Mary through town. Their large gatherings in the open markets on one of the many religious holidays were quickly approved. It was only when Bill cited the constitution of the land, which promised religious freedom, that he occasionally got permission. Of course, all the "other criteria," whatever that meant, had to be met.

The first year Bill and I often stood alone at the police-appointed street corner, trying to hand out tracts or talk to individuals. When possible, our good friend Marie Johnson, the Child Evangelism worker in Belgium, joined us. She and I tried to gather children around and tell them about Jesus. We set up our easel and told Bible stories using flannelgraph pictures. The children loved to sing and receive our materials. Sometimes, out of curiosity, one of the parents would join us and listen. As soon as a priest or nun came by, and that was amazingly often, they all disappeared, including the children.

We also tried to interest the young people of the few evangelical churches in attending special evening meetings in our home. We offered times of fellowship with funspirations, snacks, games, discussion groups, and Bible studies. Slowly but surely, some of them came and even brought friends. Eventually we rented a hall closer to the center of town, which had easier access. Some of the young people formed a core group that we could count on to help us with a special summer ministry in the towns and villages in northern Belgium.

I also held two children's clubs per week. By the end of the school year, only seventeen children had attended at different times. Only three children attended the last special party I planned before summer vacation. I wrote in my diary:

> As I look back upon the almost passed year, gratitude fills my heart. A wonder-working God is our heavenly Father! And without these signs of His loving kindness the work would be even more discouraging. "But God is faithful who will not suffer you to be tempted above that you are able…" Looking upon the work there is not much we can give over to Christ as a prize for His suffering on Calvary. But it is good to know that our whole being, our service, our love for souls lie in His hands and are all because of His finished work on the cross.

Several times, we tried to show special films. One particular time we handed out 400 invitations and rented a neutral hall that seated 150 people and was close to the schools where we invited the students. We rented a projector, and Bill made three trips to Brussels to make all of the arrangements. After all that effort, only one student came, bringing his little brother. That was extremely discouraging to us.

When my parents came to visit, they joined us in our efforts to reach the Belgian people. Daddy was keenly observant. He could not believe the spiritual darkness of Belgium and mentioned that it was easier to minister in China than in Belgium.

We continued to have visitors. Brigitte joined us for our first Christmas as a married couple. Then several of our former fellow students from Paris came to stay a few days before going to the mission field in Africa and Dutch New Guinea, now Papua. A Japanese student from EBI who could not return home came and spent the Easter holidays with us. Friends from the US and Holland were some of our other visitors. We were grateful for every visit, as we always longed for good fellowship with like-minded believers.

The local churches were small. Fifty people were considered a large group. At that time, less than one percent of the population of Belgium was believers. We were only a handful trying to reach the lost, and we remarked often about how lonely we felt. It wasn't unusual for us to beg folks coming through to please stay one more day.

The Lord was faithful to send us wonderful surprises. Many a time when funds ran out and we had nothing to eat, someone would come and bring us a food basket or leftovers. Other times we were invited for a meal at a friend's home. Over and over again, the Lord proved Himself to be true. Many times, we did not have what we thought we needed, but His grace was always sufficient.

If we ever bordered on discouragement, we would remind ourselves of what had happened three days before we married. A man from one of the local department stores arrived unexpectedly. He had large sample books under his arm and told us to sit down and look through them and let him know which pattern we liked. We were absolutely shocked. Not in our fondest dreams had we thought of ordering floor coverings for our apartment. There were too many other necessities that had to take precedence. With a big smile he assured us that everything was taken care of and that we were not to ask any questions. Someone had paid him to install linoleum in our living room.

Several months later, the merchant appeared again. Once more, he told us we were not to ask questions about who could have been so generous. In fact, he said it was a different person. This time he was to lay linoleum in our bedroom. We thought it was wonderful that the Lord would surprise us with such a much-needed item for our little home. How blessed we felt that our rough wood floors would no longer give us splinters.

About thirty years later Bill and I had the occasion to revisit our first home in the Sevillastraat in Deurne-Zuid. We were amazed to see the floor covering we had chosen so many years before still in place in both rooms and in quite good condition.

Since our tiny apartment did not include a sink or bathtub in the little room with the toilet, our good friend Marie Johnson, who lived two blocks down the street from us, invited us to take a bath in her real bathroom once a week. The rest of the time, we took sponge baths in the kitchen. Bill insisted that we buy an instant hot water heater, which he attached to the water pipes above the sink in the kitchen. I was then able to hand wash our clothes. I used Marie's washing machine for large items. She was a wonderful coworker and prayer partner and helped us greatly. Marie took us in her car to our open-air sites when needed and served with us in many of our meetings and activities. I helped her launch the first Daily Vacation Bible School ever held in Flemish Belgium. Only a handful of children attended, but they learned about the missionary journeys of Paul, memorized Scripture, and heard the good news.

Since our kitchen was so small, there was no space for countertops. So Bill built a collapsible table that attached to the kitchen wall. I was very grateful for this, for it made food preparation much easier. This wonderful contraption also taught me one more lesson about trusting the Lord.

One day shortly before noon, a Dutch family we had met in one of our many meetings in Holland came through Antwerp and stopped to visit. We were delighted to see them, but were also very glad that it was after the typical Dutch coffee time. It would have been rude to the Dutch family not to offer coffee at that particular time of day, and we had nothing to offer them. Our cupboards were bare. We had no coffee or cookies. Although the Dutch only take one cookie with each cup of coffee, I did not even have one crumb.

Bill and I had made it a strict rule that we would never reveal our personal financial needs to anyone but the Lord. We chatted with the family of four, reminisced about the ministry, and asked about their vacation, all the while hoping that they would leave. Finally, I realized that they were hoping to stay for the noon meal, which was the main meal of the day for most Europeans, the Dutch included. With a big smile, I invited them to stay, silently wondering what I would prepare.

In the kitchen cupboard, I found some flour, several eggs, some milk, sugar, and a little oil. That was all, but it was enough to make pancakes! The Dutch do not eat pancakes for breakfast, but for their main meal at noon. *Isn't the Lord gracious?* I thought. Had they been English folks, I would have had to cook fish and chips or some other dish. A German family would have liked potatoes, vegetables, and perhaps a roasted chicken. Belgians like French fries and steak with a salad. But the Lord sent us a Dutch family!

As I was preparing the pancakes, the little girl of four came into my tiny kitchen. She wanted to visit with Aunt Joy, having known us from the children's ministry in Holland. As we were chatting away, she slipped under my little table. With her shoulder, she accidentally lifted the tabletop up, and it did what Bill designed it to do and collapsed! Batter splattered everywhere, and along with it, my one remaining meal! The little girl started to cry, and so did I. I tried to hide my anguish, but in my mind I cried out, *Lord, what are you doing? What is this all about? You know that I don't have anything else with which to feed these friends. Why did you allow this to happen?* I was not only dumbfounded, but also I was very upset. I was not upset with the little girl, but with our situation…and also with the Lord.

Wondering what had happened and why his daughter was crying, the father came to the kitchen door. When he saw the shattered bowl with its content on the floor, he said to Bill, "Come on. Let's go to the store." With that, they were out the door. They returned with their arms full of grocery bags. The Lord met our need with more food than we could consume in a week!

Chapter 17

Unbelievable Answers to Prayer (1960-1961)

THE LORD WORKED a major miracle in our lives in the summer of 1960. From my earliest years as a teenager and in the many years that followed, I had always been involved with children. I loved them, regardless of who they were. Taking care of them, nurturing them, teaching them, and having fun and wonderful times of interaction with them was what I enjoyed. As a teenager in the children's home, I had always said that I wanted to have twelve children of my own if the Lord allowed me to marry.

It seemed as if my dream was not to be. Several years before I married, I was told by a doctor that I would never be able to have children of my own. I was devastated. Throughout the years, I had conferred with other doctors who gave me the same prognosis. I wondered why the Lord had given me such a love for children and the gift to work with them. When my sweet husband asked me to marry him, I told him what the doctors had said. Bill told me that he wanted to marry me no matter what the future held. He said that the Lord had assured him that we were to serve the Lord together.

Bill and I had experienced many miracles since we started our ministry in Belgium. Could the Lord not also perform a miracle as far as a little one was concerned? So, we started to pray. We earnestly asked the Lord Jesus to grant us our hearts' desire, to entrust us with a life we would be privileged to raise for His honor and glory. Miracle of miracles, the Lord answered our fervent plea! On June 28, 1960, a Tuesday afternoon at 3:35 P.M., our little girl, Gloria Grace, was born. Her name indicates how blessed we felt, and we gave God all the glory.

The Sunday evening before Gloria was born, Bill had returned from speaking at a Youth for Christ rally in Berlin, Germany. What perfect timing! Monday evening I mowed the lawn of our small yard. Although I was experiencing painful contractions, I prepared a picnic lunch early Tuesday morning for our team of six to eight people involved in our busy summer ministry. After Bill received the precious permission from local police, we would go to towns and villages where there was no Gospel witness and no known Christians. From early morning until late at night, we would go from house to house, trying to engage in conversations with the local folks, and we would hand out tracts. We would then conduct open-air services in the evenings. To save money, we always had a picnic lunch in a local park or some green space in town. That special morning, however, Bill sent the team on and then took me to the hospital.

As soon as Gloria was born, one of the attendants asked if we would have our little girl baptized. Most of the hospitals in Belgium are Catholic hospitals, and the priest was ready to baptize the babies as soon as they were born. I had a wonderful opportunity to tell the nurse that Gloria would be baptized only once, after she had asked the Lord Jesus to be her personal Savior. The nurse had never heard such a thing.

Several days later, the priest came by to see when he could baptize our precious little one. He too was absolutely shocked when he heard about our convictions, and a wonderful dialogue and discussion ensued. When I pointed out several Scripture verses about salvation and the redemptive work of Christ, he said, "You must be a catechist to know so much about the Bible and to be able to explain it so well."

I replied, "Most of these verses I already knew as a teenager, when I memorized Scripture after I became a believer in the Lord Jesus. Everyone can read and study the Bible."

As the priest and I continued our discussion, he asked to see my Bible. I asked him, "How many years did you prepare for the priesthood and how many semesters did you study the Word of God in seminary?"

To my amazement, he told me that it took him seven years of study to become a priest, of which only one or two semesters were spent studying the Catholic Bible. The rest of the time was spent studying the dogmas and doctrines of the church, along with the history and lives of the popes. He shared his belief that the dogmas initiated by a pope are just as much inspired as the Bible and that many of their doctrines are adhered to even more strictly than the Scriptures. At the end of our conversation, I told him that I hoped he had Assurance of Salvation through the blood of the Lord Jesus Christ. Embarrassed, he hurried to the door.

Before the arrival of our little girl, the Lord had provided us with a larger apartment on the first floor of a building that was not too far from our first home. Not only did we need more space with the baby coming, but also Bill desperately needed an office for his ministry work. Our new apartment had three rooms, a bath with a shower, a kitchen, and a small yard. We felt greatly blessed to have a shower! It had taken a definite step of faith to move, as the rent was twice what we had been paying. Again, the Lord was faithful and provided what we needed in His time.

Although we had no medical insurance, the Lord gave us every frank we needed for the hospital, the doctor, and other expenses before Gloria was born. In fact, we had more than we needed and were able to help other ministries.

Another great blessing was a small refrigerator. Bill shared with me that he had received a special gift with the specific instruction that it be used to purchase a refrigerator. Bill's surprise enabled me to go to the market only once a week instead of several times. We praised the Lord. In my letter to my folks I wrote:

Yes, what kind of miracles are we constantly allowed to experience! Things we can only dream about we receive, and that even as a gift without any expectations.

I soon came to realize how involved the Belgian government was in the birth of a child, regardless of one's nationality. After Gloria's birth, I had many personal calls at the door since we did not have a telephone—still a luxury those days. These calls were from insurance salesmen or folks who wanted to sell us something with regard to the birth of a child. I was completely dumbfounded when the doorbell rang and a lady introduced herself as representing the Department of Family and Children's Services (DFCS). She had come to see if my child was being properly cared for. This included seeing where she slept and where I fed and bathed her.

This lady from children's services told me that she would return to check on my baby several times during her first year. She was true to her word and seemed pleased with Gloria's progress. When Gloria started to pull herself up in her little bed, the lady from the DFCS mentioned that we needed to get a playpen so that she could start to walk around in it without hurting herself. Then she left with the remark that she would be back in a few weeks to see if I had followed through with her suggestion.

I was shocked that she had the audacity to tell us when to get a playpen and that she would be back to check on us! It was none of her business, and we did not have the money to buy one. I told the Lord how upset I was and asked for His help. Perhaps there was some way I could tighten our budget, but would that be enough for a playpen? They were not cheap.

A few days after the lady's visit, the doorbell rang again. Reluctantly, I opened it. A man stood there with a very large package in front of him. He was making a delivery from a certain department store. I told him that I did not know what he was talking about, that Bill and I hardly ever dared go into any department store. We certainly had not ordered anything! He asked my name, repeated the address, and then said, "Lady, don't ask any questions. I am to deliver this, and it is completely paid for." With that, he put his huge package down in our living room and left.

When I opened the delivery, there was a brand new playpen with a plastic mat! The mat even matched our living room decor to a tee. I laughed as I praised a wonder-working God!

Before Gloria was born we had been fervently praying for a car. Bill had been using his bicycle to visit the pastors in the area and to go to many of the police stations in the outlying cities and towns where we hoped to minister. It was not fun to show up dripping wet after being caught in the rain at the doorstep of these illustrious folks. And it rains a lot in Belgium! More than once my husband was extremely embarrassed when he was shown into the study of a pastor and he left wet traces on the fancy parquet floors.

We considered it a miracle when we received an offer from Dr. Bob Evans. Billy Graham had given him an Austin, a British car, to use for his immense ministry all over Europe. Bob Evans used that car for many years, often sleeping in it at night if he could not find accommodations in some of the remote areas of Eastern Europe. Since the car was no longer dependable for long trips, it had to be replaced. Somehow, Bob had heard about our need and offered us the car if we could get it from Paris to Antwerp. This would include paying the custom and registration fees that were required for crossing the French border. I have mentioned before that my sweetheart is ingenious. He knew how to get that precious car from Paris, France, to Antwerp, Belgium!

Bill invited some of the professors of the Bible Institute to come join us for our next Youth for Christ rally in Antwerp. One of them was invited to speak, and his wife, who was an excellent musician, would play the piano and sing. Another couple would give their testimonies. It was late at night when they arrived with two cars, our precious Austin and one to take them back. They drove in pouring rain all the way from Paris. Since the windshield wipers did not work on the Austin, they had to attach strings to them, which the husband and wife pulled back and forth as they drove. Of course, they were soaked by the time they arrived in Antwerp. This act of love was followed by a good rally and wonderful fellowship.

Now we were the proud owners of a car, but we could not use it. We did not have the funds to pay the custom officials for importing an old car or the necessary money for the registration. To make matters worse, in our area we had a city ordinance that cars had to be parked alternately according to house number and date of the month. The streets were too narrow to accommodate all the cars, and very few folks had garages. Since we were not allowed to drive it, for several months Bill and I had to push our precious car from one side of the street to the opposite side every evening, depending on the date. Many times, we could not find a parking spot on our street and had to push it around the corner. It must have been quite a sight to watch us, especially me in my pregnant condition.

When we moved to our new address, we could park the Austin beneath our living room window on the side of the house that adjoined a grassy area. Although we had struggled for months, the Lord finally provided us with the funds to be able to use that car, which was so desperately needed for our ministry. We do not always understand the working of the Lord, but we know some day eternity will reveal all the whys. Then it won't be important anymore.

It was a tremendous blessing to be able to take several of our young people all the way to Bristol, England, for a wonderful youth congress organized by Youth for Christ England. I will never forget the excitement of the young people when they came back and shared what a blessing it was to be together with so many Christ-followers. As believers, being in the minority and from such a small country as Belgium, they had never dreamed that there could be so many other like-minded young people who knew the Lord Jesus as their personal Savior and wanted to serve Him.

It was a special blessing for Bill to finally hear a testimony from one of the teenagers. She had come to trust the Lord Jesus as her Lord and Savior under our ministry. She had never mentioned it to us before. That was truly a wonderful gift. My four years of ministry in Belgium and Bill's ten were not in vain. In my diary I wrote, "To God, one soul is more than the whole wide world with all its riches." The old Austin made it fine on the long trip from Antwerp to Bristol, England, and back, crossing the channel by ferry.

In the spring of 1961, we were asked to meet with some of the leadership of Youth for Christ International from the States. Dr. Sam Wolgemuth, who was Overseas Vice President, and other leaders met us in Frankfurt, Germany. They invited us to come to the United States for further training in the practical aspects of this youth organization. They were looking for young men in leadership positions, and Bill was chosen. We took this request before the Lord, feeling strongly that we could not leave unless we found a young man, preferably a Flemish person, to take over the ministry. The Lord provided such a man. In March 1961, I wrote to my parents that the young man Mom had met when she visited would take over the ministry of Youth for Christ Belgium. Bill worked with him and trained him for the leadership role.

Much had to be done in order to be able to move to the States. Father's younger brother and his wife, Uncle Otto and Aunt Olga in New Jersey, became our sponsors, and all three of us passed our physical exams. Our furniture and belongings had to be sold. We found buyers in our little town, among them some missionaries who had just come to Belgium to serve the Lord. Our landlord was happy when our neighbors on the second floor agreed to take our flat with its pretty yard. They also wanted our car. Our visas were slow in coming, even though we made many trips to the US consulate.

In April, we and a number of our young people from Belgium attended a Youth for Christ congress in Berlin. Dad Boerop kindly let us use his Volkswagen to drive to Berlin, and my parents were delighted to keep Gloria while we were busy there. The congress was a very special time in our lives as well as in the history of Germany. Only a few months later, on August 13, 1961, the infamous wall between former East and West Germany went up. We were still privileged to visit East Germany without difficulty.

This trip to Germany also gave us a wonderful opportunity to say "goodbye" to my parents before leaving for America. We were hoping to be gone by the middle of June, but on June 17, 1961, I wrote:

> Every room in our home is a mess. The footlockers are packed, still a few pieces of furniture have to be sold, the suitcases with the last few pieces are also almost completely packed…but we are still here. We have gotten all our papers together but we still don't have a visa. For Gloria and myself we now have a tourist visa, but then we have to leave again after 6 months. Without an immigration visa I will not be able to finish my studies getting my degree and I will not be allowed to work…. So the consul here strongly advised us to wait for our immigration papers. Pray that we may receive those by the end of this month.

We had to vacate our apartment by the end of June and hoped to be able to leave by then. Friends in Holland invited us to spend a few days with them in July, and then David Barnes asked us to help at

EBI since we were still waiting for our visas. There was much work to be done, including painting all the shutters at the castle in Lamorlaye where the school had moved after we left. Bill and his good friend Allan worked while I cooked for the fifty or so summer campers. We did this for about a month.

We had notified the consulate that we now were in France. Several times Dave Barnes asked us how things were going, and we always responded with the same answer, "We still have not heard. We don't have our visas yet." One day when he asked me again I was in the yard playing with Gloria, who was now walking beautifully. Suddenly I knew in my heart that the visas had arrived but that we had not been informed. I told Dave, "I know they are at the consulate. They just haven't called us."

Dave answered, "You better tell Bill."

Bill immediately left for the American consulate in Paris, where he found our immigration visas ready. They had forgotten to call us with the good news.

Chapter 18

New Beginnings and Many Surprises (1961–1963)

ON AUGUST 15, 1961, we boarded a plane in Brussels, Belgium, and flew to New York. We finally had made it to the United States! Looking back over our years of ministry in Belgium, it was clear that the Lord had directed us all the way. It had been very difficult and extremely lonely, but God had always shown Himself strong on our behalf. We had shared the Gospel with people in the towns of Duffel, Geel, Oostmalle, Boom, Herentals, Deurne, Willebroek, and others. Only the Lord knows if there were any results. We knew for sure of only one who came to the Savior. When we visited Belgium on several occasions years later, we were thrilled to see small evangelical churches in some of the places where we had stood on the street corners preaching the Gospel. That was indeed cause for rejoicing and giving God glory.

The flight to the States was very traumatic. We ran into a terrible thunderstorm in that old-fashioned, prop engine plane. People screamed, cried, and yelled every time the plane shook, rolled, or bounced around. A priest slid out of his seat, knelt in the aisle, and started to pray with a loud voice. I just held our little Gloria in my arms and asked the Lord to take us safely to our destination.

We stayed with my uncle and aunt in Freehold, New Jersey. It was wonderful finally to meet the couple in the photo I had admired as a little girl so many years before at my father's study in Chongren, China. It was exciting finally to be in their home.

Before we said our goodbyes, Bill took a bus to the New York harbor authorities to get our car. The Lord had worked another miracle before we left Belgium. A businessman from The Netherlands, who was very involved with Youth for Christ Holland, heard that we were going to the States. He knew that we would need a vehicle in such a large country and offered to advance us interest-free funds to buy a car. We had an understanding that we would pay him back when we were able. Another friend in Belgium owned a shipping company and often did business with the States. He offered to ship our car free of charge. A few weeks before we left Antwerp, we were able to put our car on a freighter leaving for New York. The Lord worked in marvelous ways.

As I mentioned before, Youth for Christ had invited us to the States in order for Bill to join a local YFC chapter where he could observe, learn, and be challenged for further ministry among young people. According to their headquarters in Wheaton, Illinois, the Youth for Christ program in Detroit, Michigan, where Don Engram was the director, was to be our destination. The YFC leadership had assured us that housing and salary would be provided.

On the way from New Jersey to Detroit, we stopped to visit Fred, Joyce, and their two children. They were getting ready to leave for Europe to teach at the German Bible Institute, another school of Greater Europe Mission. They made their home in Indiana. It had been six years since I had seen my brother. Bill had never met him, and neither of us had met his family. We enjoyed spending a few days with them seeing the sights.

Just before we were to leave for Michigan, Fred suggested that Bill call Youth for Christ in Detroit to make sure things were in order for our arrival. He had a suspicion that things might have changed. They had, and very drastically! Bill was shocked when Don Engram told him that he had no idea we were to be a part of their program in Michigan. No one in Wheaton had told him we were coming, and no arrangements had been made.

After much discussion with personnel at YFC headquarters in Wheaton, it was decided that we should go to Kansas City Youth for Christ to work with the ministry there. We were quite dumbfounded, because much planning had gone into our move. Since the spring of 1961, discussions with YFC had been initiated. We had worked hard to prepare and to dissolve our household. We had waited months for our visas. We could not hide our disappointment at such a welcome to the United States.

Al Metzger was the director of Kansas City Youth for Christ. Since he and his staff were at a large summer camp for teenagers in Warrensburg, Missouri, we were told to report immediately to the teacher-training college, where the camp was already in progress. Sleeping in college dormitory bunk beds and sharing showers with a bunch of teenagers was not my idea of the promised beginning that was supposed to be in a home in the United States. It was difficult to make sure Gloria, who was just a year old, did not fall out of bed. I also had to transport her across the campus to the dining hall for meals and to other buildings for the meetings.

There were more surprises. Since Al Metzger had never heard of us before that day in late August, there had been no preparations made for our coming. No housing or salary were provided. Kansas City YFC had a nice, large building for their offices and other activities. It included a kitchen. A dormitory at the back of the premises had been added for campus training programs that the staff organized. A huge parking lot separated the two buildings.

The dormitory became our housing. It had bunk beds in the rooms with a tiny window above the upper bed. To cook meals for our little family and to prepare food for Gloria, I had to traverse the huge parking lot. I prayed as I used the kitchen that I would not be in the way of the folks who cooked for banquets, board meetings, "Mothers for Teenagers" teas, or other functions.

One day another protégé of "Metzger Tech," as the program under Al Metzger was lovingly called, said to Bill, "When Pauline and I first got married, a church in North Kansas City had an annex next to their church where we stayed. Our stay did not last long because we did not like it, but perhaps it is something that could tide you and Joy over for a while." So Bill called the pastor. Anything was better than our present situation.

The pastor said that if Bill would become the official church janitor, we could live there rent free. We were not even required to pay our utilities. The living quarters included a bedroom and a kitchen upstairs in a huge building that the church used for activities with several of their groups, including Sunday school. We also had to share the bathroom with the church folks. Gloria's little bedroom was a Sunday school classroom, and we had to move her crib out every Sunday morning. It was quite interesting never knowing who was in the building. However, it did give us a chance to meet and get to know the church family.

Bill was very busy with Youth for Christ activities. He had six weekly youth clubs in various schools in the area and nearby towns and drove an average of 600 miles each week. There was office work to do during the day, and there was the weekly Saturday night rally, where more than a thousand young people met each week to sing and hear a Gospel message. The salary Youth for Christ could come up with was $20.00 per month. Bill could fill his car with gas that was provided free of charge by using the gas pump the office had onsite. Again, we marveled that the Lord had allowed us to bring our own VW beetle from Europe.

As time permitted, Bill cleaned the church, kept the parking lot neat, and did whatever needed to be done in his role as church janitor. To bring in more money, he also worked the nightshift at a bakery making doughnuts. His shift was from 3 A.M. until 7 A.M.; so he did not get more than about four hours of sleep a night.

Al Metzger had hoped that I would contribute to our family's finances by working, but I told him that I had come to finish my degree. Every dime I earned would go towards my education. Youth for Christ would not be burdened with my college expenses. In September 1961, I was able to enroll at Calvary Bible College's first year since Midwest Bible College and Kansas City Bible College merged. All of my credits from EBI France transferred. Since I had far more Bible courses than I needed to graduate from Calvary, all I had to take were general courses. By taking English and American literature, speech, pedagogy, psychology, science, voice lessons, and several other classes along with my internship of practical teaching, I was able to graduate on June 8, 1962, with a Bachelor of Arts degree in Christian Education.

In order for me to pay my tuition at Calvary, I worked as secretary for one of the local pastors my first semester. Our dear pastor's wife, Ruth, kept Gloria for me without charge. They had a little boy named Timothy, and she was glad to have a little playmate for him. My second semester I worked painting flannelgraph backgrounds with oil paint and sold them to pastors, Sunday school teachers, and various ministries that worked with children. Gloria played next to me as I painted and shared Bible stories with her. Many times Timothy joined us.

When a leader from the main office in Wheaton came to visit, Bill had a chance to ask him for a raise. Although Bill worked three jobs, money was tight. When my husband mentioned that we were also supporting missionaries, the leader nonchalantly suggested that we drop that expense and quit helping them. We still trusted the Lord for our faith promise every month and supported those with whom the Lord Jesus burdened our hearts. It was such a priority to us that there was no question about dropping the support of our missionaries.

The Lord continued to supply our needs in mysterious ways. Our first Thanksgiving in the United States we were invited to dinner by three families. They were nicely spaced with one at late morning, one mid-afternoon, and one in the evening. We accepted all three invitations and ate voraciously. With our shortage of funds, it was good to get a wonderful meal. Then there were times when I would come home from work or college and find a large basket of groceries sitting on our kitchen table that had been given by an anonymous donor. I was glad at those times that the kitchen was accessible to everyone!

We joined the Faith Baptist Church of Kansas City North, which had so graciously accepted us and made us feel at home. It was a small church, but it included a very special group. The pastor's wife and I worked well together, as she played the organ and I the piano. Our children, Timothy and Gloria, were best friends. A wonderful group of elderly ladies were in my Sunday school class, which I enjoyed teaching. Bill was not only the janitor, but also Pastor Pontius asked him to preach from time to time.

It was a joy to be able to invite friends from church, college, and even from overseas into our small living quarters. Our bedroom had to serve as living room and study, as well as a place to rest. A special time for us included a visit from the Dutch businessman who had loaned us the money for the car. Amazingly, with hard work, the Lord had enabled us to pay back every cent in less than a year.

Our friend was quite disappointed that our expected living and working arrangements had not come to fruition. He kept shaking his head as he looked around our "living room/bedroom." A footlocker covered with a tablecloth served as a bookcase. Our coffee table was a huge cabin trunk that my parents had used for their travels to China. It, too, was covered with a tablecloth. Fortunately, some friends from church had given us a couch. I sat on the bed after serving coffee. A globe that hung from the ceiling, surrounded by pictures of the missionaries we prayed for and/or supported, revealed our priorities.

When our church was able to hire a young college student to do youth work, we knew he needed our place to live and that it was time for us to move on. Bill heard about a young couple in a town close by who were planning to be gone for the summer. They needed someone to stay in their home to care for it, and my dear husband quickly followed that lead. It would give us a home for the summer.

At the end of May, Bill terminated his work with Kansas City Youth for Christ. He was now able to help me clean the annex, which included more than sixty windows. Just keeping them clean was quite a chore in ninety-degree weather.

All our belongings were packed, and we were ready to move into our summer quarters when my beloved husband showed up and announced that he had received a phone call from the young couple in Bonner Springs. Their plans had changed. They were not leaving for the summer. I was flabbergasted! Our suitcases were in the car, and we had nowhere to go! All of a sudden, my husband was not so beloved anymore. Anger, frustration, and disappointment filled my heart. So much had happened so differently from our plans since we had come to the States. The Lord had always worked things out, but at that moment, I was in no mood to see what God would do. I was not only upset, but also, I was angry with both my husband and God!

I took Gloria, crossed the parking lot, and sat on the back steps of the church building. I held my little one on my lap and wept bitterly. What were we to do? Where would we go? Bill had disappeared, and at that moment, I didn't care where he had gone or if he would ever come back. I blamed him for not having checked with the young couple sooner so that we might have known a few days earlier about their change of plans. I cannot remember how long Gloria and I sat there.

It was beginning to get dark when Bill appeared with a big grin on his face. "Honey, guess what the Lord has done!" he exclaimed. To be honest, at that point I really did not believe the Lord was even interested in doing something for us. However, my curiosity was roused. Bill proceeded to tell me that he had gone to the college and looked on the bulletin board where many different kinds of ads were posted. Lo and behold, there was an ad from Vivian, one of my classmates, who was looking for a house sitter for the summer. Both her prayers and ours were quickly answered. My husband was once again beloved! I learned a valuable lesson about God's timing as my heart cried out to be able to always trust and obey Him!

We moved to Vivian's house in Overland Park in the middle of June, and Bill started his job at Sunshine Biscuit Factory one week later. Although the house was small, it was on a quiet street and had a large, fenced-in backyard. Little Gloria could run and play. Bill and I were thankful for that little home. We were finally able to be on our own and live privately as a family. Finances were also better. I loved being able to take care of Bill and Gloria, prepare for my Sunday school class, and practice the piano for Sunday services. This home even had a piano.

Gloria turned two years old at the end of June. She loved to remind us by singing, "Happy birthday, Lolly Gace. Happy birthday." She was making progress speaking but still had a hard time pronouncing her name correctly. When Bill gave her a warning about an infraction of a rule she responded, "No need spanking." It was wonderful to watch this little life grow.

At the end of June, our pastor announced that he was leaving our church at the end of July. He felt the Lord leading him and his family to another place of service. We as a church family hated to see them go, but it opened the door for further ministry for us. The church voted for and asked Bill to become the new pastor. July 20, 1962, was a special day for Bill. He was ordained a minister of the Gospel after meeting with a group of qualified men who questioned him regarding his beliefs, scriptural doctrines, and the call of the Lord upon his life.

I have always teased Bill. That summer, I joked that he got the biggest promotion of his life. He has never matched it. One day he was custodian of the church, and the next day he was promoted to senior pastor of the Faith Baptist Church of Kansas City, Kansas.

Before our pastor and his family left, I wanted to do something special for his wife, Ruth. She had faithfully and lovingly taken care of Gloria while I was finishing my last year of college. Their eldest son was getting married, and I thought it would be nice to buy Ruth a pretty dress for the occasion. She would never have agreed to let me buy her an outfit, so I just asked her to come shopping with me. We found a nice dress with a matching coat. After I explained the reason for our shopping excursion, I was glad that Ruth graciously accepted my gift.

At the end of the summer, when my friend returned from her ministry, we moved again. We were fortunate to find a rental home a few streets over, also in Overland Park, Kansas. In September 1962, Bill began to take classes at Calvary Bible College. He had senior status since he was able to get credit for the work he had done at the European Bible Institute. Bill also worked the afternoon/evening shift at Sunshine Biscuit Factory, where he put in a forty-hour workweek.

To help a little with living expenses, I decided to care for some children in our home. This also gave Gloria some playmates during the day, and she dearly loved that. She told me several times, especially at night when I tucked her in and we prayed together before she went to sleep, "I tell Lord Jesus I like a baby brother." Gloria really missed her little friend Timmy.

It was wonderful to have church friends help us furnish our little ranch-style home. We did not have to buy anything other than a few lamps. Two dear family friends paid for our telephone, which was a party-line phone. A three-minute phone call to my or Bill's parents in Europe at that time cost about $25.00. Needless to say, considering how much you could buy for one dollar at that time, we did not make phone calls to Europe.

Having a house with no stairs was wonderful for me. For many years, I had suffered with a great deal of back pain due to a fall I had incurred a long time before. That, along with an additional vertebra in my lower back, which x-rays had revealed, put a lot of pressure on my spine. I wrote to my parents that I was tempted to have surgery to fuse the lower vertebrae together, but the doctors discouraged it.

In one of her letters, my mother asked what they could send Gloria for Christmas. She had few toys, but loved a doll that no one had wanted to play with, which she had found in the annex where we had lived. It had a head from a white doll with blond hair and had blue eyes that opened and closed. Someone had placed the white head on a black body. The doll had lost one arm, but that did not matter to Gloria. She had carried her doll wherever she went and played with it lovingly. Every night that poor dolly had gone to bed with her. Gloria was heartbroken when we moved and she had to leave her beloved baby in the annex. To answer my mother's question, I wrote and told her that Gloria would love a doll for Christmas. In January of 1963, I wrote to my mother about her gift:

> Oh Mom, your package brought tremendous joy. You should see how Gloria dearly loves her "Ingrid." Great that she can also wash the doll's hair. Everyone here is very impressed with the doll you sent.

The beginning of that year I began to tutor one of my former professors at Calvary. The late Kenneth Gangel was a first-generation American. His father was Austrian, and his mother came from Switzerland. We had worked together on a team in Germany in the summer of 1954. He was the youngest member of the quartet from Taylor University. Now he was studying for his doctorate, and it was required that he read and understand several foreign languages. He asked me to tutor him in French and help him refresh his German. A fun part of this arrangement was exacting revenge on this extremely talented, but very demanding, professor of mine! In all seriousness, I was glad to help him and was proud that he was able to become Dr. Kenneth Gangel. The Lord used him mightily in colleges and seminaries in several places, like Miami, Dallas, Deerfield, and Toccoa. Dr. Ken Gangel was a renowned expert in Christian Education.

To help lighten Bill's load at Calvary Bible College, I typed all of his papers. His tremendous load included pastoring a church, working a forty-hour-a-week job, and taking seventeen to twenty-two semester hours at college. His duties of being senior pastor at Faith Baptist Church brought much joy to his heart, and he served his congregation gladly. Wonderful fellowship with church members was a blessing from the Lord. Many of their friendships have lasted us a lifetime.

One of the ladies in our church was an excellent seamstress. Every time she made a dress for her daughter, she would buy extra material and make a dress for Gloria. Since even little girls wore mostly dresses in those days, these beautiful clothes were a great blessing. At one time I counted seventeen dresses in Gloria's closet, all made by dear Dorothy Risker. Gloria was well loved by all the church members and often received other items of clothing and shoes from them. Her blonde, curly hair would bob in excitement as she lovingly cradled her new gift.

In order for me to stay at home with our little girl, I cared for four to six children and ironed clothes by the bushel. A friend of mine at church had experience with this trade, and she encouraged me to try it since most clothes in those days were cotton and needed ironing. I soon had plenty of customers who did not like to iron. It was not a particularly enjoyable job, especially when the thermometer in the summer registered over 100 degrees and there was no air-conditioning!

In January of 1963, we moved to Shawnee-Mission, Kansas, another suburb of Kansas City. It was our fifth move in a year and a half in the States. The rented house in Overland Park had given us many problems. The central heat needed repairs on numerous occasions. The water from the toilet backed up into the bathtub, and the water from the kitchen sink showed up in the bathroom sink. The hot water tank leaked, and water streamed through the garage into the street and turned to ice in the winter. Many of the repairs were done by the landlord. This saved him some money, but almost cost me my life.

I will never forget the day the landlord came to replace the hot water heater. It was cold in the house, since it was late afternoon and the central heat had been turned off to allow him to install the new gas water heater. To provide some heat, he turned on the four gas burners on the stove and the oven, setting the dial at 400 degrees. What our landlord did not realize was that the oven did not have an automatic pilot. It could only be lit with a match.

At dinnertime, I lit a match in order to use the oven to cook. When I opened the oven door to light the pilot, I was struck by a huge darting flame. With an enormous blast, I was thrown back against the wall and landed on a chair. The kitchen was small and narrow.

Fortunately, my little Gloria was to the left of me, in the dining room, and not right beside me, as she often tended to be when I prepared a meal. I was touched by the flame from the top of my hair to my knees. It singed my eyebrows, my eyelashes, and the front of my hair at my forehead. The lace on the front of my blouse disintegrated into ashes. My hands, wrists, and forearms were also burned, but my right hand, wrist, and inside the elbow were affected the most. The landlord stood right beside me when all of this happened, but he did not offer to get me medical attention.

Although I was in excruciating pain, he asked me to go see if the water in the tub in the bathroom was getting hot. By the time I got back to the kitchen, he had disappeared. I was shaking violently, but I had the sense to liberally apply Vaseline to the areas of my body that were the most painful. Then I read in one of Bill's first aid books that strong tea applied to the burned areas would be helpful. I tried that. To this day, I am amazed that the Lord gave me so much common sense and calm in the midst of indescribable pain.

During this ordeal, little Gloria petted me sweetly and kept on saying, "Mommy, don't cry. Everything will be all right." After about an hour and a half, I was able to call our friend Vivian. When she arrived with her teenage daughter, she immediately ordered me to get in her car. She left her daughter to care for Gloria and raced to the nearest hospital, where I spent two-and-a-half hours being treated in the emergency room. Still trembling and in much pain, I was given injections, and my hands, arms, head, face, and neck were bandaged. The doctor told me that I had done the right thing by applying tea to my burns, as the acidity in tea soothes burned flesh. My quick actions had saved me even worse harm.

As I mentioned my right hand and arm were affected the most by the fire. Fortunately, my face was not as badly burned. When Bill came home that night, he found a mummy in his bed. We had not been able to reach him at the factory by phone, and there were no cell phones in those days.

It took several weeks for new skin to grow over my wrists, several fingers, and the inside of my elbows. Eventually all healed well, except for my forearms and elbow, which would turn blue and purple when cold weather arrived. This was a good reminder that the Lord is gracious and granted wonderful healing and protection. It could have been far worse.

Needless to say, Bill decided that we should move. We accomplished this in just two days. Again, the Lord provided in a wonderful way. The new house was much closer to the college and was larger than the previous home. This was a real blessing, since we liked to entertain friends and fellow students, as well as church members.

The Lord also provided our furniture in a wonderful way through an ad in the newspaper. We bought a beautiful mahogany dining room table with eight chairs and a buffet, a complete bedroom set of bleached mahogany, a washing machine, and some items for the kitchen at an unbelievably low price. A lady had to move quickly and had no time to wait for someone to pay her what the furniture was really worth. Our hearts rejoiced as we became the proud owners of beautiful furniture. We were amazed at how often the Lord worked in mysterious ways to meet our needs. This one was perhaps on top of the list. Not before or since have we owned mahogany furniture.

That year, 1963, the Lord also answered Gloria's many prayers for a little brother or sister. The Lord did a marvelous thing again. I, who was not to have any children, was now expecting our second child. What a grand surprise from the gracious hand of the Lord Jesus. We were absolutely thrilled!

One of the highlights that spring was a trip to Houston, Texas, for the wedding of Rie, my former roommate and our infamous "mail carrier" at EBI. Rie had been a missionary in Papua, which at that time was called Dutch New Guinea, and had met her future husband, Dr. John Greenfield, on the field. He was from Houston, and Rie flew in from The Netherlands for her big day. Since none of her family could attend, she asked Bill to represent her father and escort her into the church. I had the honor of being her matron of honor, and Gloria was her flower girl.

We had instructed Gloria that she had to walk very slowly down the long aisle to the front of the church. She listened and obeyed perfectly. The wedding guests smiled and then laughed as Gloria rocked a little back and forth with each step. When she got too close to the church pews on either side, she would stop, smile broadly at the people and press her little flower basket closely to her chest. When she finally stood beside me, she smelled her flowers. Then she began to sneeze over and over again, as I did when she picked a flower in our yard and brought it to me.

During the prayer, I sensed that Gloria was getting restless. When I peeked to see, I found little Gloria had headed for the organ and was just about to sit down on the organ bench. As quickly and as quietly as I could, I went to get her, hoping not to disturb the solemn moment of prayer. From the snickers and titters of the congregation, I gathered that there must have been others who did not close their eyes during prayer. What joy children bring into the world!

On our way back to Kansas, we enjoyed a drive along the Gulf of Mexico and through Louisiana, Mississippi, and Arkansas. I still remember how surprised we were at gas stations and rest stops where we saw signs at water fountains that read, "Whites only." Our black brothers and sisters could not quench their thirst where we could get a drink of cool water. In my eighteen years in China, I too was a minority among the millions and millions of Chinese, but I was never deprived of fundamental privileges or social rights. Perhaps even the contrary was true. Bill and I just could not understand this discrimination.

On June 7, 1963, Bill graduated with a Bachelor of Arts degree in Biblical Education with a major in missions. I planned a surprise party for him, and it was wonderful to have many friends rejoice with us. With his unbelievably busy schedule, Bill was still able to make the dean's list and honor roll his entire senior year.

Bill had been in touch with the director of Youth for Christ Europe about the possibility of our returning to that continent to work with the ministry in Holland. We did not get the green light, however, for the Dutch were afraid that, having been in the States, Bill would bring American ideas to the work. This would not have met with their approval.

Then we wondered if perhaps God might want Bill to teach in one of the few Bible colleges in Europe. In order for him to be able to do that, he would need a master's degree. For this, he decided to attend Columbia International University and Seminary, which was called Columbia Bible College and Seminary (CBC) in those days. It was located in Columbia, South Carolina. Bill registered for the fall of 1963. To get several advanced courses out of the way, Bill took some classes in summer school at Calvary in Kansas City. That way he would only be required to take thirty hours of classes at CBC in Columbia, write his thesis, and hopefully be done in one year.

It was a great blessing to spend a lot of quality time with our little girl. Gloria especially loved helping me in the kitchen baking cakes, cookies, or pizza. I would give her some dough, which she rolled around and around until it was almost gray. She would then put it into her small play pie forms and "bake" small pies or cakes for her doll. We would talk about anything that was on her mind—the baby we were expecting, observations she had made about her friends, or Bible truths she had learned in Sunday school.

Bill and I were amazed at the depth of interests Gloria had and how sensitive she was to the things of the Lord. Our prayer continued to be that we might instruct her in the right way according to the Word of God and that she might find the Lord Jesus as her Lord and Savior at an early age.

That summer my pregnancy started to become difficult. I had to stay in bed or lie down a great deal. The doctor warned that I would lose the baby if I did not take care of myself. For several weeks it did not go well, but the Lord lovingly undertook and encouraged us each day as we looked forward to the birth in October. Because of the many difficulties, the doctor was concerned that the baby might not be a healthy, normal child even if I carried it to term. It was not an easy time, but we kept on trusting the Lord.

Chapter 19

Multiple Tasks and Opportunities (1963–1966)

OUR TIME IN the Kansas City area came to a close. In July, Bill resigned as pastor of our little church. A short time later, the Lord was gracious to send a minister from Ohio who took over the reigns. My husband finished his summer school classes and achieved high grades. In order to pay our college bills, we sold our Volkswagen and got a pre-owned 1955 Pontiac.

Since we had gone through extremely difficult financial times since coming to the United States two years earlier, it was only natural that my parents were concerned. In a letter to them, I wrote:

> Please, please don't worry about us. We have absolutely no debts, have been able to pay our college bills, own a 1955 Pontiac, have more clothes than we can put on all at once (as Daddy used to say), especially Gloria who has twenty-four dresses and none of them were bought by us. We are so grateful to the Lord for everything, although we cannot be spendthrifts.
>
> All this not to brag, but to put you at ease. A fourth of our income (one whole week's earnings) goes back to the Lord for His work. So please, please, we have so much to be thankful for. We don't want to dishonor the Lord Jesus with our worries, OK?

Bill planned to drive to Columbia, South Carolina, with the Pontiac and a trailer that would hold most of our earthly belongings. Because of my condition and the doctor's concerns, we entertained the idea of Gloria and me staying in Kansas City until the baby was born. I hesitated to go to a new doctor in a new town, but then the Lord blessed in a way that changed our plans.

Our church had a going away party and a baby shower for us. Their love and generosity included wonderful gifts for the new baby, needed items for our move, and a cash gift. This changed our plans drastically, and we checked into Gloria and me flying to Columbia—not a common travel arrangement in those days. My doctor was cautiously optimistic. He certainly would never have agreed to my riding in a car for 1,800 miles on bumpy roads. At that time, there were few interstate highways as we know them today.

Bill worked until August 30, and we had several folks who helped me pack and get things organized. On August 31, 1963, we moved out of our rented home in Shawnee Mission, and a young couple, who were newlyweds, moved in. They also bought most of our furniture and paid three times as much for the beautiful pieces than we had.

Our little family went to stay with a doctor's family. I had known the wife in China. Her parents were also missionaries with the China Inland Mission. Bill left the next day, Tuesday, September 1, 1963. He drove carefully, pulling the trailer through the serpentine roads of the Smoky Mountains, which included 6,000-foot elevations at times. On September 3, he made it to our new destination.

Friday night Bill called and asked me when Gloria and I planned to follow him. "Tomorrow, of course," I replied. We were almost 2,000 miles apart, and we needed to be with him. Gloria was greatly excited about flying on an airplane and had lots of questions. We changed planes in Atlanta, Georgia, never dreaming that city would have a great part in our future someday. Flights in those days were not as fast as today. We left Kansas City at 1 P.M. and arrived in Columbia at 7 P.M. Kansas City time, having had a one-hour layover in Atlanta.

Several weeks before our move, Bill had checked with the college about housing. Many of the married students stayed in two locations that included cheap government housing. We were fortunate to be able to rent a townhouse in one of these places called Hendley Homes.

I was amazed at how much Bill had accomplished in our new home before Gloria and I arrived. He had hung makeshift curtains and purchased several pieces of furniture from a former student. The college gave us a dining table with six folding chairs. It did not take long for us to feel at home. Since Bill was an ordained minister attending seminary, we were privileged to get a home with three bedrooms upstairs. Bill felt blessed to be able to use one of them as his study. Our rent was $33.00 per month, which included utilities.

Besides those from Columbia International University and Seminary, many of our neighbors were students at the University of South Carolina. We made friends quickly and developed a strong bond with them, helping each other in any way we could. We women shared recipes for inexpensive dishes and told each other about our latest discoveries to help save money. Several of these friends from the mid-60s still remain our friends today. In a letter to my parents at the beginning of October 1963 I wrote:

> We have to say we are very happy here and the beginning here was much better than in Kansas City.

Gloria made friends quickly. It was convenient to watch her since a large play area with a sandbox and swings was right in front of our house. Gloria had quite an imagination. She would cook meals for her friends playing in the sandbox. She would gather them around and pray before their "meal." My heart was touched, and my prayer was that our little girl might be a true witness. It reminded me of the times when I was three and four years old and would play cooking meals with my Chinese friend Loo-deh' in our sandbox in Chongren, China. I did not pray for the meal with Loo-deh'. I must not have been as spiritual as our little girl was!

Bill soon found a job as a stock clerk in a local grocery store. Fortunately, prices in the South were much cheaper than in the Midwest; but wages were also much lower. CBC had a strict rule that students could only work a certain number of hours depending on how many semester hours they took. Bill could only work thirty hours per week since he was taking a full load of fifteen semester hours at seminary.

In correspondence with my folks, I wrote:

Yes, in the last weeks we again experienced the wonderful help of the Lord. So again, please don't worry. He is the same here as He was and is in Kansas City, Belgium, or for you, in Germany....How marvelous! When we did not have one cent left, we received $10.00 from a church in Kansas City where Bill preached about six weeks ago. Then again nothing was left on a particular weekend. I had to pay the milkman and lo and behold, we received $5.00 in the mail. How great is God and how wonderful that we have to depend on Him completely with body, soul, and spirit—with everything!

One of the local doctors had graciously taken me under his wing. He was a believer and the official doctor of the college and seminary. All of us were very surprised that I carried the baby until the latter part of October. On October 24, Bill and I were watching the late night news when my labor pains started. As arranged beforehand, Bill rushed to our widowed neighbor lady next door and asked her to stay with Gloria.

At 2:22 A.M. on October 25, 1963, Arlita Ann was born at South Carolina Baptist Hospital. The daughter of one of my mentors in Shanghai was named Arlita. I have always loved that name, and Ann means grace. It was truly God's grace that allowed us to have another little one to raise for Him.

When my sweet husband was shown his newborn baby girl, he immediately looked her over carefully, counting each finger and toe. We both prayed diligently that our baby would be healthy after the many concerns of the doctor in Kansas City. The only thing Bill found was a small brown spot on one of Arlita's legs. The Lord had done a marvelous thing—she was well and healthy.

Little Gloria, who was three-and-a-half years old, was very excited. She told everyone who would listen that she was going to teach her sister to walk and talk as soon as she came home.

I was able to go home after a week in the hospital. What a joy it was to see Gloria and to be together again. She would not leave my side, but played with her dolls and treated them just like I treated baby Arlita. It was sweet to watch.

I also rejoiced that my sweetheart was home every evening, unlike Kansas City, where he came home at midnight or later every work day of the week and left the house before 7 A.M. to get to the college. Even if Bill was upstairs in his study working hard on his assignments, it was a comfort to know that he was home.

At the beginning of December 1963, I worked in the evenings at a discount store in the automotive department. It was part-time work during the Christmas rush, and Bill was able to watch the girls. This helped financially a bit, and I also learned something about auto parts. It was quite comical that many times customers overheard other customers asking for a particular item and they helped me know what to advise them.

I also started selling Avon cosmetics there in Hendley Homes. About sixty percent of the renters were college or university students, and the rest were low-income people. There were even some people who had served prison time. One of our friends came home from college one day and was greeted by a, "Hello, preach." When asked how he knew our friend was a preacher, the man smiled broadly and replied, "Well, sir, you preached last week in prison where I was and where I heard you. I was just released a few days ago."

It was amazing how well the sale of Avon was received in our neighborhood. Several times the Lord allowed me to be sales person of the month. A number of our household goods, including a coffeemaker, a hand mixer, and some Pyrex dishes were the result of sales awards. There were a lot of surprises too. Many times I would go to an apartment to deliver an Avon order and the apartment would be empty. It was likely that they had suffered eviction. One day a lady with a gun answered the door after I rang her doorbell. She had not been sure who was calling and so pointed the gun at me. She was somewhat embarrassed when she found it was me.

I wrote to my parents:

Selling Avon is really in a missionary territory. In so many houses where I go there is heartache and heartbreak…the father and husband is in prison…divorced people in dire need…oh, so very poor people, (how rich are we in comparison!)…students…those who do not need to worry about anything and others who work hard, etc. How open they all are. As if they are waiting for someone to listen to them!

The girls were a joy to my heart, and it was wonderful to watch them thrive. Gloria was a very sweet, obedient, and sensitive little girl. Many times before I could rebuke her about an infraction, she was already sorry and would let me know how she felt. She was a happy child and loved to hear stories and to be read to. Her many questions revealed a keen mind. Gloria longed for the day when her sister would be big enough to play with her. Arlita grew quickly and delighted us with her smiles and gurgling laughter. She was a very sunny, yet quiet baby. Over and over again, I rejoiced and praised the Lord for the miracle of our two little ones.

The folks at Hendley Homes got to know our girls, as they accompanied me when I delivered Avon orders. Our church family dearly loved them both. We had joined Colonial Heights Baptist Church and had become active immediately, singing in the choir, teaching Sunday school, and helping out in any way we could.

Uncertain about our future, we pondered. What did the Lord have in store? Were we to go oversees again to serve the Lord in Europe or some other mission field? Were we to serve the Lord in the States? Bill and I seriously considered these questions, as the future seemed to lay dark before us.

Bill's job situation changed, and he only had work once or twice a week. I became the breadwinner by selling Avon. The Lord knew our needs and supplied. Quite unexpectedly, in March 1964, I received a call from the State Employment Office. I had applied for a position as a substitute modern-language teacher, but nothing had come of it. Now they wondered if I was still interested in employment.

I was greatly interested in employment, and after an interview, was chosen with three other ladies from a pool of about ten women to work in an office. Half of the buildings of Columbia College, a women's institution of higher learning, had tragically burned in February. The college had hired a New York fundraising firm to help raise one million dollars to rebuild the school. Another fundraising effort was to take place in the fall. My job involved secretarial work. I was thankful for my shorthand skills.

After only four days on the job, I was given a raise. I was humbled and deeply moved by the Lord's goodness. My work entailed creating advertisements, designing and printing fliers, drawing, planning, and arranging, along with taking dictation and writing letters. When I got my first paycheck, I was amazed at how much it was. We had been able to live on very little money since coming to Columbia in September of 1963. Now I received a salary that covered our expenses.

Besides work in the office, I also typed Bill's master's thesis, "What Makes an Effective Missionary Church?" Unfortunately, his professors kept the thesis a long time before they shared with Bill what changes he had to make. That did not leave me much time to type the final draft. We nervously awaited news to know if his thesis had been approved.

At the end of May, immediately before graduation, we learned that his thesis was not accepted. Bill had already ordered and paid for his cap, stole, and gown and was deeply disappointed. It was another lesson in learning that out of our disappointments we sometimes realize God's appointments. Bill was able to condense his thesis into an article and it was accepted and published in World Vision's Magazine that summer. He was even paid for it. Had the thesis been accepted by the seminary, it would have been placed in the library in book form and not been read by too many. Instead, Bill's great burden and concern as outlined in his thesis was circulated widely.

Knowing there would be great demands on his time once he was established in ministry, Bill decided to try again to complete his master's degree. At about this same time, I was asked if I wanted to continue to work for the college. It had been decided that the office would stay open during the summer in order to be able to get ready for their next fundraising phase of $5,000,000.

We saw the continuation of my job as coming from the hand of God. I was asked to take over the management and leadership of the office until our new boss arrived in the fall. With this assignment, I also got another raise. I had excellent rapport with my three colleagues, and it was actually wonderful to have added responsibility.

Bill spent a great deal of time in various libraries of local educational institutions doing research for his next thesis. While I was at work, a neighbor and friend of ours took care of the girls. Since my raise, we were earning more than the allowable amount in order to be able to live in government housing. So we decided to have a lady come in to take care of the children and help with housework. Those deductible expenses allowed us to meet the requirements of the housing authorities. Thus, Louise came into our lives. The girls loved her dearly, and she was a tremendous help.

My parents sent money for us to buy Gloria a tricycle for her fourth birthday. She had prayed for one for a long time, especially since many of her little friends had one. From earliest childhood, we had taught our girls that we do not always get what we want. The Lord promises to supply our needs. Sometimes that includes our wants, but Gloria seemed to understand that our first priority was giving to the Lord's work so that boys and girls could hear about the Lord Jesus. Sometimes our desires have to wait.

In one of my letters to my parents at the end of June 1964, I wrote:

> Yes, you were a tremendous example to us for teaching us to sacrifice for Christ's sake. Over and over again you expressed it in your letters to us and in the few months we were with you when we were children. God bless you, dear ones! May we impart this same teaching to our precious treasures, the girls. So that they too might not become bitter or resent the Lord. Recently, Gloria said to us: "I want the Lord Jesus to come into my heart. I don't want to be naughty anymore. I believe in the Lord Jesus and some day I will be with Him in heaven." And then she prayed that the Lord Jesus would forgive her naughtiness. When she finished she beamed: "Now I can go to heaven, I believe in Jesus." Then Bill had a wonderful opportunity to explain to his daughter the plan of salvation and pray with her.

One of the highlights that summer was a week's paid vacation in Florida, our first vacation since coming to the States three years before. A young couple, friends from seminary, stayed with the girls. The sun, surf, and sightseeing were refreshing, and we came home invigorated.

For some time we had been inviting my father's youngest sister from New York, Aunt Katie, to come visit us. After Uncle Willie died, she was able to come. It was wonderful to finally meet the lady of whom my father had so highly spoken. We had an instant connection. Aunt Katie was a fun-loving, cheerful person, and the girls loved her. When she left, Gloria cried buckets of tears. I was so glad Aunt Katie had come to visit and had felt so at home with us.

While Aunt Katie was with us, we had some wonderful talks. Bill and I were saddened to learn about her childhood. Having lost both her parents at a very young age, she was placed in an orphanage in Germany. My father, a young teenager at that time, and his brothers could not take care of her. Although the orphanage was "Christian" in name, my aunt did not have many favorable memories. This experience turned her completely against anything with the name "Christian."

The same year that my father left for China, his brother Otto immigrated to the United States. He got established in his new country, married, and then sent for his younger sister. Katie lived in New York and married a young man of German descent. She had gone to cosmetic and beauty college and had become a hairdresser.

Aunt Katie really listened when I shared how I had grown up separated from my parents most of my childhood years in China. Only when I accepted Jesus Christ as my personal Lord and Savior could I truly accept His leading in my life.

Bill and I prayed that Aunt Katie might see a difference in our lives and in our home. We also prayed that she might be refreshed by the presence of the Lord. Over the years we stayed in close contact with her and visited her as often as we could in New York and then in New Jersey. She wanted us to send her a Bible, and we were glad to do so. It was a thrill for us when she wrote before she died, "Thank you for having shown me the way to God." I still have that card.

Before Arlita turned one, she had to have surgery on one of her eyes for a blocked tear duct. She did well, and the operation was a success. It was a joy to watch her grow. She was not a fussy baby. We celebrated her first birthday in Hilton Head, South Carolina, at the beach house of the Chairman of the Board of Columbia College for whom I worked.

In 1964, Bill was asked to become the director of Youth for Christ in Columbia, South Carolina. He was happily occupied ministering to the youth of our city while working on his thesis. We still sought the Lord's will concerning our future and explored different doors of ministry in Europe.

At the beginning of January 1965, I wrote a letter to my folks:

We only want to walk in the Lord's path and do His will. We can really feel at home here, but we also know that in the last fifteen years I constantly had to move around…When I think about the almost eighteen years I spent in China, then I realize that since then I now have lived the longest in America in one stretch.

Which makes me wonder where I really belong. I was in Germany two-and-a-half years with interruptions, in Belgium four and France three years with interruptions, then more than one year in Switzerland, a few weeks in Sweden as well as in Holland and a few months in England, then visits to Italy and Denmark.

We can truthfully say that we are citizens of heaven…But now we also have to think about the children and their future. Again, the Lord has to lead and direct.

Would God again lead us to another country?

At the end of the college's fundraising drive, the Director of Development and the President asked me if I would join the staff of Columbia College and work in the Development Office. During the campaign, I had opportunity to work for both gentlemen. I gladly accepted the offer. I had also done a lot of work for the Chairman of the Board of Directors of the college, Mr. T. J. Harrelson.

Once my responsibility in the rebuilding fund office across from the State Capital in downtown Columbia ended, I moved into the Development Office at Columbia College. I enjoyed working for the development director. He was a kind, elderly gentleman, whose hobby was growing roses. Anyone who loves flowers, especially roses, is my friend. It was also my privilege to work for Dr. Speers, the president of the college. Whenever his secretary was sick or on vacation, he called for my services. All I had to do was walk across campus and enter his suite of offices.

The end of May, we moved again. This time we found a rental home down the street from our church. Bill's second thesis, "Do Belgians Have an Adequate Opportunity to Hear the Gospel?" was accepted. He was glad finally to get his Master of Arts degree. On graduation day, he looked distinguished in his cap and gown with his stole over his shoulders. My brother Fred, Joyce, and their four children came to help celebrate. It was their first furlough year from teaching at the German Bible Institute.

Although Bill had been looking into taking a pastorate, nothing materialized. We realized that the Lord had other plans for him when our church, Colonial Heights Baptist Church, needed a youth pastor. Bill had a lot of experience working with young people, first in Belgium and then with Kansas City and Youth for Christ Columbia. He was hired.

Bill had seen a prayer request for a regional representative in a Greater Europe Mission publication and had inquired about it. We wondered if the Lord was leading in this direction, but we received no response. Then in June of 1965, we heard from the General Director of the Mission, who wondered if Bill was still interested in the position. Although Bill answered in the affirmative, we heard nothing for a long time. We continued to pray, however, and sought the Lord's leading.

The Youth for Christ ministry was going well. Bill had some wonderful coworkers who helped him with rallies in the city and other ministry opportunities. The work among the church youth also brought much joy, and Bill had a wonderful rapport with the Senior Pastor of Colonial Heights Baptist Church.

Gloria had been in kindergarten at Hendley Homes. In the fall of 1965, we enrolled her in the kindergarten at our church. On one occasion, the kindergarten teachers decided to have a picnic and party for the children in one of the nearby parks. Gloria was very excited as I drove her to the park. A few blocks before we reached our destination, she asked me to stop and park along the curb. We could see some of the children who had already arrived. When I explained to my little girl that we would have to walk a good distance if we parked that far away, she said, "Oh Mommy, that's all right. I don't mind walking." Thinking that was strange, I questioned her further. She explained, "You know, Mommy, our car doesn't look so good. It is old."

Gloria was right. Our car was old. It was the 1955 Pontiac we had bought in Kansas City. I did not want to embarrass my five-year-old, so I parked the car and we walked to her party. I have always believed that little ones have deep feelings and emotions just like adults, and they are important and are to be respected.

When Halloween night arrived that year, both girls were sick with bad colds. They had looked forward to going "Trick or treating" in our new neighborhood, which was so different from the large government housing complex. There was no way, however, that I could let them go with fevers, coughs, and runny noses. In those years, Halloween was not about witches and ghosts but was a fun evening for children to meet neighbors and get a big stash of sweets. I did not want to disappoint the girls, so I bought all kinds of different candy and goodies and surprised them. I told them we were in a pretend neighborhood. I hid behind every door of our house. When I heard, "Trick or treat!" I flung the door wide open and gave them some candy. By the time they had been to every door, they had quite a lot of treats in their baskets and were glad they "trick or treated" after all!

The year 1965 ended with an unforgettable New Year's Eve celebration for the young people of the church and for our little family. The last day of the year, the Senior Pastor always had a wonderful midnight service, which led his congregation into the New Year with a recollection of highlights of the past year, songs, and prayer. The service started at 11 P.M. and ended a little after midnight. Of course, we had to be there too.

We felt that we should attend as a family. So I put the girls to bed at their usual time and then woke them up at 10:30 P.M. to go up the street to church for the service. They were excited to go to church so late at night, but the young people of the church were even more excited. Their youth pastor, Pastor Bill, had planned an all-night youth activity. After the service, the whole gang went bowling. Then they went back to the church for a lock-in for the night. Games, movies, snacks, and devotions kept them busy. Early in the morning, Bill took them all in a bus he had hired for a surprise breakfast. All the windows were blackened so no one could see where they were going. When they arrived, they found themselves at a very special, popular restaurant in Sumter, South Carolina, about forty miles east of Columbia. Of course, my sweet husband rose in popularity among the youth!

In 1966, I became our church's secretary, as their longtime secretary had to move. I was sad to leave my job at the college, but I knew this job at my church would present more ministry opportunities. My official title was Secretary of the Senior Pastor, Bookkeeper, and Purchasing Agent. I was also encouraged to do some counseling with women when the pastor was not available. I was thankful for this opportunity and enjoyed it immensely. The Lord was gracious and allowed me to help many women who were despondent and discouraged. It was a thrill after much prayer and counseling to see those who were facing divorce rejoice in their newly-found love for their spouses. My salary at the church was noticeably smaller than at the college, but the rewards were greater as I looked into smiling faces or listened to excited voices on the phone of those whom I had helped. I also thoroughly enjoyed teaching Sunday school and singing in the choir.

In the spring, we finally heard from Greater Europe Mission in Wheaton, Illinois. Bill was asked to come up to their headquarters for an interview. We had no money for an airline ticket, but our dear doctor, a personal friend and board member of Columbia Youth for Christ, loaned us the $250.00 for Bill to fly to Chicago. Next, we both had to appear at Candidate School in Wheaton for the board to decide if we would be accepted.

In June of 1966, Bill and I drove to Wheaton to Candidate School for our final candidate interview. The girls stayed home with friends who were kind enough to care for them. It was also a special joy for me to meet again with Esther Wilhelm, one of my best girlfriends from Shanghai, China, days. She lived in the area and came to visit us. We had not seen each other in many years, but we still had a special bond. Not long after that meeting, she became very ill with cancer. Esther was a great blessing to all who visited her, and we all felt a keen loss when the Lord took her home.

At the end of Candidate School, each candidate had to meet personally with the Board of Directors of Greater Europe Mission for an in-depth question-and-answer period. When it was our turn, I could not believe the enormously thick file that had been assembled for each of us. We answered questions about our goals, the Lord's leading in our lives, and whatever else was on any of the Board Members' minds.

The distinguished gentlemen must have been satisfied, because we were told that we had been accepted by GEM and were now official candidates. It was now time to busy ourselves with raising our prayer and financial support, as well as expenses for whatever ministry we would be involved in as Area Representatives. When the directors asked us what city we had considered as our home base, we replied, "We have prayed about Atlanta, Georgia." They smiled. When we asked them what area the Lord had laid on their hearts for us, they responded, "Atlanta, Georgia." That sealed it for us. Atlanta became the hub for the Southeast and later became the New York of the South and convenient to travel out of.

Rejoicing in the Lord's leading, we drove back to Columbia, South Carolina, knowing where God wanted us to serve and in what ministry. Bill's territory as Area Director would be eleven Southeastern states. He was to recruit young men and women for the mission field in Europe and visit seminary, college, and university campuses.

In order for these young missionaries to be sent forth, they needed believers and churches to stand with them prayerfully and financially. Therefore, Bill had to share the need of Europe with individuals and churches throughout the Southeast, hoping the Lord would burden their hearts to help the young people get to the field. First, however, he had to try to raise support for his own family and for the Southeast office.

At this time, Bill had been working with the Billy Graham Organization in the Film Department for several months, in addition to doing his youth work. That work dovetailed beautifully with our new ministry. Some wonderful Christian movies were being shown in theaters across South Carolina. At their conclusion, an invitation was given, and local churches and counselors were ready to help new converts find a home where they could be spiritually fed. This took a lot of organization that had to be completed weeks ahead of the showings. Bill was the Assistant to the Regional Director of the Billy Graham Association Film Ministry. When they were done in South Carolina, they moved on to Georgia with the film ministry. This was the first time Christian films were shown in movie theaters on such a grand scale.

Chapter 20

Finally Home (1966–1968 and beyond)

IN JULY OF 1966, Bill terminated his ministry as youth pastor of our church and left for Atlanta, Georgia. He continued his work with the Billy Graham Association (BGA) Film Ministry, which was now showing films in theaters in Georgia. This provided him with an opportunity to minister on Sundays in various churches and help raise our support. On weekends, he came back to Columbia to help the young man who took over the leadership of Columbia Youth for Christ. The girls and I spent a week with Bill in Decatur, Georgia, a suburb of Atlanta, and surveyed the area that was to become our new home.

At the beginning of September, we packed all of our belongings and, with the help of several friends, moved to Atlanta. We were soon able to purchase a small ranch-style home in Decatur. Our parents helped in a wonderful way and gave us $1,000 towards the down payment. The yard was large and was a great play area for our girls and the many neighborhood children who joined them.

September of 1966 was a milestone for Gloria, as she started first grade at Rehoboth Elementary School. Riding the bus was a new experience for her, but she adjusted well and enjoyed school. Her fertile mind was eager to learn, and her teachers enjoyed having her in class. With Gloria in school, I had wonderful special times with our younger daughter.

Arlita, almost three years old, was such a great companion, always wanting to help Mommy. As little as she was, she wanted to be where I was and help me in her way. She had such a happy disposition. When I took her with me to run errands, people were always amazed at what a sweet little girl she was. I was so thankful for the extra special blessing the Lord sent us in our second daughter.

From earliest childhood Arlita had an interest in fashion. Dressing up in Mom's clothes and shoes was a delight to her. I will never forget the day Arlita went shopping with me in a large department store. Busily looking for good deals, I all of a sudden realized that my little girl was no longer with me. Quickly I called her name, looking everywhere, but no Arlita. Panic gripped my heart. Where could she be? As I was searching I came to the millenary section of the store. I could not believe what I saw. There she stood in front of a mirror with a huge, wide-brimmed hat on her head, turning this way and that way. The sales ladies and I had a good laugh.

Bill and I have always believed the Word of God and have heeded its words as the instruction guide for our lives as well as for raising our children. Unfortunately, in our society today we have become lax in scripturally training up a child in the way he or she should go, according to Proverbs 22:6. There we are promised that if we obey Scripture, our children will not depart from God's way. In many instances today, children and youth are undisciplined, spoiled, and angry individuals who cannot control themselves. Therefore, they act out their hostilities. In teaching and training our two precious gifts from heaven, Gloria and Arlita, I found it very helpful to read one chapter from the book of Proverbs daily.

When our pastor from Columbia felt led of the Lord to serve as an evangelist, he relocated to Atlanta for easy travel in and out of the city. Once again, he asked me to be his secretary for his revival ministry. Since he had no office, I worked out of our home with no pay.

By the fall of 1966, we had been immigrants in the United States for five years. Dutifully, as was required by the Immigration and Naturalization Service, we registered at the post office every January, keeping our green card up to date. After five years as a resident, an immigrant can request citizenship, provided he or she diligently studies the government-recommended texts on civics and history and passes the citizenship test. It was also required in the 1960s that one be able to read, write, and speak English.

For some time we had considered this step. After years of uncertainty, we now knew that the Lord wanted us to remain in the US. We felt strongly that we needed a unified home and country where we belonged. The four of us had come from three different continents and had been born in four separate countries. Bill was born in The Netherlands, I in China, Gloria in Belgium, and Arlita in the US. As soon as we reached the milestone of five years of uninterruptedly living in America, we applied and studied for citizenship.

Bill and I easily passed the examinations. On January 25, 1967, we, along with Gloria, were sworn in as citizens of the United States of America. Bill and I came to America with Dutch passports, and Gloria was included in mine. I had promised Bill that his people would become my people. So when we married, I had become a citizen of The Netherlands. Now we were part of, "WE THE PEOPLE."

At the beginning of 1967, Dad Boerop had a severe heart attack in Belgium and was hospitalized for three months. He was released in April, but his progress was slow. For months he was under the strict care of a cardiologist. It was wonderful how the Lord took care of both Mom and Dad Boerop. Dad Boerop believed the Lord could provide everything for all circumstances. They did not believe in taking out any kind of insurance. It was amazing how his heavenly Father provided for them. After three months in intensive care, all bills had been paid.

God honored Bill's parents' faith, and they were an example to us of trusting the Lord to meet every need. They believed literally Jesus' words in the Sermon on the Mount, the Beatitudes. The verses in Matthew 6:25–34 have always been special to them and to us. Here the Lord Jesus speaks of not worrying about what the next day will bring, what to eat or drink, or what to wear. His eye is on the sparrow, and the lilies of the fields do not labor or spin; yet he cares for them. Verse 33 is the key, "Seek ye first the kingdom of God and His righteousness, and all these things will be given to you as well."

After the film ministry with the Billy Graham Association terminated, Bill looked for another job while continuing to raise our support. A pastor introduced my sweetheart to a businessman in his church, who, among other things, was involved in the mobile home business. He needed someone to help with selling mobile homes, so he offered Bill the job. It was Bill's only offer of work, so he took it. Thus, my husband became a mobile homes salesman.

We celebrated Gloria's seventh birthday on June 28, 1967. Birthdays were always special days in our home, and we celebrated them in extraordinary ways. It was a tradition for the birthday child to be served breakfast in bed with her favorite breakfast food. The family would gather around the bed with the food tray and birthday presents and would sing the birthday song. Bill would then pray, thanking the Lord for His blessings in the past year and asking the Lord's guidance and protection for the birthday child in the year to come. The rest of the day, the girls were exempt from all of their chores. Dinner at a restaurant or a surprise outing were also part of the day. A birthday party with the girls' friends was scheduled according to the activities on the family calendar.

On Gloria's seventh birthday, I wrote to my parents:

Today is Gloria's birthday. She had a wonderful birthday party with eleven friends. Thank you for the greetings you sent. She is always happy to hear from you or Bill's parents. Yes, our big girl, Gloria (I can hardly fathom that already seven years have passed since she came to us in Antwerp), brings us much joy. She really loves the Lord Jesus, truly knows she is a child of God, and is very concerned about her little sister that she too might go to heaven.

She cannot understand that spiritual things seemingly don't concern Arlita as much. Not too long ago she said to me, "We have to teach Arlita more about the Lord Jesus, so that she will accept Him and believe in Him. Otherwise only we will be in heaven and she won't be with us and the Lord Jesus."

I continued:

It really took something to make Gloria see that Arlita still did not comprehend the things of the Lord and she also would go to heaven if she has no understanding yet. Gloria thinks that she should be ready by now to accept the Lord. This notion comes perhaps from the fact that she herself was almost four years old when she accepted the Lord and Arlita is now almost four years old. This also gave us the opportunity to point out that not everyone has the same experience nor does everyone come to the Savior at the same point in their lives.

Sometimes it seems that our Gloria won't be with us long…she is so tender hearted and so focused on heavenly matters. It often amazes me and makes me ponder these things. We truly have no difficulties with her. Oh, yes, she is a real child who can also be disobedient but immediately she is sorry. Sometimes when she sasses me or talks back, immediately, before I can say something she says: "Oh, Mommy, I am so sorry, I shouldn't talk to you like that." Right now she is struggling with being so easily offended.

A few evenings ago, as we were reading her Bible, we talked about that. And immediately she tries to remember and improve her attitude. Talking about reading the Bible. We were so surprised when the other day she read whole paragraphs out of her children's Bible. I could not do that when I finished first grade. She also loves to read to her sister so that Arlita also starts to "read." Arlita memorizes a few lines or verses and then "reads" them to us (she pretends). It is hilarious.

My letter went on:

When I write about the children, I am truly thankful that I am allowed to have them with me. Occasionally, when I go shopping with them, perhaps to buy a pair of shoes or a dress, I sometimes think that my mom and dad did not have this joy when I was seven years old, to buy me some necessities. I was not with them. On many, many occasions the Lord has used this experience, especially when I am allowed to minister in meetings, ladies gatherings, and among the young people, etc. Many people never think about what so many missionaries sacrifice to serve their Lord. You are a wonderful example to so many.

Over the years, I have had many physical challenges. Two problems have included severe back pain and debilitating migraine headaches. I remember the day I was in so much pain with my back that I collapsed in a store when Bill and I were shopping. I have a high tolerance for pain, but that day I could not hold back tears from the unbearable suffering. I often considered surgery but knew the doctors warned that the outcome might not be good.

At one point in my life, I also suffered terribly with migraine headaches, which included blurred vision, tingling in my left arm, vomiting, and excruciating headache pain. Sometimes the attacks came every few weeks and lasted for three to four days. A darkened room and total quiet seemed to be helpful. Bill understood what to do to help me because his father had severe migraine headaches when Bill was growing up. Once when Bill was out of town, I woke up on the floor one night, having fainted in our half bath. Little Gloria was bent over me crying. Today I only have occasional migraine headaches.

We prayed a great deal about Bill's job selling mobile homes. It included much disappointment when anticipated sales fell through due to lack of loan approvals. Other times, buyers would fall through on their promises. It was very stressful, as Bill worked on commission. A real irritation was his sales manager's talking mynah bird. He could only repeat one phrase, "What are you doing? What are you doing?" The bird drove Bill crazy with his insistent question, and Bill was tempted to wring the bird's neck. My husband struggled with feelings of wasting his time when he longed to be on the front lines serving the Lord full time. He was anxious to go to colleges, universities, and seminaries to challenge young people to go overseas and serve the Lord, especially in Europe. Bill wanted to find churches and individuals who would faithfully stand with these folks in prayer and through financial commitment.

In desperation, Bill cried out to the Lord. There had to be something better. A friend at church approached my husband and asked him if he wanted to join his sales force selling life insurance. We both prayed about this offer. Bill felt that selling insurance could not be worse than selling mobile homes. At least this opportunity would give Bill complete charge of his own time. He would be setting up appointments with prospects, as well as making calls on pastors and individuals to find partners for our ministry. So my husband promoted himself from a mobile home salesman to an insurance salesman.

One of the highlights of the week was Saturday morning sales meetings, which included breakfast. The company was very family-oriented and encouraged the sales force to bring their families to these gatherings. We were strong believers in doing things together as much as possible; so most Saturdays the girls and I joined our now more successful salesman. The sales force loved the girls.

The Lord answered our prayers, and Bill's endeavors as an insurance salesman were much more successful than his endeavors selling mobile homes. One month he was even awarded "Salesman of the Month."

It was wonderful to see how quickly the Lord undertook and answered our prayers for young people to hear God's call for the mission field of Europe. With his new job, Bill had been able to increase his travels for Greater Europe Mission. Eleven states in the Southeast was a large territory, and he was progressively more absent from home.

In October of 1967, I wrote to my parents:

> These last days it was a special joy to entertain a missionary candidate for five days in our home. This past spring he was called into the service for the Lord through Bill's ministry and influence.
>
> He and his wife are the first couple through whom we can multiply ourselves.

Gloria learned a lot from speaking with the missionary candidate. She opened up to him and told him she was not happy about her daddy traveling so much and being away from home. The young man understood, but he knew the wisdom of Gloria seeing the larger picture. He spoke to her tenderly:

> Gloria, some day when we are in heaven, some Italian boys and girls will come to me and thank me that I came to Italy to tell them about the Lord Jesus. But I will tell them, "Don't thank me, thank that little girl Gloria, over there. She let her daddy come to my church and tell me about the many boys and girls in Italy who don't have a chance to hear that the Lord Jesus loves them and died for them. She let her daddy go so that I could hear about you in Italy needing the Lord Jesus. Those boys and girls will then come to you, Gloria, and thank you."

I think this experience gave our elder daughter a better understanding of why her father was gone so much during her growing-up years.

The girls and I sometimes joined Bill on his weekend trips if the city was close enough for that to be feasible. I was often asked to sing solos and speak at ladies' luncheons at the missions conferences of some of these churches.

It was wonderful how the Lord used Bill to help ministries and missionaries from other organizations. On November 16, 1967, I wrote to tell my parents that we rejoiced that we were able to help Werner. He and his family had taken an assignment with Youth for Christ to help the youth ministry in Jamaica. Bill introduced my brother to a Sunday school class in a local church in Atlanta. This meeting resulted in someone providing a much-needed vehicle for my brother's time in Jamaica. Bill helped others raise funds for their ministries. It did not matter what organization someone worked for as long as the Gospel was expedited. He often said, "We all work for the same company, only a different subsidiary."

I kept busy working as a secretary for Bill and for our former pastor. Letters had to be written, meetings had to be arranged, and many phone calls had to be made for my husband's itinerary. Teaching ladies' Sunday school classes and working with the youth at Rehoboth Baptist Church was a great blessing to me during the eleven years we were members there. I was also one of the regular soloists for the Sunday morning services, and I sang in the choir. We made some wonderful, life-long friends in that church.

A week before Christmas that year we drove to Miami, Florida; parked our car at a friend's home; and flew to Kingston, Jamaica, to spend the holidays with my brother and his family. Before they left for Jamaica, they had spent a few days with us in Decatur, and we had planned this wonderful trip. Their four children and our two girls got along fabulously. We took trips to places like the straw market, Ocho Rios, and the Dunn's River Falls, the rain forest, and a club where we could swim. The weather was nice and warm. We ate our turkey dinner on Christmas Day with the breeze blowing through the open windows, as there was no air-conditioning. I loved the tropical fruits and lush plants and flowers. Those ten days in Jamaica were truly a memorable time.

We had invited my parents to visit us for several years. Before leaving for Jamaica, we learned that Mom and Dad were planning to come visit us in the summer of 1968. That thrilled us and excited the girls greatly. We had shared with them every letter their grandparents had written. The girls had received packages and gifts from them, but now they would be able to meet them face to face. This would be Arlita's first time to meet them. With much anticipation, we looked forward to the summer.

The spring of 1968 brought another first-time experience. For many years, I had been singing solos in churches, special meetings, and gatherings. Many times friends and even strangers had urged me to make a record, but I had always hesitated. Now the time seemed right. Through a friend, I learned about a nearby studio in South Carolina. It was owned by a Christian who truly believed the Lord could be honored and folks could find the Lord through recorded music. That impressed Bill and me, since this was also our fervent belief. We made this possible project a matter of prayer.

Not long after getting in touch with the studio, everything fell in place for me to make a record. Our desire was that it be unusual. Since the Lord blessed me with a wide range of vocal ability and I could sing anything from contralto to the highest soprano, I wanted to record duets and trios as well as solos. Focusing on God's love for the world, I felt a need to sing songs in different languages. At that time, it was very unusual for an artist to be able to do that, and I knew I could only do it with the Lord's help and a great deal of practice. I began to accompany myself on the piano and to practice morning, noon, and night. I thank the Lord for my family, who patiently listened to me as I struggled with the second or third part of the melody as I was trying to learn the various parts for a duet or trio. It must often have sounded very strange not having anyone sing the melody with me.

After I went to Anderson, South Carolina, the recording was completed in three days. Each session, I asked the studio owner to pray for a successful time of recording. He was very talented and would play the piano or the organ and add special touches. By the process of multiple recordings, he added another voice or instrument. When it was all done, Arlita asked me, "Mommy, who is that singing with you?" I answered, "That is Mommy, me, and myself singing." It took her a while to figure that out!

The record was also a personal testimony. It began with the song "God So Loved the World." I focused on God's love for mankind. Then several songs related how I did not always know the Lord Jesus as my personal Savior. Only when I accepted Him as the One who shed his blood for me was I able to testify, "Free, I'm Finally Free." God's loving care was represented by the song "His Eye Is on the Sparrow." The focus then turned to peoples of other nations, including the Chinese, Swedes, French, Dutch, and Germans, with songs in their languages. So many of them are lost and in need of the Savior. The record ended with the plea, "Lord Send Me."

The much-anticipated day of June 30, 1968, finally arrived, and my parents flew into the Atlanta airport. There was great rejoicing and excitement. It had been seven long years since Bill, Gloria, and I had seen my folks. Now they were here with us in Decatur, Georgia! As soon as we entered our little home on Hudson Woods Trail, my father broke into the doxology, just as he had done so many times many years before in China. We all sang, "Praise God from whom all blessings flow. Praise Him all creatures here below. Praise Him above ye heavenly host. Praise Father, Son, and Holy Ghost. Amen."

We had not told my parents that I had made a record. It was truly a surprise. When Mom and Dad heard the Chinese words, they were flabbergasted. They began to sing along and then asked, "Is that you singing? Is that really you?" Not having heard me sing in a long time, they could hardly believe that it was actually their daughter's voice on the record.

My parents' stay of three months went by all too quickly. It was a glorious time filled with precious memories, a time we will always treasure. We took trips to many scenic attractions in Georgia, Tennessee, and North and South Carolina and documented all of it with photos. We attended numerous Christian activities, and my dad even joined our senior pastor, Reverend Lester Buice, and our minister of music, Baynard Fox, on visitation several times. One of our many highlights was a Christian Women's Club luncheon that Mom and I attended at the Governor's Mansion, where Mrs. Maddox, Georgia's First Lady, greeted us.

Innumerable fun times at our home will always be treasured memories. We were able to celebrate three birthdays during that time:

Mine was in July. Daddy's was in August. And Mom's was in September. We spoiled my parents as much as possible, providing them time to relax and do what they enjoyed most. Since Dad had not seen his younger brother and sister in New Jersey and New York in over forty-three years, they planned a few days with them before returning to Europe.

So it was on September 26, 1968, that our wonderful visit came to an end. Before they left, I presented Mom and Dad with a scrapbook detailing all of our exploits and memorable times. They told us repeatedly in the following years that it brought them much joy as they relived our precious times together.

Not long after my parents left, we were blessed with another big surprise. One afternoon the doorbell rang, and a friend from church told me that she wanted me to meet her at a furniture store not too far from our home. She proceeded to say, "My husband and I learned that you and Bill have been sleeping on the floor in the living room these past three months while your parents were here. Not having a couch in your living room, you slept on the carpeted floor on blankets. Now we want to buy you a pullout couch, which you can use as a queen-sized bed at night. You need a place to sleep with the many visitors who always come to stay with you."

I was overwhelmed! How did this dear lady know that we had slept on the floor these past few months? As far as I know, Bill and I never mentioned it to anyone. It was true that we did not have much furniture in the living room, but we were so happy our folks were with us that we would have slept in the laundry room off the carport. We looked at that dear lady's gift as a wonderful provision from the Lord. It seemed too good to be true that I could select a brand-new couch with colors and style according to my taste.

That couch gave us wonderful service for almost thirty years. We had it reupholstered several times, but it was constructed with such good craftsmanship and solid oak wood that it was almost indestructible. Countless friends, family, and folks from all walks of life, including many of God's full-time servants, slept on that pullout couch throughout the years.

In the fall of 1968, Gloria entered third grade at Rehoboth Elementary School, and our sweet little Arlita started kindergarten at Rehoboth Baptist Church. It was a privilege for me to be asked to help with the music at the kindergarten and teach the little ones some phrases in a foreign language. To my delight, I was in the classroom with our younger daughter several times a week. Arlita was a sweet, happy little girl whose beautiful, large blue eyes and big smile charmed teachers and visiting parents alike.

One of the ladies in the Bible study class I taught came to me laughing one Sunday morning. She was a substitute teacher in Gloria's elementary school, and she shared with me what she called a priceless experience. One of Gloria's classmates had come to her the previous week complaining that Gloria had used a bad word in class. In fact, she had sworn and said "hell," according to little Johnny. Knowing our family, the substitute teacher could not and would not believe it.

My friend took Gloria aside and asked her privately what had happened. With much concern in her voice, Gloria told her, "Nothing happened. I just told Johnny that if he did not believe in the Lord Jesus, he would go to hell."

Gloria's teacher exclaimed, "Honey, if you used the word 'hell' in that context, warning Johnny that's what will happen, then you go right ahead and warn people about their future without the Lord Jesus."

Although we both laughed about the incident, I was glad that Gloria was so concerned about her little friend at school. It reminded me of a time a few years before. While living in Columbia, South Carolina, we were exiting our church one day with our pastor. Gloria turned to him and asked, "Uncle John, do you know the Lord Jesus as your personal Savior?"

He very sweetly replied, "Yes, Gloria, I do know the Lord Jesus, and I am glad you know Him too."

Chapter 21

Struggles and Pitfalls in Ministry (1968 and beyond)

BILL CONTINUED TO travel for Greater Europe Mission and was often gone for three or four weeks at a time to churches all over the Southeast, which included Kentucky, North and South Carolina, Alabama, Georgia, Florida, Tennessee, Virginia, and West Virginia. Bill enlightened people in local churches about Europe with its dark spiritual condition and lack of a true Gospel witness. Many became burdened to pray for this needy area of God's world. Young men and women began to answer the call to serve the Lord overseas, and churches started to financially help those who were willing to go. Bill was thrilled and enjoyed his work immensely.

When Bill came home from his travels, he was tired and exhausted. At times, he was home only three or four days before he had to head out again. Traveling mostly by car also took its toll. The girls and I were delighted to have him home, but it also caused some friction. While he was gone, I was responsible to run the household on my own. I made the budget work, paid the bills, and even had to fix things in our home or find an inexpensive plumber, electrician, or handyman to do so.

Being in charge of the household also included being the spiritual leader of the family. I had to discipline the girls as well as be their loving counselor. When Bill came home, I wanted to shift gears and let him take over. So often, however, he was so weary and drained that he was not in the mood to take over or be in charge of anything. He tried his best, but time usually ran out for him to accomplish what needed to be done. All of that was a real challenge to our relationship. I knew that my most important responsibility was being mother and father to our children in Bill's absence during their growing-up years.

It was difficult not being directly involved with my husband's ministry. There were few weekends the girls and I could join him. During our years of serving the Lord in Belgium, I had worked alongside Bill every day, being totally part of the ministry. We had been deeply entrenched in reaching the Belgian young people and had relied upon each other when facing the appointments and disappointments of the ministry. Now the situation was extremely different, and I often felt like an outsider.

Many times when my husband was out of town, I did not have an address or phone number where I could reach him. I only knew the name of the church in a particular city where he was speaking that weekend. He did not even know in whose home he would be staying until after he arrived at his destination. When I needed to call him for advice, counsel, or an emergency, the church office was usually closed.

Although Bill had to raise all his support, including his ministry expenses, the mission had a rule that Bill could only call me once per week with mission funds when he was traveling. I was so upset and hurt by this rule, especially since our budget was very tight and did not include phone calls. So Bill and I resorted to a wonderful arrangement. After my sweetheart got to his destination, he would call me person-to-person and ask for Bill Boerop. Recognizing my husband's voice, I would tell him, "Sorry, Bill Boerop is not here." Then Bill would say, "Would you please have Mr. Boerop call me at this number ___." Thus, I had a number where I could reach my husband if I needed to get in touch with him, and it did not cost the mission.

I have often said that it is amazing that more couples in ministry do not split up. With their rules and regulations, mission societies often cause great strain in a husband and wife's relationship. We give all the glory to God that we were not one of those casualties as Bill traveled for eighteen years with two mission organizations throughout the Southeast and later nationwide. Whenever it was at all possible, Bill and I made it a point to spend extra time together. Some of the Atlanta hotels had special weekend rates that were enormously low. If we could afford it, we got a babysitter and spent some wonderful time away from home.

My sweet husband often brought me flowers for no special reason except that he loved me. He continues to do that to this day. He has always let me know in many different ways that he loves me and that I am a priority in his life. Bill was a great help to me in coping with not being directly involved in his ministry by reminding me that we had a great task to fulfill. The Lord Jesus had miraculously given us two children to disciple, train, teach, and lead to honor and love God and to become good, upright citizens. The lion's share of that responsibility rested upon my shoulders. That made me remember over and over again how blessed I was to have two daughters to raise. I had a family, and they were with me. It also made me think of my parents, who did not have that privilege during my growing-up years.

Although Bill was gone a great deal of the time, he spent much quality time with us as a family. We made it a priority to spend every occasion we could together, and to make it a special event. The occasions included Bill's coming home, his leaving, the girls doing well in school, and special achievements. When he was home, Bill would often grill his special hamburgers and we'd have a picnic in our large backyard. We went for nature walks at Stone Mountain Park and looked for special plants and leaves. Friends let us use their cabin and boat for swimming and water skiing on Lake Lanier. Going to our pastor's home to swim in their pool was another fun time. There were many more happy times. Family and friends, even strangers who came to stay with us, were always impressed that the Boerops liked to celebrate even the smallest occasions.

In my letter to my parents on March 4, 1969, I wrote:

Bill had three good weeks in Florida and the week in Alabama was also blessed. But he was also very tired. Every day he had to speak three or four times, and in Birmingham, Alabama, he was in eighteen meetings in one week. The girls and I flew to Birmingham on February 21, and immediately, I too was engaged in ministry.

It was wonderful to be involved and get to know the dear believers personally. Then Bill was home for three days before he left for three weeks in Kentucky, Tennessee, South Carolina, Virginia, and North Carolina, as well as again Toccoa Falls, Georgia, where you, Daddy, served with Bill when you were with us. The end of this month he will be home again and will be here a bit longer.

In that same letter, I shared with my parents that the mission wanted Bill to visit all the fields where Greater Europe Mission had ministry efforts as well as all their schools. This was a four-to-five-week assignment for August of 1969. The leadership felt that Bill could better relate the need for workers in Europe to the many churches, colleges, universities, seminaries, and other places where he had the opportunity to share if he had visited there recently. Of course, he had to raise all the expenses for this trip. Once again, the Lord proved Himself all-sufficient.

In my letter I continued:

One church already sent $100.00 with the remark, "For a special purpose in Bill's ministry." They had no knowledge about the mission's decision. So we are convinced that all the money will come in. This morning we again received $25.00 for his trip.

The miracle is that a lady wants to pay for my round trip ticket to Europe. She already sent the funds to the mission. That made us laugh. I can go and Bill has to stay. No, it is more important that he goes! But we believe that we all can go, because someone else wants to pay half the fare for the girls' trip to Europe. Now we are praying for the other half, as well as for all expenses for Bill, also in Europe, where he will have to travel all over.

Chapter 22

Joy and Sadness (1969-1970)

THE LORD ANSWERED prayer, and all of the funds came in so that we were able to travel to Europe in August of 1969. Bill had great fun showing Gloria and Arlita where he grew up in Holland. They visited his childhood home and school and saw windmills, canals, little towns and villages, and larger cities. We had the joy of introducing the girls to Bill's parents, Arlita for the first time. They were amazed at how Gloria had grown since they had seen her eight years previously. It was also wonderful to meet some of our Belgian friends again and to see how the work of Youth for Christ Belgium had continued under the leadership of the young man to whom we had entrusted the ministry. We were also able to visit France, Switzerland, and Germany.

The highlight of the trip for me was a family reunion that my parents organized. Both of my brothers and their families were in full-time Christian work in Germany. Fred and Joyce and their four children, Werner and Inge and their four children, and Bill and I with our girls joined Mom and Dad in an old farmhouse that had been converted into a restaurant. It was a great joy to see my parents surrounded by their three children and spouses and their ten grandchildren. It was the first and only time that we would be together like that.

August 27, Dad's birthday, the girls and I took a train to Frankfurt, where my dear friend Brigitte met us. We spent the night with her and then left for the Frankfurt airport the next morning, where we caught a flight to Amsterdam. There Mom and Dad Boerop and Bill's Aunt Marie met us at the airport. In those days, people could still go to the gate. We were able to spend several hours with Bill's family before flying back to the States.

After we arrived in New York, we took a short flight to Philadelphia, where the girls and I were able to spend two wonderful days with my friend and mentor from Shanghai, Anna Swarr. She was working again as secretary in the main office of the US headquarters of the Overseas Missionary Fellowship. Then, finally, it was time to end our wonderful trip and go home.

Bill stayed in Europe and visited the various fields where Greater Europe Mission personnel were serving the Lord. This included visiting nine countries in six weeks. While Bill was still in Europe, he visited my brother Werner, who was in the hospital. We all were shocked when we heard that he had cancer because no one at our family reunion had any idea. The next weeks and months were difficult. Many prayers were lifted up at our church, in my Sunday school class, in our home, and around the world.

We asked the Lord to heal Werner, not just for the sake of his wife and four small children, or for us as a family, but for the multitudes who still needed the Savior. Werner was the Lord's servant and faithfully proclaimed the Gospel message of hope. We had to commit him completely to the Lord's will and trust our Savior to raise Werner up since "the harvest is plentiful, but the workers are few" (Matthew 9:37b). Many dark days followed.

My father and several other Christian leaders gathered around my brother's bed to pray. Suddenly, Daddy spoke up, "Son, I have served the Lord for twenty-five years in China and now almost twenty years here in Germany. I am an old man, and you are still young. I wish I could have your cancer. I wish the Lord would let me carry this burden for you."

Werner got better. The Lord healed him completely and used him mightily around the world for many years.

The fall of 1969 was very important for Arlita, who started first grade. We celebrated her birthday at a dairy farm in the area. Ten of her friends and our girls enjoyed the many animals and had great fun when each got a turn at milking Rosy the cow. Farmer Mathews had a great time demonstrating how to milk Rosy and squirting the children with milk from her udder. Cake and ice cream were served on picnic tables set up at a beautiful lake. A drive through the gorgeous property in an open wagon ended the party.

A few weeks later, Bill and I came home from an out-of-town engagement and went to pick up the girls at a friend's house. Before we could get to their house, which was next to our church, the police stopped us and would not let us through. In my December 4, 1969, letter to my parents, I wrote:

> Our old church was still burning. The fire started at five P.M. and the next morning it still was smoking. The fire fighters could not go home because it was such a huge fire. Apparently the fire started right next to the baptismal, close to the room of Bill's office, which also went up in flames. Bill turned white as a sheet when he realized how bad the fire was. He turned to me and said, "My whole life is gone." Seven years of studies, all his notes, messages, books, all of our files for the whole Southeast, which I had just completed for each state, all copies of correspondence. But I immediately said to him, "The Lord has brought us this far and He will continue to bring us through."

For some time the leadership of the church had let Bill use some rooms in the old church building as an office. Since church services and most other activities were held in the new building, the old one was used for a few Sunday school classes and youth Bible studies on Monday nights. Now the whole building was a heap of ashes.

When we saw our pastor and our minister of education, they told us that they had retrieved everything of importance out of Bill's office. They worked until the ceiling started to burn. The only loss was materials kept in another room. These included supplies such as envelopes, letterheads, pamphlets, and brochures that had recently been printed.

We thanked the Lord that all the important materials were saved. The supplies could be replaced.

As a result of the fire, the church offered Bill the press box on the football field as his office. Since football season was over, we could temporarily use the press box until we found something else. It was a very unusual office, but it had large, bright windows and even a telephone.

On Christmas Eve that year, we had a wonderful experience as a family. After the girls went to bed, Gloria shared with Arlita what she had learned in Sunday school. They had talked about the War of Armageddon. When Gloria told Arlita what this was all about, she asked her, "Don't you want to fight on the Lord Jesus' side?" It was not long before they both found Bill. Gloria asked her father, "Daddy, how do you lead someone to Jesus? Oh, I know!" With that, she quickly ran to her room and got her Bible.

During one of our evangelistic crusades, the evangelist had shared with the congregation how to lead someone to Christ. Gloria wrote the steps and all of the verses down in her Bible. Now Gloria told her little sister, "You have to realize that you have sinned and ask the Lord Jesus to come into your heart." Then she went down her list and showed her Bible verses: "For all have sinned and come short of the glory of God" (Romans 3:23). "For the wages of sin is death, but the gift of God is eternal life in Christ Jesus our Lord" (Romans 6:23). "I tell you the truth, whoever hears my word and believes him who sent me has eternal life and will not be condemned; he has crossed over from death to life" (John 5:24). Then we talked to Arlita. What a joy it was when we all knelt together and Arlita prayed to receive Jesus as her personal Savior. Gloria immediately said, "Now we all belong to Him." We thought it was wonderful that the Lord allowed Gloria to lead Arlita to Jesus because she had prayed for her younger sister and been concerned about her soul for a long time.

In February, we were able to host my brother Werner after his bout with cancer only five months before. He was restored and able to serve the Lord again. As always, Bill kept on traveling. In the first seven weeks of 1970, he was gone five-and-a-half weeks. His itinerary also included Mississippi and Louisiana. On one of his trips to New Orleans, someone broke into his locked car and stole two suits and his tape recorder, camera, and shaver. These are some of the trials that come with traveling.

Besides teaching a ladies' Sunday school class, I taught two home Bible studies and worked with the young people of our church on Sunday and Monday evenings. I also continued my ministry as a soloist in our church, as well as in other churches in the area. I spoke often at ladies' meetings, luncheons, and missions conferences. I was usually able to sell some of my records, and I was told that they were a blessing to people.

On one of Bill's trips to North Carolina he turned on the radio and was surprised to hear his wife singing "His Eye Is On the Sparrow." The next day, while traveling in Virginia, he again heard me sing. Several of the radio stations in the Southeast played my record from time to time. Bill said those days when he heard me sing he was especially homesick. The Lord in His kindness let him hear my voice and be encouraged through the songs I sang.

It is wonderful how the Lord often wants to use us in unexpected ways. For some time a lady, Margret, had come to my house selling Avon cosmetics. From time to time, I bought a few things; but on one particular day, I did not intend to buy anything. Somehow we began to talk about the Lord Jesus, and I told her what He meant to me. I shared how I found the Lord and then asked her if she had peace with God and knew she was His child. As we talked further, she admitted that she too wanted to become a child of God instead of just being a creature of His. We prayed, and she accepted the Lord! She ended up selling only one lipstick to me but gained eternal riches in finding the Savior.

Margret became a very special friend. She went with me to all of my home Bible studies and was a tremendous help in recording the lessons I taught. We spent a lot of time together as I discipled her. She was a devout listener to good Bible teaching on the radio. If she did not understand something, she came to me with her questions. Margret had beautiful artistic inclinations. Making Christmas decorations together was fun. I have kept them all these years and still hang them on my tree every year. Margret was also a wonderful seamstress and made some stylish dresses for me. Her husband was not a believer, but she lived her Christian life before him, and eventually, he too found the Lord. Three days before he went to be with the Lord, they both sat at my table and had lunch with me.

The year 1970 brought us many challenges. In the spring, Bill and I tackled the job of enlarging our little home. Since we had moved there in September of 1966, numerous visitors had stayed with us. Having two bedrooms and one-and-a-half bathrooms presented a real space problem. We decided to close in our carport, but we did not have enough money to hire someone to do it. With the occasional help of some friends who knew more about such things than we did, we went to work.

I cleaned bricks, put up siding and crown molding, and framed doors and windows. Bill and I worked hard and transformed our carport into a large family room with a corner that served as my office. Our small den became another bedroom. Although it had taken longer than we expected with Bill's travels, we were thrilled and thankful when it was finally finished and marveled at how wonderful it turned out.

In April, I got a strep-staph infection in one of my large toes. I developed a fungus at the root of the toe, and it turned into blood poisoning. In my letter to my parents on April 20, I shared the following:

> It happened so quickly that Bill had to take me to the emergency hospital. The red stripe had already crept five to six inches up on my foot. I had to take strong medication and keep my foot elevated higher than my heart for forty-eight hours lying down. Instead of the medicine curing me, I thought it would kill me, because at twelve o'clock at night, I collapsed. My whole life passed before my eyes. Quickly I thanked the Lord that He had saved me and that He was having a prepared place for me. Then I fainted or collapsed.
>
> Later on the doctor told us that the poison had already entered my system and that's why I felt so bad. Praise the Lord that Bill was at home. Now my toe is almost okay. When I saw the doctor again, he was amazed that my body reacted so favorably to the medicine, in spite of the initial reaction. But we also let him know that God answers prayers, for the folks at our church had prayed for me during the prayer meeting.

I went on to tell my parents that Bill had been in a terrible car accident on his last trip. He was driving in the rain on the way to Alabama with bald tires on his car when it skidded and spun around across the road into the path of an oncoming car. The gas tank lay next to the car, and the trunk was pushed into the front seat on the driver's side. The door and center support collapsed like an accordion and pushed Bill across the front bench. He stepped out of the car on the passenger's side. His car and the equipment was a total loss. His left arm was bruised, and he had a puncture wound on his forehead.

With blood streaming down his face, Bill had walked over to the other driver and introduced himself, "Hello, I am Bill Boerop." I am not sure what the other man thought. His car was also a total loss. Both were taken together to the hospital for x-rays and check-ups. The other gentleman was from Greenville, South Carolina, and had sprained his knee. Besides Bill's bruised arm, the puncture wound, and pulverized glass in his hair, he was all right. Bill thanked the Lord for sparing their lives and then had a wonderful opportunity to share the Gospel with the man. He said he did not believe in Christ, but wanted to go to church more often. My husband made it a special point on his next trip to Greenville to look him up and follow up on their talk. Only the Lord knows if the young man became a believer. We hoped and prayed that he would.

We wanted to celebrate Gloria's tenth birthday in a very special way, like the Chinese do. She had a pajama party with seven of her girlfriends. After a picnic with hamburgers and watermelon, we played lots of games. Then we had ice cream and birthday cake. A little later, I told a story. Soon after 10 P.M., we read Psalm 23 and prayed with the girls before they got into their sleeping bags, which were spread out on the living room and dining room floors. We had moved the furniture to make room for them, and they had a great time. After enjoying homemade pancakes for breakfast the next morning, the girls played more games. Then I took them all to Vacation Bible School at our church. The parents gladly agreed to this, and we were grateful that the girls were exposed to the redeeming message of the Lord Jesus Christ.

My parents sent money to the girls for their birthdays, for special occasions, and for good grades. We taught our children to be thankful for kindnesses shown to them and to express their appreciation. A note of thanks attached to one of my letters was always well received. Here is one example,

> Dear Oma and Opa,
>
> Thank you so much for the money to buy the beautiful dress and the money for good grades. I'm going to day camp at our church. One present I got was a diary I can lock, a pocket book and badminton set.
>
> With much love, Gloria.

After her first year in school Arlita wrote,

> Dear Oma and Opa,
>
> Thank you for the money for good grades.
>
> I love you so much, Arlita.

For many years, my father had a desire to go back to the area where he fought in France in World War I and was a prisoner of war for a little more than a year. In the spring of 1970, Fred made my father's dream come true. He took him to France, where they explored the area in Northern France close to the Belgian border. Daddy had been captured by the British in September 1918 and handed over to the French. He then was housed in tents in a prisoner of war camp in one of the smaller villages in the area of Arras and Cambrae. The prisoners had to clear the area of artillery shells. Although the war officially ended in November 1918, my father was not released until early in 1920. I was very glad Dad and Fred took that trip. Neither knew then that it would be Daddy's last trip.

The fall of 1970 was very busy. An international team of alumni from EBI were to travel with Bill from the end of September to the middle of December to raise interest in what the Lord was doing in Europe, particularly under the ministry of Greater Europe Mission. Bill was in charge of setting up the itinerary and getting bookings made, as well as traveling with the team. Our good friend and director of EBI, David Barnes, also traveled with the team. They were completely booked for those two-and-a-half months. I was asked to find matching dresses for the girls and matching shirts, ties, and slacks for the guys. It was fun to scour Atlanta stores for the appropriate clothing. When the team was in the Atlanta area and Bill was not traveling, we all joined them for some meetings.

The fall brought sad news about my father. For several months, he had felt pressure in his chest. When some tests were finally performed, Daddy found out he had lung cancer. Mother told him when he was in the hospital in October. He had a difficult time believing it. Daddy wrestled through the shock of the diagnosis and finally could say to the Lord, "Agreed!" We as a family remembered Daddy's prayer at Werner's bedside almost exactly one year previously, "I served the Lord for twenty-five years in China and now almost twenty years here in Germany. I am an old man and you are still young. I wish I could have your cancer. I wish the Lord would let me carry this burden for you." Now Werner was well, and Daddy was dying of lung cancer.

Sad days and weeks followed as my father lay in a hospital bed in Germany. I wanted to rush to his side, but we did not have the finances. Then in December, just before Christmas, we received a call from Fred and my mother. Daddy had gone home to be with the Lord on December 20, 1970. I was devastated. I was the only one of Daddy's three children who did not see him again after our one and only reunion in 1969.

Word spread quickly among our friends about my father's death, and they rallied the funds for me to fly to Germany on December 22 for the funeral on Christmas Eve. It was a long flight that required us to pass through London, England. Since some of the airline personnel were on strike there, I had to wait at Heathrow Airport. I prayed fervently that I would be able to make it to Karlsruhe, which is an hour-and-a-half drive south of Frankfurt. Finally, we were cleared to leave England.

After a journey of fourteen hours, I arrived in Frankfurt. One of the flight attendants led me to first class and told me to be ready to leave the aircraft as soon as we landed. Everybody had to wait until I was escorted off the plane unto a van that was waiting for me at the foot of the stairs on the tarmac. Never before or since has a driver raced me through the runways at an airport, skillfully avoided arriving and departing planes.

My brother Werner had a friend who was employed at the Frankfurt airport. He had set things in motion so that I could arrive on time for my father's funeral. Both of my brothers and one sister-in-law met me at the airport, and we raced to Karlsruhe.

Fortunately, in Germany there were no speed limits on the autobahns. As we raced down the autobahn, my sister-in-law Inge pulled out some black hose she had in her purse. She pointed to my skin-colored hose and said, "You know, here in Germany folks still wear black to a funeral, and your hose won't do. To spare you some embarrassment, I brought a black pair of hose for you. You can change right here in the back seat of the car. There won't be any time at the cemetery." Dutifully, as we were flying down the expressway, I changed my hose for the black ones. That was an experience I hope I never have to repeat!

We arrived at the cemetery five minutes before the funeral started. Mother had begged the preacher to wait until I got there. The interment crew was getting anxious, as it was the middle of winter. With Christmas coming and the ground freezing, it would have been impossible to bury my father after December 24. Although it was a nerve-wracking trip, I am extremely thankful that the Lord allowed me to get there in time in spite of the strike in England. I acknowledged once again that without the Lord and His help we could do nothing.

As soon as I stepped out of the car, my mother fell into my arms with a sigh of relief. "Thank God you made it safely!" she breathed. I was so glad to be there for her. As I entered the little chapel, it was difficult to imagine that my father was actually gone. They had not yet closed the coffin, so I was able to see the earthly remains of my father one last time. Had I met him on the street, I would not have recognized him. He had lost so much weight. Fred must have seen my distress, for he stepped up and said, "You know, Joy, this is not father. It is only his shell. Dad is with the Lord."

It was my privilege to stay with mother in her apartment for the remainder of December and most of January. Bill had looked forward to us being together as a family for Christmas, especially after his prolonged absences from home traveling and on the road with the EBI team. But he was very understanding and felt that Mother needed me at this time of transition.

Mother shared with me about Dad's last days on earth. Two weeks before he died, he would go down to the entrance of the hospital and hand out tracts to the visitors. At first, this greatly alarmed the nurses, because he would ask them to disconnect the numerous tubes that were attached to his dying body. When Dad saw how upset they were at this request, he would say, "Now, now. Don't be upset. I'll be fine and will be back soon. I must be about my Father's business while there is still time." He never stopped witnessing for His Lord. When he had an option to be moved from a ward with several sick men to more private quarters, he refused. He still had a job to do witnessing to the men in his ward.

One of his roommates had already lost one lung during an operation. He came to my father and thanked him for showing him the way to Jesus. Then he added, "Mr. Burklin, it won't be long now and we both will meet again at the feet of Jesus." What a tremendous legacy is mine to have had a father who was a true missionary until the day the Lord called him home.

Chapter 23

Discipler, Hostess, and Tentmaker (1971–1975)

WHEN I RETURNED from Europe, I found that Bill had moved his office to a new location. He had found some space in the back of a real estate office where he could spread out. Since I had been gone for almost five weeks, Bill had hired a young lady from our church to help with his secretarial work. I lost my job and always teased Bill that he might regret his decision to fire me. He now had to pay his new secretary, while I never had received a salary.

To help with the cost of closing in the carport and the additional furniture that was needed, Bill and I asked the Lord to show us if I should find a job. I knew it would have to be one in which I could regulate my own hours, as Bill and the girls came first. My responsibilities with my Bible classes, as well as opportunities to speak at Christian Women's Club luncheons in our area and in neighboring states, were another strong consideration. Occasionally I also traveled with Bill to some missions' conferences in his territory. Thus, our consideration of gainful employment for me became a real matter of prayer.

Soon a friend of ours mentioned a new company in the Atlanta area that needed sales people to help sell shares in the company to get it off the ground. I liked the fact that I could set my own hours, so I studied hard to meet the requirement of being licensed by the State of Georgia.

I will never forget the day I went to the State Capitol to the office of the Secretary of State to take the necessary test. I was extremely nervous, especially when I saw that I was the only lady in the room. All the other hopefuls were men. I failed the exam by only a few points that first attempt but was successful on the second and became a licensed securities' sales person.

The Lord was good. He gave me many opportunities to make presentations, and people bought shares in the company. Soon after I started this job, I wrote to my mother in March of 1971:

> I am now a licensed sales lady. What is so wonderful about it is that I can arrange my own time and have to work only a few hours per day. When I was with Bill in Florida for ten days, I could minister with him. When I came home, the Lord was so good. In two weeks I earned almost as much as Bill's monthly mission salary. The Lord is faithful. This weekend I was told, "because of tremendous performance, etc., etc.," I was asked if I did not want to consider becoming a manager of one of the divisions. I would get a certain percentage of the sales the folks under me made. Not bad, eh? When I was in Europe, Bill replaced me with a secretary. So now I have the time and can still be at home when the children are here.
>
> This week, my home Bible study was well attended, but one of the ones at church suffered since I was gone for some time in December and January.

Our little family made Mom's being a sales lady a real matter of prayer. Arlita often prayed, "Lord Jesus, help Mommy to sell a lot of chairs today." She could not quite grasp what shares in a company were. We are glad that the Lord knew what she meant. The Living Bible describes it this way: "For we don't even know what we should pray for nor how to pray as we should, but the Holy Spirit prays for us with such feeling that it cannot be expressed in words" (Romans 8:26 TLB). The Lord certainly heard and answered many of Arlita's prayers.

The end of April, Bill and some professional and businessmen went to Europe for two weeks to get more acquainted with the work of Greater Europe Mission. Bill counted it a privilege to be their guide.

The girls grew and thrived. Gloria was always inquisitive and pondered much about life in general. We had some wonderful talks and times of interaction. Arlita was a sunny child who always looked on the bright side of things. She often kept us in stitches sharing a funny perspective of life as she observed it. I thought it important to be open and honest with the girls. If they did not feel like going to Sunday school and church on a particular Sunday but wanted to sleep in, I told them that I too sometimes felt that way, but I had a ladies' class to teach and would not neglect that responsibility. We agreed that the Lord had a special blessing in store for us, so we went to see what it was that particular Sunday.

As I have said, there was much laughter and fun in our home, but there was also correction and discipline. We used a paddle that we kept hidden on the large bookcase in Arlita's bedroom. One day when I went to get it, it was gone! I noticed that Arlita had been watching me. Before I could say anything, she confessed, "Mommy, I took it to school and gave it to the teacher. I thought she needs it more than you do." That was in the days when the teachers had more discipline and order in their classrooms.

For some time we begged my mother to visit, or even to come live with us in America. A wonderful opportunity came when Fred and his family planned their furlough. Fred taught at the German Bible School and came home every four to five years to visit supporting churches and individuals. In June of 1971, Mom decided to join Fred and his family and travel with them to the States.

On April 25, 1971, I wrote to Mother:

You should have seen us yesterday when Joyce shared the news with us that you will come with Fred and his family!!! Praise the Lord!!!!! The children jumped a mile into the air. Then both of them thanked the Lord for this answer to prayers. Gloria was immediately concerned— she is usually very considerate of the feelings of others—and asked the Lord, "Please help us to make Oma feel right at home."

Some time ago she cried bitterly. She was concerned she would not know how to act towards you, now that Daddy is with the Lord, and she does not want to hurt you. Yes, that is our Gloria. The other night, when Arlita was already in bed, Gloria cried relentlessly. When

Bill went to her, she told him that she missed Opa. She remembered going on walks with him, helping him in the yard, and then the fun in the pool. We are so grateful that both our girls got to know and love you both.

Bill was able to get a car for Fred to use during his deputation tour. A friend of ours in Atlanta had a car dealership and was glad to make a car available for him and his family. Since Bill also had to be at GEM's headquarters in the Chicago area in the middle of June, we both drove the car to Wheaton, Illinois. On June 17, 1971, my mother arrived safely with Fred, Joyce, and their four children at the Chicago airport. Bill and my brother and family had to stay in Wheaton for candidate school of the mission. They had to help fledgling missionary candidates better understand what their task overseas was all about.

Mother and I flew home to Atlanta. Some wonderful weeks followed. Although Mom's visit this time was much shorter than when she and Daddy were with us in 1968, we were able to spend quality time together. She went with me to my Bible studies, shopped with us, spent time with the girls, told stories as we shelled peas, and enjoyed all our normal activities. We had a great time visiting friends, entertaining with picnics, and going on special trips. It was wonderful to share each other's lives.

Fred and his family spent ten days with us. Knowing they really needed a vacation, Bill and I wanted to do something special for them. We treated them to seven days at the Stone Mountain Inn, which is a hotel in Stone Mountain Park. The park includes a large entertainment area with lots of activities. It documents some of the history of our nation during the Civil War. I kept their four children during that week, and the cousins had a great time getting to know each other better. After their visit with us, Fred and his family left to visit friends, churches, and family in the Midwest.

Our next guest was a friend from my Shanghai days. Our new family room and the added space in our little home was a real blessing.

One highlight of that summer was our vacation in St. Petersburg, Florida. A friend of ours invited us to stay one week free of charge at a conference center in her city. It was wonderful to be able to take my mother with us. We stayed at the center, where Bill, the girls, and I enjoyed the tennis courts and pool. Mother enjoyed walks on the beautiful property, the sunny weather, and the many tropical flowers and trees. It reminded her of the area in South China where she lived for many years.

When we had invited Fred and Joyce to stay at Stone Mountain Park at our expense, we did not expect anything in return. We never dreamed that someone would give us a free vacation. We thanked the Lord for His goodness in allowing us to have that wonderful time in sunny Florida. We all needed those days together.

The summer went by all too quickly. Joyce had to take her children back to Germany for the beginning of the new school year, and mother traveled with her. Fred stayed to raise more support, and Bill was able to introduce him to several churches in his Southeast territory.

Once again, in August, Bill attended the annual conference of the mission, which was always held in beautiful Switzerland. No provision was made for the wives and children of the area directors. Bill was also able to spend a few days in Belgium with his parents on that trip. Upon returning, he relocated his office once again.

In the spring of 1972, we had the joy of hosting Bill's parents. It was wonderful to see how Dad Boerop had recuperated from his heart attack in 1967 and was now able to fly. They stayed with us for three months. During the girls' school hours, I sometimes took Bill's parents with me to some of my appointments, especially if they were in some of the outlying towns. That gave them an opportunity to see more of the area. We would have lunch at a hotel, and then I would install them at a shady place around the pool or in comfortable chairs in the lobby. They loved to read and always had books with them. When I finished my presentations, I rejoined them for coffee or tea, and then we would drive home. They loved these little outings.

As a family, we also took them to places like Stone Mountain Park, the Cyclorama, and the Atlanta Zoo. We also enjoyed trips to Tennessee and Florida. The girls had a great time visiting with their other "Oma and Opa" and getting to know them better. Bill's parents also got a better understanding of our life's task and our ministry.

In July of 1972, Bill wrote in a prayer letter:

Greetings from Wheaton, Illinois, and the Greater Europe Mission's annual CANDIDATE SCHOOL. It was exciting to see The EUROCORPS leave for a summer in Europe after three days of orientation. These seventy college students will share the workload of our missionaries there. Ask the Lord to speak to them. We trust a number to join our permanent force in the years to come.

Explo '72 was conducted for a few days in the summer in Dallas, Texas. It was an endeavor by Campus Crusade for Christ to mobilize young people for evangelism. They also invited mission agencies to bring displays and help recruit young people.

Bill continued his letter:

EXPLO '72 was a tremendous inspiration. We helped distribute ten thousand copies of a special edition of the regular G.E.M. Report. Already we have received some inquiries about summer, short term, and career opportunities. Pray that scores of young people follow through on the Great Commission so clearly presented at Explo.

The interest in Europe and G.E.M. ministries there continues to increase in the SOUTHEAST. This is a direct result of your prayers on our behalf. Some churches will have their first missions conference. Individuals for the first time have come to know the joy of involvement in world evangelism. Pray for a constant flow of new contacts. Several business and professional men have formed an ADVISORY COUNCIL for the Southeast. We thank the Lord for each of these men who are working with me in some very tangible ways.

Bill was deeply burdened for the young folks he was trying to impact to surrender and make a complete commitment to serve the Lord full-time.

In the fall of 1972, Bill traveled with another European Bible Institute Alumni Team throughout the Southeast. Again, the purpose was to make the need of Europe, one of the darkest mission fields, known. There were still 40,000 towns and villages in France alone where there was no Gospel witness. This was the sad truth in villages, municipalities, and cities in Belgium, Spain, Italy, Portugal, Austria, and other countries. Bill knew they could not hear if there was no one to tell them.

It was wonderful to see how our two girls grasped the importance of their father's mission and work. One morning during family devotions as we were remembering our regular missionaries, Gloria prayed, "Lord, give them all the money they need or make the dollar stronger." This prayer touched our hearts. Who would dare believe that the Lord could simply improve the world's economy so that His work overseas could go on?

To teach Gloria and Arlita to be practically involved and to personalize missions, we placed a world map on the wall that they viewed when they ate their meals at the breakfast bar. We put photos of missionaries we knew around that map and indicated with some red string where they were serving the Lord around the globe. The photos included their names, their mission agency, and the country where they were working. After dinner, using three by five cards with all the pertinent information of these laborers for the Lord, we would pray for one missionary or family at a time. We interceded regularly for about thirty folks.

When we received prayer letters from these faithful servants of God, we read them together and then asked God to help them in their work. As mentioned in other places in this writing, we also helped support a number of these friends. At times, the girls shared some of their pocket money. Later, they shared their hard-earned funds to help someone who had a special need.

It was a thrill for the girls to meet some of the folks they had prayed for as these missionaries passed through and stayed in our home. In 1973, we earnestly started to look for a larger home to help accommodate our many guests. We also prayed much about this. Since Gloria would finish the seventh grade and her elementary-school years in early June, we felt it would be a good time to move. With no middle schools in the area, she would be entering high school, and Arlita would be going into the fifth grade.

Soon after we listed the house, the realtor brought a lady who absolutely fell in love with the royal blue carpet and the custom-made, blue, lined drapes in the living and dining rooms. She walked in and exclaimed, "This is my house. I love the color blue!" She had not even seen the rest of the house. The realtor had a difficult time trying to convince her that the house was not hers until she made an acceptable offer, applied for a loan, was approved, and signed the closing papers. Never in my wildest dreams had I thought that our choice of color for the carpet and drapes in the main living area would clinch the sale of our little ranch-style home in Decatur. We truly saw the hand of God in it and once again felt that our heavenly Father must have a sense of humor!

We found a home and welcomed the four bedrooms and three baths. Now we had a lot more space. Folks from across the US, as well as many from overseas, enjoyed time with us. That house in Stone Mountain, which was only two miles from our beloved Stone Mountain Park, became our home for the next twenty-four years.

Gloria, Arlita, and their dad enjoyed a week of summer camp at Children's Bible Mission Camp in Alabama. Bill made it a point to spend time with his girls, and I was glad they had those special times together. Some of their "dates" included going to concerts, a movie, a favorite restaurant, or even the Opera when the New York Met came to Atlanta in the spring. The girls loved these times with their dad.

That year, 1973, Billy Graham came to Atlanta with a crusade. It was my privilege to take my friend Margret, the Avon lady, with me. We enjoyed singing in the choir. I also continued with my home Bible studies, as well as with the ladies' class on Sunday mornings at our church. There were several of the gals who played tennis. I have always loved the game. In order for me to get to know these ladies better, I joined them in playing two or three times a week. It was wonderful to play at some country clubs, apartment complexes, private courts, and parks. Although it was a fun time, inevitably they would also ask questions about our previous Sunday's lesson or share prayer requests and family concerns. I met for lunch with the ladies in our class who did not play tennis.

At the end of the summer, both girls had to go to a new school. Arlita quickly adjusted to fifth grade at Hambrick Elementary School and had wonderful teachers, whom she loved. Going to high school was more daunting for Gloria. When I talked and prayed with her before she went to bed one night, she confided that she was very apprehensive about entering eighth grade. In those days we did not have any middle schools in our county. Eighth through twelfth grade were considered high school. It was very daunting for a thirteen-year-old to enter high school. The drug culture was beginning to expand into the schools, and promiscuity was becoming more prevalent.

I assured Gloria that the Lord Jesus was right there in school with her. In fact, He promised to go before her and never to leave or forsake her. God had a purpose for her. As His child, she was to be a witness for Him, a bright and shining light as she had been in elementary school. Then I quoted: "Being confident of this one thing, that He who has begun a good work in you will also perform it unto the day of Jesus Christ" (Philippians 1:6 KJV).

The Lord Jesus had begun a good work in our children when they accepted Him as their Savior, and He would also keep them in the palm of His hand. This was a promise my little one could cling to. As a parent, I claimed it many times over the next few years, especially during the rough and unpredictable teenage years.

Bill was asked by the General Director of Greater Europe Mission to become the coordinator of celebrations for the mission's 25th anniversary. Founder's luncheons and banquets were to be held across the nation in 1974. This position required a great deal of travel as Bill set up the banquets and then attended them all across the United States.

From time to time, we asked the girls to communicate with our prayer partners and supporters. In the fall/winter of 1974, Gloria, now fourteen years old, wrote:

Dear Friends,
This has been a very busy year and I'd like to share some of the highlights with you. It was especially busy for Dad. As you know he has been in charge of most of the twenty banquets. From the kickoff banquet in Chicago, until the successful finish last month, all banquets went well. The attendance total, an average of 300, was surpassed. Pray for Dad as he continues his regular job. He needs much wisdom and guidance with all there is to be done.

Mom had surgery twice this year. The second one was successful and we thank you for all your prayers. Continue to pray for complete healing. Also pray for much strength as she has many added responsibilities with Dad traveling.

These last few weeks we've been fortunate to have Grandma Burklin with us. We are looking forward to our first Christmas together! (Mom and Grandma spent their last Christmas together seventeen years ago.)

Arlita is enjoying sixth grade with many outside activities. Please pray that she may be a witness for Christ.

Pray too that I live for Christ daily in school, cheerleading, and other activities. Next summer we are planning, the Lord willing, to go to Europe. (I hope to be able to speak some French by then)...I personally thank you for standing behind us.

A blessed Christmas to you all and may God be with you in this coming year.

Gloria, for the Boerops

In September 1974, Mom came once more to be with us. Since I had to have major surgery and would not be able to fully run the household, she agreed to help us. She traveled to the US alone for the first time on September 25 and arrived in New York, where Bill met her at the airport. Mom felt great, so they decided not to spend the night in New York but to fly to Atlanta that same evening. What a surprise it was for me when Bill called from the airport to say that they were on their way home.

Mother was a great help. Not only did she manage the household, but also she helped Bill with mailings for the Southeast office. Mom folded and inserted prayer letters in envelopes and got them ready for mailing while I helped from where I lay in bed. Those were also great times of sharing. We would sit on the upstairs deck, which was right off the master bedroom, and have a cup of tea or coffee together as Mom shared life experiences, beginning with her youth. It truly was a good time. I recuperated slowly, and after a few weeks was well again.

Over the years mother had been in touch with her relatives in Salamanca, New York, which is just outside of Buffalo. Her mother's brother, who was to take over the farm in Germany, decided to immigrate to the United States instead. In the latter part of the 19th Century, around 1875 to 1880, he came to the New World and settled in upstate New York. Mother had always wanted to visit with her family in upstate

New York, but it had never worked out. She told me that when she had recently written to one of her cousins at the last address she had, the letter had been returned stamped, "DECEASED." She deeply regretted that she would never meet them.

I decided to investigate to see if there might possibly be some descendants of my mother's uncle in Salamanca who were still alive. I picked up the phone and dialed directory assistance for Salamanca. At that time, calls were operator assisted. I told the operator that I was looking for a Mr. Rettberg. I was shocked when she told me that there were many Rettbergs in Salamanca! She commented, "It seems the whole town exists of only Rettbergs." I asked the operator just to give me one of them. Much to my surprise, I was connected to the wife of one of Mom's first cousins. We were very excited and felt this was an answer to prayer. We made arrangements for Mom and our family to visit them after Christmas.

It had been a long time since mother and I had celebrated Christmas together. It was, as Gloria said in her letter, 17 years. The year dad died, we were too grief stricken to celebrate. Bill and the girls had never spent this special holiday with her. We made the most of it and had a meaningful Christmas. We also shared this sacred holiday with friends who did not have family in the Atlanta area.

Since mother was to fly back to Germany the first week in January of 1975, Bill planned for us to drive to Salamanca, New York, a few days after Christmas. Mother could not wait to finally meet her relatives. What a meeting it was! We found that mother's Uncle Rettberg had ten children who had numerous offspring. No wonder the whole town was mostly inhabited by Rettbergs! Only one first cousin and another cousin's wife were still living. Had Mom and Dad been able to visit in 1968, five of her cousins could have met them.

We stayed in the home of one of the cousins, and many of the Rettberg family from all over the town came to visit Mother. Several of the extended families who lived in a town nearby invited us for lunch or dinner. It was a busy time of getting acquainted. Mother was thrilled the most when the Rettberg clan organized a welcome party for her on New Year's Eve. They rented the fellowship hall of the Methodist Church in town. Folks came from all over the area, until there were wall-to-wall people. As we looked at Mom and her only living cousin sitting side by side, we were amazed at how much they looked alike. They could have been mistaken for brother and sister. It was a wonderful evening!

When we walked back to our sleeping quarters a little after midnight, it started to snow. Gloria and Arlita had been praying for snow, and the Lord graciously answered. They had seen very little snow in Atlanta, but now it came down in large flakes that formed a breathtaking landscape. We were all mesmerized and drank in the beauty of God's creation.

On New Year's Day, following a good-old-American tradition, we all watched a football game. My mother joined her cousin in cheering for his team. We laughed as she shouted with excitement about a touchdown, then exclaimed delightedly over an extra point scored by *their* team. You would have thought Mom had watched American football all her life when she expressed disdain over a penalty flag. Actually, this was the first football game she had ever watched! She really had a wonderful time. I am so glad that we were able to fulfill her longtime hope and dream of finally meeting her family in Salamanca. After that visit, Mom was able to stay in touch with the Rettbergs of Salamanca for several more years.

It had been more than ten years since we last drove in snow country, so we were very cautious driving without winter tires or chains. We made it safely to Aunt Katie's and her husband's apartment for dinner. It was so good to see Aunt Katie, who had married again after her first husband died. We all were glad for the visit and had a good time.

We said our goodbyes the next day at J.F. Kennedy Airport, as Mother was flying back to Germany. The Lord was good to give us three-and-a-half months together, and we praised Him for this precious time. The farewell was made a little sweeter for our family with the anticipation of a summer visit to Europe, when we would see Mom again.

Bill's travels continued. He faithfully visited churches, sharing the need of Europe and introducing young men and women whom the Lord had called. They needed prayer and financial partners, and Bill continually invited churches to come alongside and help. He also visited seminaries, colleges, and universities, trying to interest and challenge students to heed the call: "As my Father hath sent me, even so send I you" (John 20:21 KJV). We were humbled each and every time people responded.

That year Bill also hosted the G.E.M. representatives' seminar in Atlanta. This allowed the representatives to interact and receive input from Christian business and professional men. They greatly appreciated this. Then he had to work out the details and itinerary for our summer trip. We were asked to visit several of the fields where G.E.M. missionaries served. It would be a good opportunity to see the work of some of those who had surrendered to the Lord's call under Bill's ministry.

In June 1975, Gloria completed ninth grade, and Arlita completed sixth grade. They were busy with activities such as cheerleading, piano, Bible studies, youth choir, and youth meetings at church. They loved to spend time with their friends. Both looked forward to their second visit to Europe.

It was Arlita's turn to write our prayer letter, and her anticipation of our trip to Europe was well documented in her writing. It also shows the tremendous sense of humor with which our daughter has been blessed. In May 1975, as an eleven-and-a-half-year-old, she wrote:

> Hi! This time it's my turn to write. I'd rather talk to you all on the telephone…but then, that would cost too much. I don't know much about writing prayer letters, but this time I want to tell you about the really "fun" things in our family!
>
> It seems that Daddy really has "fun" traveling…going to Alabama, Tennessee, Virginia, North and South Carolina, Florida—oh, yes, he always goes to Florida in the winter—.the last time he liked it so well we didn't see him for almost three weeks. I guess he could be gone all the time because there are so many new churches that want to hear about people in Europe that need Jesus.
>
> At home Mother has "fun" entertaining the many friends that are passing through from all over. We had company fifty-nine days out of the last three months…from eleven different countries or states! Mother enjoys cooking, washing clothes, and cleaning house for them (with the help of Gloria and me), but has the most "fun" showing them around beautiful Atlanta. She also has "fun" teaching her Sunday School class, and "thinks" she does a good job with Gloria and Me! (We don't always agree with her!)
>
> Recently Gloria had a lot of "fun" being in the hospital for ten days. They gave her all sorts of tests, and when they couldn't find anything wrong with her (they should have asked me!) they finally

took out her appendix. She is fine again, but doesn't think it's so much "fun" to catch up on all her schoolwork, exams, etc. She needs your prayers, and so do I, when she gets frustrated!

I think it will be so much "fun" to go to Europe this summer. I can't wait to see my cousins and Uncle and Aunt from Africa. I don't even know them, since they are missionaries there. Also to see some of the countries where our missionaries work will be neat.

It will be "fun" to meet those again in Spain, Italy, Portugal, Germany, Belgium, and France who are working in Europe because God used my Daddy to tell them to go.

Some of the travel money has already been promised. We are praying for the rest. It'll be so much "fun" to see how God answers prayers! It was "fun" to write to you!

Love ya, Arlita

Chapter 24

The Trip of a Lifetime (1975)

THE DAY OF our departure for Europe finally arrived. My dear husband, always the eager beaver to serve the Lord, planned several days of ministry in St. Petersburg, Florida, on our way to catch our flight in Miami. We flew out on July 7 via Nassau in the Bahamas to Luxembourg, where my brother Fred picked us up on July 8. He drove us to Mother's apartment in Karlsruhe-Durlach. After a short visit with her, we began our tour through Europe. Bill had arranged for us to pick up a car in Germany. What a blessing and thoughtful foresight that proved to be. We drove 5,000 miles in forty-one days and visited nine countries, something we could never have done had we tried to use the trains.

Some very special memories from that trip often come to mind. As we drove through the Black Forest in Southern Germany, we decided to stop at St. Georgen, where I had lived when we came from China. I thought it might be interesting for my family to see where I had worked as a secretary about twenty-five years previously. As we approached, I could not believe how the factory had grown. There were expanded buildings everywhere. It was after hours, but I introduced myself to the guard at the gate and explained that I had worked there many years before. I told him we were visiting from America. He smiled and immediately picked up the phone and made a call. Then he said, "Lady, it is all right for you to go upstairs. The VIPs are in the conference room."

When we all walked up the stairs, I was amazed. Gone was the old drab building and the crowded offices. Beautiful modern halls revealed bright offices with large windows. The Papst brother who had been my colleague greeted me with a big hug and then ushered us into the conference room, where his two brothers and another former colleague of mine were having a meeting. Our little family could not believe the warm reception I received from these men. They treated us to coffee, drinks, light sandwiches, and cakes.

We soon learned that the young men I had known were now the executives of the company. Their father, who had hired me, had been pulling back and was letting the younger men slowly take over. After a wonderful time of reminiscing and sharing about our lives, we were invited by one of the brothers to dinner in one of the wonderful, quaint restaurants in town. He also made sure that we stayed in the best hotel in St. Georgen at his expense. With a twinkle in his eye Bill said, "You must have been quite the employee in those days. You must have done something good!" I praise the Lord that after so many years I was still remembered as a faithful, diligent worker.

Our travels began in earnest with Switzerland and Austria. We stayed in some charming bed and breakfast inns in these beautiful countries. In Italy, we visited ancient sites in Venice, Florence, Pisa, and Rome. In Rome, we were treated by one of our missionaries to the Opera *Carmen* in an open-air theater. In Monaco, it was an unforgettable thrill for us to experience a concert with the Monte-Carlo National Symphony Orchestra. In Spain, we visited one of the newer Bible Schools of Greater Europe Mission, where a couple served who had been challenged under Bill's ministry.

When hunger nagged, we sometimes stopped at a little grocery store and bought some bread, cheese, and fruit, which we would eat at a park. Cokes were not readily available; so we made our own drinks by mixing "cassis," black currant syrup, and water. Gloria and Arlita did not like it, but it was all we could find in some of the towns and villages.

We still remember a unique Sunday luncheon experience in Spain. Having been invited to have lunch after an early morning church service, we were quite surprised when our hosts stopped on the way to their home and went shopping for the ingredients for the meal. A chicken from the yard was killed; potatoes were peeled; and vegetables were washed and cooked. Finally, about four in the afternoon, we sat down to eat our meal. Since we had left the house at 8 A.M., we were quite hungry by that time!

Another surprise and culture shock for us was how late the Spaniards ate at night. Often we did not sit down for dinner until midnight or even later. This was quite an adjustment for the girls. It made them appreciate more what it cost a missionary to live in a foreign land. Now they were truly able to pray for them with better understanding.

When we visited Lausanne, Switzerland, I did not want to miss showing Bill and the girls the area and the house where I had worked so hard as a governess in the early 50s. We were able to go into the actual house where I had lived and worked. The once-beautiful house had been converted into three apartments, one on each level. We could only see the entrance and the spiraling white-stone staircase.

In Switzerland, Bill also showed us the fancy hotel in Leysin where, for the past six or seven years, he had joined Greater Europe Mission for their annual field conference for their missionaries. This year it was to be in Belgium. It would be the first time I was invited to the G.E.M. conference. It would have been nice to be able to attend the conference and stay at the Leysin hotel as in the past, but those were sacrifices that had to be made.

Since it was my birthday, my dear husband took us higher up into the mountains to a wonderful chalet-restaurant for a delicious fondue meal. We were serenaded by several Swiss men who played alpenhorns. These nine-foot horns produce wonderful melodies, skillfully played by these musicians. It was a never-to-be-forgotten birthday celebration.

In Paris, we met some former EBI classmates who served the Lord in Dutch New Guinea and were on furlough. The sights in Paris impressed the girls, but they were ecstatic when we discovered a McDonald's Restaurant. We did enjoy our Big Macs!

When we worked in Belgium with Youth for Christ in the late 50s, we befriended a family who had a girl a little older than our Gloria. Over the years we stayed in touch and were excited we could meet again in 1975. We invited Gloria's little friend, Beatrix, now a teenager, to join us for a once-in-a-lifetime experience. Youth for Christ Europe had organized a youth conference called Eurofest with Billy Graham as the evangelist. What a thrill it was for Bill, Gloria, and Beatrix to join 8,000 young people from all over Europe for a week of Bible studies, workshops, and evangelistic meetings. It was a wonderful opportunity for Gloria's friend to hear the true, unadulterated Gospel of Jesus Christ. She and Gloria engaged in some earnest discussions.

During the days of Eurofest, Arlita and I spent time with Bill's parents, who were on vacation in The Netherlands. After the congress in Brussels, both girls stayed with Grandparents Boerop. Bill and I attended the annual field conference of G.E.M. in Brussels at a building the mission bought, which had formerly been a monastery and seminary. We joined with 425 missionaries, Eurocorps, and short-term missionaries for great meetings and wonderful fellowship. The only drawback was four showers for 425 people. We heard one phrase over and over again, "This is not like the beautiful hotel in Leysin!"

A family reunion with Bill's folks followed in Ede, The Netherlands. We had not seen Bill's sister in fifteen years and had never met her British husband or her three girls, who had been raised in Nairobi, Kenya, East Africa. It was a time of getting reacquainted and getting to know each other. Sights we visited included a 235-foot-deep well that was over 160 years old and was used for watering the army's horses, a large park with animals foreign to Holland, the windmills, and thousands of bicycles. Ubiquitous cups of coffee in the morning, cups of tea in the afternoon, and coffee at night were also new experiences for our daughters.

The highlight of our time together came when Dad Boerop invited us all to celebrate our reunion in a multiple-centuries-old farmhouse that was now registered as a restaurant. It is amazing how Europeans have been able to take care of old buildings that are many hundreds of years old. The specialty of the house was a variety of savory or sweet pancakes for lunch or dinner. It was the first and last time Mom and Dad Boerop were surrounded by their son and daughter and their spouses and their five grandchildren.

A visit with my family in Germany was next on the agenda. We visited with both of my brothers' families in their homes. Mom and our three families met for the Burklin reunion at a Chinese restaurant, where we had a wonderful meal. Since mother would be turning eighty shortly, we also celebrated her special birthday. It was the only time my mother was together with her three children, their spouses, and her ten grandchildren. She often mentioned what a wonderful, special evening that was.

On August 21, 1975, we left Luxembourg via Air Bahama and flew to Nassau. After two days in the Bahamas, we had another week of meetings in Florida, and then finally arrived back home in Stone Mountain, Georgia, on August 30. Those eight-and-a-half weeks were treasured experiences that we as a family will always cherish.

In Bill's first prayer letter to our supporters after our return, he wrote:

> Scores of impressions linger on in our minds—the growing nationalistic spirit in most countries—the difficulty in getting through when sharing Christ with adults steeped in philosophies and religions—the joy of seeing a growing response to the gospel among young people—praise for safety and strength—joy of time spent with loved ones, some of whom we had not seen in fifteen years—challenge and inspiration of staying with a Belgian family we ministered to fifteen years ago—our girls' culture shock—the hundreds of towns passed through that have no gospel witness—the unbelievable practices still prevalent to try to find peace with God, such as ascending the holy stairs in Rome on knees and kissing certain steps—the overwhelming evidence of the soundness of "training Europeans to evangelize Europe" (almost fifty graduates of the European Bible Institute alone were engaged in Eurofest in an official capacity, from chairman on down).

Chapter 25

Faith, Guidance, and Fulfillment (1976–1978)

OUR BUSY LIVES continued. Gloria was in the tenth grade, and Arlita was in the seventh. We continued to have a great deal of company. In 1976 we were challenged at church to give a special missionary offering. Bill and I felt God tugging at our hearts, even though we were already supporting several servants of the Lord. In faith, we wanted to participate but did not have the funds. Just when we were praying earnestly about the amount God had laid on our hearts, our washing machine broke.

Very unexpectedly one day, the mailman brought a check from Bill's former employer. Bill had occasionally received some residuals from his sales as an insurance salesman. The check was the exact amount we had promised by faith! Bill and I decided to quickly write the check for the Lord's work before we would be tempted to spend it on a washing machine.

Several days later, Bill visited a friend we both knew well. Coming home from that visit, Bill asked me to come outside and look at his car. My first thought was that he had been in an accident. When I went outside, I noticed that the trunk was propped open. Walking to the back of the car, I was shocked to see a washing machine in the trunk!

My husband told me that our friend had asked him how I was doing. Bill mentioned that I was fine and had just gone to the Laundromat to wash some clothes. Our friend asked, "What is Joy doing going to a

Laundromat? She cannot lift wet clothes into a basket and cart it home with her bad back. Is your machine broken?"

When our friend learned that we did not have a useable washing machine, he told Bill to go to a certain address and pick up a good, used washing machine. He was not in the washing machine business, but the Lord was! It was humbling to reaffirm that we could trust the One who had asked us to be a channel with our faith promise offering, and we praised Him that we had obeyed the tugging of the Holy Spirit. The Scriptures promise that He will supply *all* our needs, and He does. It is not always *all we want*, but it certainly is *all we need*. Another favorite verse of mine is: "But seek ye first the kingdom of God, and His righteousness; and all these things shall be added unto you" (Matthew 6:33 KJV).

It was always our joy to help appointees to the field. Bill considered it a privilege to arrange meetings in churches and to challenge believers to help them with prayer and financial support. It was also fulfilling for him to assist missionaries home on furlough with their financial needs of erasing deficits and securing much-needed additional monthly support. Increased regular gifts for some of the Bible Institutes resulted in more training opportunities for European young people who were eager to serve the Lord.

Bill faithfully presented the need of Europe across the Southeast, and God gave us numerous folks He led to Europe to reach and train Europeans to evangelize. We could truly see God's hand leading us so differently than we had thought He would so many years before when we first came to the United States. Had we gone back to Europe with Youth for Christ, we could only have served the Lord full time in one or two countries. Had we gone with G.E.M. to teach in one of their Bible Institutes, we would have been serving Him in one country only. Now we were blessed to see men and women serving in at least ten different countries across Europe.

The end of the school year in 1976 was exciting for Gloria. We received word that she would be allowed to skip the eleventh grade due to her good grades. At the same time, the end of the school year was traumatic for Arlita. Graduating from seventh grade was a milestone, and her classmates wanted to celebrate with a dance. It was amazing to us how quickly times had changed. When Gloria had graduated from elementary school three years earlier, they had a lovely party for the whole seventh grade. There was no talk of a dance.

Bill and I felt that seventh graders were too young to have a dance. In those days, most boys and girls did not even like each other. We discussed this with Arlita, pointing out that there would be many wonderful experiences ahead of her when she got older.

That night when I tucked Arlita in bed, she began to sob, "But Mom, I really want to go to the dance. All my friends are going. I will be the only one in the class who is not going." I tried to assure her that I understood what it felt like to be left out. I remembered how awkward I felt my first few years in Europe when it was difficult to fit in. Between her sobs, Arlita shared that some of her friends whose parents were also Christians were being allowed to go. She surmised that perhaps it was because her mom and dad were believers that we were not excited about the dance.

I had a wonderful opportunity to share with our precious girl that her dad and I felt that going to a dance at such an early age was not in her best interest. We were trying to raise her and her sister in a way that was pleasing to the Lord. Activities we are involved in can put pressure on us that we don't know how to handle. Sometimes that results in not honoring the Lord. We then prayed together. Arlita was still not too convinced and kept on crying. I hugged her tightly and cried with her while my heart ached for her. It would have been much easier to agree to let her go, but that would have jeopardized our convictions.

Many years later, Arlita and her friend Linda were laughing and reminiscing about school days. I heard Linda say, "You know, Arlita, do you remember the dance we had when we graduated from elementary school? We had no fun at all, and it was so stupid. We didn't know what to do. No one danced. We all stood or sat along the walls and stared at each other." With that, she laughed heartily.

"Yes, I remember, the one I was not allowed to go to," replied my dear Arlita. Linda got quiet for a minute and then she said, "I wish my mom had not let me go either. She should have had the guts to say 'no.'" Arlita sat up straight and smiled.

I breathed a prayer, "Thank you, Lord Jesus, for giving us the wisdom we desperately need as parents."

That summer we had the privilege of hosting the daughter of one of my former colleagues from the company in Germany where I had worked as a secretary. Our trip to the Black Forest the previous year had resulted in our inviting Martina Papst to stay with us for six weeks during the summer vacation. She fit well into our family, and we all had a wonderful time.

In our 1976 Christmas letter, we wrote:

> We celebrate the unspeakable gift of God, His Son, our Savior, the Lord Jesus Christ. It is an appropriate time to look back and see the many gifts God has showered upon us as a family this past year... Many of these gifts are wrapped up in the lives of our two girls, Gloria and Arlita.
>
> Gloria, an exuberant 16-year-old senior in high school, is enjoying her last year at home to the fullest. We see little of her—school activities, volunteer work at a nursing home, being a sales girl in a dress shop (she is very eager to save up towards college expenses), church, and meeting her friends (the other night we had about twenty in our basement for Bible study) keep her 110 percent occupied. We do praise God for her and know that He'll lead her, also into the college of His choosing.
>
> Arlita is experiencing what high school is all about. Already in eighth grade, she had to choose between the good and the best—friends who are popular, but lack in reputation, and those who want to make their lives count. She experienced definite answer to prayers—made cheerleading and was voted captain the other day. She has become a responsible little gal, who likes to play the piano a little better, thinks school is a necessary evil, and loves to babysit. Pray with us that God may be able to continue to form and mold her.

It was a joy for me to attend football and basketball games when the girls were on the cheerleading squad. Gloria cheered for the varsity team and Arlita for the junior varsity. Occasionally they had the fun of cheering together. I loved watching my girls, and nothing kept me from it. They pretended not to see their mother cheering for the football team or proudly applauding some dangerous contortion or pyramid in their routines. Years later, they shared with me how much it meant to them to glance at the bleachers and see me cheering them on.

Bill attended whenever he could and would always dress in the school colors of red and white. The girls teased him mercilessly about his red pants and white golf shirt. Even his broad belt was the right color. We knew it meant much to the girls for him to honor them and their school with his attendance. On weekends before a game, our whole family got involved in supporting the team. We helped the cheerleaders make tags and banners, sell doughnuts, and prepare breakfast for the players. We were always creating something to help cheer the boys on to victory.

On a trip to California, we had the privilege of meeting one of my friends from Shanghai days whom I had not seen in more than thirty years. He was one of the former G.I.s who came to the children's home almost every day after work. He taught us to play softball. It was a great blessing for us to stay in his home and meet his family. We have remained in touch to this day.

My employment as a securities sales person came to an end when the issuance of stocks for my company was completed. When Gloria applied to Wheaton at the beginning of her senior year in high school, she received early acceptance and a small scholarship. With her entering college in the fall, I decided to look at work options. It would have been impossible to send our girls to private colleges on a mission's salary, but we felt it was in their best interest.

In the spring of 1977, Gloria entered the Miss Stone Mountain High Pageant. It was exciting to watch as she was voted second runner-up. The pageant gave her an opportunity to share her faith in Jesus Christ through the talent competition. She sang praise choruses in different languages as she accompanied herself on the piano. This event encouraged Gloria to enter the Miss Georgia National Teenager Pageant, which proved to be an invaluable experience.

On June 8, 1977, Gloria graduated from high school. It was Bill's privilege to be the speaker for the baccalaureate address. It was an excellent opportunity to communicate the Lord's greatness and goodness to more than 300 graduates.

Our friends in the Black Forest invited Gloria to spend six weeks with them in Germany. It was a wonderful opportunity for her to immerse herself in another culture before she left for Wheaton College. She had a wonderful time with Martina and her family.

Gloria spent the remainder of the summer working in a dress shop. She earned so many prizes competing with other salesgirls that she was able to accumulate a nice college wardrobe. Warm clothes were necessary for the cold winters in the North.

Arlita babysat for our neighbors that summer from 5:30 A.M. until 4 P.M. It was a long day, but our diligent thirteen-and-a–half-year old was a dependable worker. Not once did I have to wake her in the morning or challenge her to take her job seriously. As young as she was, Arlita was a real testimony of faithfulness and hard work.

When a friend approached Bill with a real estate job for me, I hesitated. I liked the fact that I could set my own hours for the many ministries with which I was involved, and I knew nothing about selling houses. Having to go to classes for several months and then pass an exam was another scary thought.

After much discussion with Bill and prayer for guidance, I agreed to try the job in real estate. I went to class every day for two months, five days a week, six hours per day. Then came the day of the dreaded exam. I went into it thinking that if I failed, I would take it that the Lord had something better for me than becoming a licensed real estate agent.

After weeks of hearing nothing, we came home late one night from an outing to find a letter in our mailbox from the Secretary of State. I had passed the exam! My dear husband and the girls whooped and hollered. Bill declared, "This calls for a celebration. Let's get some ice cream!" My niece was with us that evening and was quite amazed that we would celebrate so late at night. We assured her that the Boerop family was always ready to celebrate, no matter what hour it was!

I sold real estate for twenty-five years and helped scores of families find homes. Many of them came to me over and over again throughout the years if they needed a larger house or if their jobs warranted moving out of town or to a different area of Atlanta. This job certainly provided for both our girls to attend good Christian colleges. These resources were also a great blessing in allowing us to help many ministries as well as in providing for the ministry of our calling. Without these resources, we could not have entertained as many people in our home throughout the years.

On Labor Day weekend, we all traveled to Wheaton, Illinois, to move Gloria into her dorm room at Wheaton College. It was a big step for her, as she had just turned seventeen the end of June. It was also a big adjustment for us as parents and especially for Arlita. The girls had always been close. Arlita and I cried all the way back to Atlanta. Bill and I missed our firstborn, but we were glad that she quickly fit in and loved Wheaton. Bill wrote in a prayer letter:

> Gloria started her college life. Her communications indicate great excitement and enjoyment at Wheaton College. We must admit that we miss her. Her absence was accentuated by my extensive travel this past fall. You can imagine how glad we are to have her home for the Christmas holidays.

Arlita started the ninth grade and was once again thrilled to make the cheerleading squad. Bill continued with the Greater Europe Mission appreciation dinners. About 4,500 people attended twenty-six dinners from Augusta, Georgia, to Spokane, Washington, and from Canada to Texas. Bill not only organized these dinners but also was often the main speaker. They were a great challenge, but also were a wonderful opportunity to get more folks involved in what God was doing in Europe.

Spending Thanksgiving as a family at a friend's lake house was a real blessing. We have always loved the water. One of Bill's greatest thrills is to race a boat across the water. During the summers all four of us had enjoyed water skiing and boating. We especially loved early morning breakfasts across the lake on our "special island" when Bill would cook for us. It was great fun to once again have breakfast on "our" island that Thanksgiving in November. We loved hearing Gloria share about her first experiences as a college student.

The beginning of 1978 was hectic, to say the least. I spoke at twenty Christian Women's Club luncheons in Georgia and surrounding states. We gave praise to the Lord as a number of ladies indicated their desire to accept the Lord Jesus Christ as their Savior and wanted to follow Him as their Lord and Master.

In February, Arlita and I joined Bill for a missions conference in St. Petersburg, Florida, at a church that was strongly missions minded. Bill used that church over and over again as a model to show pastors and church leaders what their home churches could do in reaching the world for Christ. Northside Baptist Church in St. Petersburg had incorporated the Faith Promise plan for giving. That was a new concept for Arlita. When the challenge was given to trust the Lord in faith for a certain amount per month to give for reaching the lost, her heart was touched. She wanted to participate. When she revealed to me how much her faith promise was, how much she wanted to trust the Lord for in the next year, I could not believe it. She had not had much opportunity to make extra money lately, as babysitting was slow and small jobs were not materializing. I thought there wasn't any way, humanly speaking, that she could fulfill her promise; but I said nothing.

When we returned home, the phone began to ring for Arlita. She was in high demand for babysitting and small jobs as well. Every month she sent her faith promise gift to the church in St. Petersburg. At the end of the faith promise year in February, 1979, she had been able to fulfill her promise. The Lord had honored her faith and used her as a channel to provide resources for His work around the world. Arlita was so encouraged that she doubled her promise for the next year. She told her father jokingly, "I have to go to St. Pete for the next mission's conference and check on what they have done with my faith promise." It was wonderful to see our ninth grader grow in the Lord. She learned to commit big and small things to the Lord in prayer and was a great testimony to her peers.

A few days after Gloria came home from college, she was thrilled to find a full-time summer job in a dress shop. On June 5, Bill's parents arrived by direct flight from Brussels and stayed with us for five weeks. They were a real inspiration as they shared with us how the Lord had provided for them during their more than thirty-year ministry in Belgium. Our prayer was that we as a family might also practice the same principles of childlike trust and commitment that both sets of parents had modeled before us.

Chapter 26

Major Decisions and Events (1978–1981)

IN THE FALL of 1978, a great number of missionaries and short-term volunteers in Bill's territory needed help obtaining prayer and financial support. There had never been as many workers at one time needing Bill's help in arranging meetings for them in churches. He worked diligently, and the Lord answered many prayers. Besides the Midwest, where G.E.M.'s headquarters were located in Wheaton, Illinois, the Southeast became the strongest area for the mission as far as missionary recruits and financial giving were concerned.

When Bill had begun his ministry with G.E.M., he had started with an "office" in our den, which consisted of an old typewriter on a small table. Through the years, many gradual upgrades had finally resulted in lovely permanent quarters with adequate desks, office equipment, and a part-time secretary in a well-located, modern office complex. In 1968, there had been forty-two participating churches. Now, in 1978, there were more than 450 churches. Bill was responsible for the oversight of eleven states. In those same years, in three southern states alone, the financial income for the mission had increased from $50,000 a year to $250,000. Scores of missionaries, candidates, and Eurocorps workers had come from Bill's territory. This had not come about without a great price to my dear husband. Years of hard work and travel had taken their toll.

In November 1978, Bill experienced total burnout. The doctor told him it was mandatory that he take six months to a year of medical leave due to total exhaustion. Bill took off three months. Friends of ours offered him their second homes, condos, and penthouses in Florida, and Bill tried to rest spiritually, physically, and mentally. He called me regularly to let me know how he was doing. I surprised him for his birthday in December, and we had a wonderful weekend together. To celebrate Christmas as a family, the Lord allowed us to go on a cruise with our girls. This was especially good for Bill. He resumed his work in February, glad to be back at the task the Lord had given him. He felt God had renewed his strength, and our prayer was that God would improve his ability to pace himself.

The summer of 1979, Gloria spent six weeks in Israel with a Wheaton study group. She attended the Institute of Biblical Studies in Jerusalem and also journeyed to Rome, Italy, and Cairo, Egypt. In Cairo, she was approached by a man who offered to give her father one thousand camels in exchange for her hand in marriage! Egyptians loved her blonde hair! The time abroad was an enriching experience for Gloria. We were deeply thankful for my work in real estate that also allowed Arlita to go on this same special pilgrimage with Wheaton College four years later. Although she was a student at Taylor University, Arlita received full credit for the summer session due to a consortium between the two schools.

In the spring of 1980, the Lord opened another door of opportunity for Bill and me. In his April prayer letter, Bill wrote:

The Lord gave direction regarding a major decision I faced. You prayed, I searched the options. God opened the door. THANK HIM WITH US!

On May 1, I will assume the position of Director of Ministries with CHRISTIAN NATIONALS EVANGELISM COMMISSION. The overall thrust of my responsibilities is world missions promotion. This will be in North America and overseas. CNEC assists nationals in thirty-five different countries. These gifted and dedicated national Christian leaders carry on various significant ministries....

It has been a privilege to serve the Lord and Europe, through Greater Europe Mission, these past fourteen years. Hundreds of Christians across the Southeast have become aware of Europe's spiritual need. Many churches are involved now to help meet this need. Scores of missionaries were recruited. Financial support from this area is close to a million dollars now. The Lord has done this. THANK HIM WITH US! I want to thank my three girls, Joy, Gloria, and Arlita. Without their sacrifice and support, I could not have done it. I want to thank you for your share, through your faithful prayers. The Word of God is now more available in Europe because of you. Continue to pray for the continent and the ministries of Greater Europe Mission. I trust you will continue to pray for us as you have in the past.

That spring Gloria became engaged to Douglas Darr, a senior at Wheaton College. He was from Dallas, Texas. They planned to get married in the spring of 1981, after Gloria graduated in February of that year. Even before our girls were born, we had prayed for the young men they would one day marry.

Arlita's senior year was extremely busy, as she was president of her class, cheerleading captain, and on the homecoming court of Stone Mountain High School. Arlita was extremely proud to have her dad escort her onto the football field. No one, however, could have been more proud than her daddy was. We were grateful that Arlita's many achievements did not come at the expense of her testimony.

That fall Bill held several pastors' seminars, where he challenged them and their church leaders to launch meaningful world missions outreaches in their local churches. He never dreamed what the Lord had in store for him as a result of these pastors' seminars.

God did many miraculous things for us, but they did not always come without challenges. In early 1981, while on one of his assignments at a church in Birmingham, Alabama, Bill felt compelled to call me, although he had just left us that morning. He and Don Hillis, a true missions statesman and personal friend, had come together to pray for their families. As they knelt in prayer, they felt particularly burdened to pray for Arlita and me. Bill asked me if anything unusual had happened at 1 P.M. Atlanta time. He shared with me that he and Don had been especially prompted to pray for Arlita and me at noon, Birmingham time.

I tried not to bother Bill with problems or difficult situations while he was out of town, knowing there was little he could do. Most situations were resolved by the time he came home anyway. This time we knew the Holy Spirit had interceded on our behalf. Driving to a 1:30 P.M. eye doctor appointment in the rain, our car had hit a slippery spot in the road and spun around three times at 1 P.M. The car had gone in the opposite lane and veered back, hitting a guardrail. For a split second, we had sat on top of the rail. Then the car was jerked back, as if pulled by an unseen hand, and we were back in our lane facing the right direction.

When our car had begun to slip, I had shouted out to Arlita, "Pray, honey, pray!" When we finally came to a stop, I was shaking uncontrollably. I stepped out of the car and looked over the guardrail we had just straddled. We could easily have fallen down a twelve-foot embankment if the car had not jerked back. Arlita and I thanked the Lord for sending His angels to protect and keep us from harm. We experienced what the Scriptures promise: "For He will command His angels concerning you to guard you in all your ways; they will lift you up in their hands so that you will not strike your foot against a stone" (Psalm 91:11,12). They certainly had lifted our car up in their hands and placed us back on the street. Miraculously, the car started when I turned the key, and we actually made it to our appointment on time.

Bill believed that there were some strong churches in northern Europe that could, and should, become supporting and sending churches. He and the International President of Partners, International, traveled together to Europe to explore the potential of seeing some of them become meaningfully involved in World Missions. This trip was a great blessing.

Bill's trip to Guatemala to attend the World Missions Conference at the Central American Seminary was historic for him. Several hundred students and pastors responded with real commitment to the challenge of world missions.

On April 25, 1981, Gloria and Doug were married at First Baptist Church of Atlanta. After a honeymoon in Cancun, Mexico, they moved to Dallas, Texas, to start their new lives together. Doug was employed by Texas Savings and Loan as a supervisor.

The Lord had truly led our daughter all the way, teaching her precious lessons, especially during the tough teenage years. In spite of some of my shortcomings in rearing her, the Lord was faithful in keeping His promise. He who had begun a good work in our children would also perform it until the day of Jesus Christ (see Phil. 1:6). He gave me unspeakable joy through the privilege of raising two beautiful girls.

Arlita celebrated her graduation from high school on June 10, 1981. We were extremely proud of her when she received one of six local radio station awards, which recognized leadership abilities, citizenship, and moral standards. She never compromised her Christian testimony.

To celebrate her graduation, we had a special surprise for her at Stone Mountain Park. A treasure hunt took her all over the park before she was finally led to a parking lot where she discovered her prize—a Triumph TR 7, her first car. It was exciting to see her joy and surprise. Arlita was now ready to begin her college experience at Taylor University in Upland, Indiana.

It was unfortunate that at that same time a damper in our joy came with the threat of my having another surgery due to thoracic outlet syndrome. A nerve on the left side of my neck was pinched and was causing unbearable pain in my shoulder and down into my arm. This caused a thirty-percent decrease in strength in that arm. For thirty days, I had to have daily treatments at the doctor's office, and I had to be in traction three times per day for twenty minutes each at home. If the traction did not work, I knew I was facing a surgery that would incapacitate me for six months. I prayed diligently and trusted the Lord to intervene, because I had exciting plans for the end of August. I was planning to go back to China for the first time, joining both of my brothers and a tour group. The Lord answered prayer, and I did not have to have the dreaded surgery.

That summer was extremely busy as Arlita worked a job and we busied ourselves with the many things that had to be done to get her ready for college in the fall. Because of my visit to China, I would not be able to make the trip to move Arlita into college. This was especially traumatic for me because I had experienced too many situations during my childhood years without my mom and dad present. Our little family cherished each and every experience of each other's lives. When I said "goodbye" to Arlita at the airport on my way to China, sadness overwhelmed me that I would not be able to see her in her new college surroundings. After Labor Day, Bill and Arlita left for Taylor University in Upland, Indiana.

Chapter 27

Back to My Roots (August–September 1981)

ANTICIPATION OF MY upcoming trip to China mounted as I worked on and finally realized an end to the great volume of necessary paper work. On August 24, 1981, I arrived in Beijing, the capital of China, along with my two brothers and a tour group. I flew via Frankfurt, Germany; Geneva, Switzerland; Athens, Greece; and Bombay, which is now called Mumbai, India.

A lovely twenty-one-year-old from the China Travel Service, Comrade Liu, was our guide. All Chinese were addressed as "Comrade" at that time. She met us at the airport and took us to the Friendship Hotel. In two-and-a-half days we saw: Tien Amen Square; Mao Memorial Hall, where Mao Zedong is enshrined in a glass coffin; the Forbidden City; the Temple of Heaven; the Naval of the Universe; a dance performance called "The Silk Road Episode"; three of the thirteen Ming Tombs; and the Boulevard of the Spirits, which is a street lined with huge animals carved out of stone. I even got to "ride" one of the camels, which is no longer allowed. We also saw the Great Wall; the Summer Palace, including the Marble Boat; and the Friendship Store, which at that time was only open to tourists.

Although I had lived in China for eighteen years, I had never been privileged to visit the sights I was now seeing. I was thrilled to be back in my native land and to have my Chinese understood by some. On

August 27, what would have been my father's birthday, we were going on to Shanghai, the city where I spent twelve years as a child and teenager. I wondered what I would find and if there were still some folks I had known so long ago.

I could hardly wait! As the plane lowered the landing gear, and its large wheels touched the runway, my excitement grew to a fever pitch. More than thirty-one years before I had said good-bye, never dreaming that I would see my hometown again. Yet, here I was! The Lord in His goodness gave me this great gift of returning.

Early the next morning we went by taxi to see some of the places we had known as kids. In 1981, things were still completely regulated by the government, especially visits by tourists. We thought it was safer to go on our own, not letting our tour guide know what we planned to do, since she might not agree to our sightseeing plan.

The first place we visited was the children's home, where I had lived when I came to Shanghai as a five-and-a-half-year-old. No one came to the door when we rang the bell, so we went on to our next stop, which was the school I had attended. It had become a social club of some kind, and we could walk around freely. I found my homeroom, which had been turned into a barbershop. The gym was now a huge meeting place, which I am sure was used for mandatory lectures on Marxism and Lenin's doctrine.

The building that had once hosted the radio studio and station was still standing. It brought back memories of my singing on a children's broadcast when I was a teenager. I distinctly remember the last time I sang on the radio before the Communists closed the station to religious programming.

Then we moved on to the children's home at Great Western Road, where I had lived the longest period of time. It had been changed into an even larger house than the double house I knew. Thirty-five families now lived in the home. Some of the Chinese invited us in when they heard we had lived there many years before. Every room, little nook, and cranny had a family living in it. With the one-child policy in China, still strictly adhered to today, the families were small; but each still had barely enough space to move.

One of the families invited me into their tiny living space. As I looked around, I was surprised and delighted to see a Chinese Bible lying on a small dresser. When I asked them if they were believers in the Lord Jesus Christ, they beamed and responded affirmatively. It was extremely meaningful for me to find a Christian family in the same space that was part of what once had been my bedroom. It was there that I had received Christ as my Savior many years before. It was frustrating that my Chinese was not good enough anymore to share this with them. All I could do was tell them how happy I was that they knew my Lord and that we were family. Asking them if we could pray together, I joined with the husband, wife, and daughter as we committed each other to Him.

Someone had gone to get our "Amah" when they found out who "these foreigners" were. We greeted each other excitedly. She invited us to her home close by, at the end of the alley, where she lived with her son's family in a small, dark place. She made us some tea in the kitchen, which was an open concrete area with a makeshift roof, about four-feet wide and six-feet long. When she served us, I was amazed that Amah had a western tea set, which looked faintly familiar. Perhaps it was china Aunt Wehmeyer could not take with her and had left behind when they had to leave China.

Of course, we also had to visit the Jessfield Park, our old play area when we lived in the home on YuYuen Road and had no yard in which to play. The Chinese quickly gathered around us, and we could tell that they had not seen too many foreigners lately. It was fun to walk around and see some areas that still had flowers, bushes, and trees. One thing I noticed immediately when I arrived in China was that it had become a drab, austere place. Even the people dressed in gray or dark-colored Mao suits. Very seldom did we see any colorful clothes. Many plants, trees, and flowers had been destroyed under Mao's orders, especially during the ten-year Cultural Revolution of the 60s and 70s. Walking through the streets reminded me of what we had seen in East Germany just before the wall went up in August of 1961.

From the park, we moved on to the former Shanghai Free Christian Church. Now it was a factory and a warehouse that was filled with goods confiscated from the citizens during the Cultural Revolution. Some of these irreplaceable and prized possessions were exquisite pieces that were thousands of years old. I was sad that I could not revisit the place where I had been nurtured and taught about the Lord as a teenager. We tried to go into the side building, which had been our educational building, but someone immediately shouted that we had no right to be there. We retreated quickly when that person told us that he had already called the police.

We had to make one more stop, knowing we could not miss seeing the former headquarters of the China Inland Mission. However, we were refused entry, as C.I.M. had become a hospital. When President Nixon visited Shanghai on his visit to China in 1972, he was shown several local places, including this hospital. I wonder if he was ever told that this western-looking structure had at one time been the headquarters of the largest mission in China.

By 11 A.M. we were all back at the hotel to meet Comrade Liu. The rest of the day and the next morning were spent experiencing more of Shanghai. There was lunch at a Sichuan restaurant, a three-and-a-half-hour boat ride on the Huangpu River, the Bund, a carpet factory, and the formerly famous Park Hotel for lunch on the second day. We saw the Jade Temple with its white jade Buddhas, one sitting and the other reclining. People prayed to them by kneeling with their heads touching the stone floor while incense burned. In the afternoon of August 29, we boarded a train to Hangzhou in Zhejiang. Comrade Liu left us after introducing our new guide, Comrade Chee, who stayed with us the remainder of our time in China.

On Sunday, August 30, we were able to attend our first church service in Hangzhou. It was a tremendous thrill for me to worship once again with Chinese believers in China! After the service, I met one of the deacons, who had come to some of the meetings for students at the C.I.M. in Shanghai when he was a young student. He knew several of the directors and missionaries of the mission whom I had known.

After seeing the sights in the city known for its many lakes, we boarded the train again. This trip would take us further south to Nanchang, the capital of the province Jiangxi, where my parents worked for twenty-five years and where I was born.

I had hoped and prayed that my brothers and I would receive permission to go into the area where our parents had served the Lord. It was territory that was still closed to foreigners. We praised the Lord when we arrived in Nanchang and found permission had been granted by the authorities. Eagerly, we received our stamped papers to visit Nancheng, Nanfeng, and Ningdu. The remainder of the tour group went on a side trip to the Lushan Mountains.

The hotel in Nancheng where we stayed was considered the best in town. It had changed little from when we lived in the area thirty-five years before, except that we had not had electricity or running water. There were mosquito nets over the beds and a single light bulb that hung from the ceiling on an electric cord. The bathroom facilities were in the outside courtyard and consisted of cubicles of squat toilets in a row with no flushing mechanism. A long sink with running water and individual faucets was close by.

After dinner, we decided to take a walk down to the river in remembrance of when we had done that as a custom long ago. It had been a welcome relief after bearing the heat of the day. We reminisced, and as we turned to walk back to the hotel, we saw a Chinese walking towards us who reminded me of our cook from Nanfeng, who also had a peculiar walk. He stopped in front of us and asked if we were the children of Lin Muh-si. What joy to affirm that we were and that it was our former cook, Foo Min-Seng! He took us to the former mission compound. It had been totally destroyed by a Japanese air attack. As mentioned elsewhere, Mr. Wyss, a Swiss missionary, lost his life during that air raid. It was sad to see the ruins of the mission station that had been my mother's first home when she started her missionary career as a single lady in 1926.

Min-Seng took us to see his home. We walked through alleys to a dilapidated structure made from bamboo mats and wood. In a tiny room with a small table, he lit an oil lamp. His bed consisted of some boards across two sawhorses that were covered with tattered pieces of padded cloth for blankets. Pointing to it, he laughed and said, "Mui yoo 'Wantzen,'" the German word for bedbugs. No bedbugs! He knew how we hated them and that on most travels in China we had encountered them.

Min-Seng's dirt floor was all too familiar. I had seen these in many homes when I escorted mother on her visits to families in our towns.

Our former cook told us that he was now the pastor of a small flock that met in his home. He lamented that he did not have a Bible, but said he shared the biblical stories he remembered from the time when he worked for my parents. Mother's faithful daily morning devotions with her helpers and Dad's messages in the little church had borne fruit. Before leaving our friend, we invited him to go with us the following morning to Magushan, our summer retreat of long ago. In the past, he had been there for summer holidays with our family and eagerly accepted our invitation.

The next morning I was coming back from the outdoor bathroom facilities when I noticed a large group of Chinese standing in the courtyard of the hotel pointing to one of the balconies and laughing. I could not believe my eyes! Werner was standing on the balcony in his swimming trunks taking a shower with a water hose! Most of the locals had never seen a foreigner, much less one showering right before their eyes!

After breakfast, we waited for Min-Seng and finally inquired about him. We were told that he had arrived at the hotel at 6 A.M. and had been sent away. An official informed us that we had permission to see the sights but not to visit with people we knew. We would have loved to have spent more time with him, but his life was not his own.

The trip to Magushan was an emotional time for me. The hour-and-a-half ride in a minibus was certainly in stark contrast to the eight-hour trips we had experienced when we were carried in a sedan chair or had to walk the winding paths up the many steps hewn into the rock. Now there was a paved road winding up to the village, and then we walked the last section. We went on a narrow path right through some blueberry bushes, which reminded me of the many berries we had picked in this very area. One of the bungalows was still standing, although most of the flooring and siding had been removed. It was difficult to remember exactly where our cabin had been.

We were surprised to find some of the locals who knew us as teenagers. One lady, who had also been a teenager with us, had helped some of the missionary ladies on washday. Another one invited us into her home and served us the ubiquitous hot tea. Her brick stove, which had a large opening in the front, was as it had been many years ago. It was still fed with sticks and dry grass, which resulted in it smoking up the whole area and making the walls pitch black. A variety of animals, like chickens, ducks, pigs, and dogs, still wandered in and out of the open door. Some were happily at home right under the table where we were served.

Not much had changed in China since we had lived there, especially in the more remote areas. The villagers were now making a living working at a sawmill. The mountainside was regretfully almost void of the wonderful forest we knew. Tea and wine were produced at a commune in the area. We stopped to get some tea, and Comrade Woo, our guide for this side trip, presented us with a packet of Magushan tea for mother. We passed the teahouse, where we rested on our way up the mountain, and smiled at the waterfall where we swam. It was sad for me to see our beloved Magushan as it was now.

In Ningdu, we found that the mission house was now a museum. Chairman Mao had spent a few days there on his infamous "Long March" in the early 1930s through South China. Although major renovations were taking place, they allowed us to enter the house and see our living quarters, now displaying relics from Mao Zedong's time. Our guide showed us where the revolution against Chiang Kai-shek was signed when Mao passed through. It was the room that used to be my parents' bedroom.

Lai-Sao had been our cook when our family moved to Ningdu in 1946. She had come from Ruijin, the city where Mao Zedong had started his Communist regime. Lai-Sao had joined the Communist army at that time and become the wife or concubine of one of the generals. She had moved around with the troops. Many years later, after she came to work in our house, Lai-Sao accepted the Lord Jesus as her personal Savior. After several months of instructions for new believers, she was baptized along with Fred, Werner, a Chinese teacher, and me.

The church in Ningdu was still being used by a small band of believers. As we walked through, we came to the spot where we were baptized by Daddy in May of 1947. I walked on to an adjoining area where I had once taught Sunday school to children. I was fifteen years old then. It seemed like a lifetime ago.

At 5:30 in the morning, local news blasted from loudspeakers all over town. The same thing occurred in the evening when the news came from Beijing. This was a way of indoctrinating the people through the years with Communist propaganda. I thought it was a terrible thing to disturb the peace and privacy of the Chinese people with such an intrusion twice a day.

When we mentioned that we would like to see Tsui-wei-feng, our guide was amazed that we knew so much about the area. He had never seen some of the spots we visited. He laughed, "It seems as if you are my guide instead of me being yours." When Comrade Woo saw the large rock with its deep crevice on one side, he could not believe that we had climbed all the way to the top as teenagers. Now he was happy to rest a while on one of the lounge chairs that were set out near the Taoist temple while we explored the area.

One of the priests, who now had enough freedom to be a Taoist priest again, poured us some tea. As we chatted, he told us that he had remembered us from the past. Daddy had talked to him at length, and I am sure presented the Gospel to him.

On September 3, we left for Nanfeng. Our first stop was the former mission station, which greatly saddened us. All the wonderful orange trees that had been in the garden were gone. Nanfeng had been famous for its many different kinds of wonderfully sweet oranges. Merchants had come from near and far to buy and sell these golden treasures.

The mission house where my parents were confined for more than five years during World War II was now rundown, and the side yard was completely gone. I found my former bedroom upstairs off the side verandah but had to look through barred windows. Several families must have moved into this house. Downstairs was the open entrance where Dad, after showing us some Chinese posters used for evangelism, had once asked all three of us if we knew the Savior. Although he and Mother were prevented from having much physical contact with us, they bathed us all in prayer continually. For me to stand at this spot was like standing on holy ground.

Adjacent to the mission compound was the church. It was now a carpenter's shop. Planks of wood, sawdust, and large beams were lying everywhere. There was no sign that this had ever been a house of God. The news spread that some foreigners were in the area, and scores of children, young people, and men and women of all ages quickly gathered.

On September 4, 1981, we left Nanfeng for the capital Nanchang to rejoin our group. Our two-and-a-half day excursion had been emotionally draining, but also exhilarating. I was deeply grateful that the Lord had allowed me to revisit so many of the places dear to my heart and even let me meet some of the people I had known thirty-five years previously.

That evening the China Travel Agency invited our tour group to a special banquet. Since we were leaving Jiangxi, our "home territory," they wanted to honor us. The authorities had been extremely surprised when my brothers and I had expressed interest in going into the interior. They had asked, "Why do you want to go there?" They were shocked when we had answered in Chinese, "We want to go home." They must have wondered what foreigner would ever call that remote, impoverished area "home."

Our calling the interior of China our "home" must have pleased the Chinese officials, because they treated us to a fifteen-course dinner with special Chinese delicacies. The turtle soup had unmistakable turtles floating in the bowl. The eel, frog legs, and numerous non-descriptive dishes were perhaps tasty to those who dared to try them. The final "pièce de résistance" was Peking duck, a famous culinary delight for those in the know. Onions, some veggies, and specially prepared duck were rolled into what is the equivalent of a thin pancake or tortilla. It certainly was a memorable meal and an evening we would never forget.

We traveled on to Changsha, the capital of Hunan, by train. No one knew of the mission hospital where we had gone as children or the Mission School for the Blind of another mission. We were surprised when we were told that there were no churches in Changsha. That city had been a stronghold of several mission agencies, including the C.I.M. affiliate. I was disappointed that we would not be able to go to church that Sunday and meet more Chinese Christians.

I had a very interesting conversation with the elevator mechanic. Most hotels and inns in the interior were two-story buildings, but the one in Changsha had nine floors and an elevator. The mechanic shared with me that he would have loved to become an engineer, but the

Chinese government had other plans. He was not allowed to study at one of the universities. The authorities had decided his future, as they did the future of all Chinese people. Everything was regulated by the government. It made me sad to think that there was so much wasted talent in that vast land. Young, gifted people with special abilities were enslaved by a tyrannical ideology.

We visited the silk needlepoint factory and the Park of the Martyrs, a memorial to soldiers of several wars. The Hunan Provincial Museum housed over 3,000 valuable relics, the most treasured being a mummy that was over 2,000 years old. We found all these sites very interesting. Our kind guide, Comrade Chee, bid us farewell after he saw us safely situated on the train to Canton, which was 450 miles further south.

After arriving in the subtropical capital of Guangdong, a Comrade Loo guided us on a sightseeing tour in his town and then led us safely out of China to Hong Kong. The first thing I noticed about Canton was that there were far more tourists in this town than we had seen since leaving Shanghai. Many foreigners who visited Hong Kong took quick side trips to Canton so that they could say they had visited Mainland China. In 1981, Hong Kong was still a British colony. The city of Canton showed definite signs of Western influence, especially architecturally.

Our city tour included visiting Dr. Sun Yat-sen Memorial Hall, which seats 3,000; the Pagoda of Six Banyan Temple; and a local church, which was once a Southern Baptist Church. All denominations had been done away with in China, and there were only churches sanctioned by the government. We also enjoyed spending an afternoon shopping at the Friendship Store.

September 9, our last full day in Mainland China, we visited the art center in Foshan on the outskirts of Canton. Skilled Chinese amazed us with their exquisite work, which included jade carvings, lace-looking paper cuttings, weavings, Chinese scrolls with artistic script, and much more. We then went on to the temple of "Worship of Ancestors," and concluded our evening with an acrobatic show.

We arrived in Hong Kong on September 10, where we were taken by a European lady to the Furama Hotel, a five-star establishment. I was overwhelmed after having spent almost three weeks and after traveling 2,000 miles in a still very-primitive China. Since we had the afternoon free, I did not waste any time in phoning one of my friends from our Ambassadors for Christ youth group in Shanghai with whom I had stayed in touch. It had been more than thirty years since I had seen Elsie. We spent three wonderful hours together, and she shared with me her experiences during the initial years after the Communist takeover. Her family was eventually able to leave China and settle in Hong Kong.

A wonderful American breakfast buffet the next morning was followed by sightseeing to places like Repulse Bay, Happy Valley, and Aberdeen. I enjoyed a sampan ride to see the homes of the "Boat People," folks who lived on boats their entire lives. A visit to the famous "Peak" with its wonderful view of the harbor was truly unforgettable. In the evening, I invited my brothers to a fabulous dinner at the hotel's revolving restaurant, "La Ronde," to celebrate the end of a fantastic trip "home."

September 12, 1981, our last day in Hong Kong, finalized our visit to the Orient. Elsie picked me up at the hotel, and we went across to Kowloon by ferry to her apartment. It was a joy to see her husband, Sam, and her mother again. I had known all three before Elsie and Sam were married. Since September 12 was Moon Festival Day, we had a lovely lunch with moon cakes for desert after a delicious meal of homemade noodles. It was a wonderful time of fellowship and sharing. I had often wondered if I would ever meet my friend again. The Lord graciously surprised me. I returned to the hotel just in time to join the group for a two-hour harbor trip on a junk, a typical boat of the Orient, our last excursion on the agenda.

That evening marked the end of my long-awaited trip back to the land of my birth. It was a trip that had been preceded by much hope and prayer. As I settled back in my seat on the long flight home to my adopted land, the United States of America, my happiness knew no bounds. My heart burst forth in worship with my father's oft-sung words:

> Praise God from whom all blessings flow,
> Praise Him all creatures here below,
> Praise Him above, ye heavenly host,
> Praise Father, Son, and Holy Ghost
> Amen!

Wedding Day, June 21, 1958

Serving the Lord together in Holland

Singing God's praises in Germany

The Boerop family in 1966, Decatur, Georgia

Bill and Joy with teenage daughters at Stone Mountain Park, Georgia

Happy couple before cancer struck in 1989

Joy teaching in Brazil

Plenary speaker at Mission 83 in Switzerland

Missions Congress in The Philippines

Author with ladies participating at World Thrust seminar in India

Bill and I celebrating 50th wedding anniversary with family

Conclusion

FOR MANY YEARS, I wondered where I belonged. Was it China, Europe, or the United States? Many of us missionary kids feel like an enigma, or even an anomaly, in the various countries where we have lived. I have lived, not just visited, in seven countries on four continents. At one time I asked, "Will I ever feel like a real citizen of one country and feel at home? If so, which one will it be?"

I thank the Lord that I did find my home. Before I became an American, I had the choice of remaining a Dutch citizen since I married a Dutchman or becoming a US citizen. What a blessing it is that the United States welcomes people from around the world, allowing folks from every tribe, nation, and tongue to become naturalized citizens. To be entitled to full, inalienable rights, I had to make a commitment to the United States and swear an Oath of Allegiance. As a result, I possess all the rights and privileges bestowed upon me by my new country.

I believe that those of us who have chosen to belong to the United Sates appreciate it more than those who were born in the US. I am proud to be an American and a citizen of the United States. My dear husband often says to a congregation when he shares his testimony, "I have chosen to be an American. Most of you cannot help it; you were born in this country."

There are many parallels between becoming a citizen of the United States and obtaining citizenship in heaven by becoming a believer in Christ. I had to make a choice. Philippians 3:20 tells me that my citizenship is in heaven once I have repented and turned to God. My allegiance has to be to Him because I am no longer just His creature but now I am a child of God. With that comes all the rights and privileges of being adopted into the family of God: "You are no longer a slave, but a son, and since you are a son, God has made you also an heir" (Galatians 4:7). After our US citizenship ceremony, there was rejoicing and celebrating. So it is if someone comes to Christ. There is rejoicing in heaven:"There will be more rejoicing in heaven over one sinner who repents than over ninety-nine righteous persons who do not need to repent" (Luke 15:7).

Looking back over the many years since we came to America in August of 1961, it is amazing to see what the Lord has done for us. He has led us all the way through the good times and through the bad. My heart is filled with adoration, joy, and gratitude.

During our time in Kansas, a lady from the State Taxation Department came to the church annex where we lived. She was personally investigating and assessing how much state tax we owed and asked about our possessions, including fur coats, jewelry, our home furnishings, and appliances. I told her that we owned none. All the furniture, equipment, and appliances she saw in the building belonged to the church. Not believing me, she asked to see our apartment. When I led her upstairs to our one bedroom, kitchen, and communal bath, she exclaimed, "You don't own anything, not even a lamp?" It was difficult for her to believe that we did not own anything.

Since that time the Lord has allowed us to live in three different houses we called our own. In the past years, He provided various cars for us to do His work and to help others in need. We were able to share our homes with people from all walks of life and many different countries. God gave us a host of friends in the US, as well as around the world.

It is one of the blessings of our nation that with persevering hard work, diligence, and sacrifice, everyone has the opportunity to better their lives. Multitudes of immigrants who have come to this land with absolutely nothing but the clothes on their backs have done that, prospered, and been greatly blessed. The Lord Jesus Christ has graciously allowed me to be a part of this group, even as a former missionary kid, a missionary wife, and a missionary mother, teaching our children and grandchildren to reach the world for Christ.

Epilogue

IN DECEMBER OF 1982, the European Student Missionary Association held a student congress in Lausanne, Switzerland, called MISSION 83. Bill had helped start this organization in the mid-50s, when he was a student at EBI. He became the second president at that time. It was still dear to his heart, and he was thrilled when he was asked to address pastors and those who were planning to go into the ministry.

I was one of the plenary speakers and talked about China and my life as a missionary. It was a joy to have Arlita, who was a sophomore at Taylor University, attend this congress with us. After the New Year, 1983, we visited with my mom, who was now living with Fred. Arlita had a chance to spend quality time with her grandmother, and I was deeply grateful to the Lord that we had that visit.

There were many memorable moments and days in 1983. In the spring, Leni, my friend and mentor from the children's home in Shanghai came to visit us for six weeks. Bill and I celebrated our 25th wedding anniversary with a trip to Acapulco, Mexico. Arlita joined the Wheaton College study group and went to Israel, and Rome, Italy.

Bill attended the Amsterdam '83 Congress for Itinerant Evangelists, a historic event where 4,000 evangelists from all over the world accepted Billy Graham's invitation to come and learn together. On his flight home, his parents joined him in Amsterdam. They stayed with us for six months while their apartment in Holland was being renovated. In August our children arranged a wonderful "drop-in celebration" in honor of our silver wedding anniversary. More than sixty friends came by our home to wish us well.

In 1984 I was able to travel and minister with Bill. It was a year filled with opportunities for ministry here in the States, as well as overseas. I spoke at ladies' conferences, Christian Women's Club meetings, and youth and pastors' gatherings. I served the Lord gladly wherever He opened doors. It was wonderful to work alongside my husband at many of these opportunities. Ministry in Brazil in December of 1983 was followed by ministry in Guatemala and El Salvador in the spring of 1984. Bill also started world briefings and pastors luncheons to keep pastors informed of what God was doing in other parts of the world and to get them involved beyond their own ministry.

April 5, 1984, is a day I will never forget. It was the day the Lord took my dear mother home to her eternal resting place. When she was so ill with all kinds of tropical diseases after leaving China in 1950, none of us ever dreamed that the Lord would allow her to live to be almost ninety years old. She was a great woman of prayer, who trusted the Lord implicitly. I was deeply thankful that she and I had a special time together on my last visit to my brother's home. Although it was winter, she wanted to go for a walk. I was amazed at how well she did, being in her late eighties. We talked, laughed, and reminisced. When we passed a large sleigh in front of someone's home, she joked that she could be the horse and wanted me to take her picture.

For some time Bill had been burdened with the fact that so few churches were truly interested in reaching the lost in the unreached nations of the world. The churches that had a burden for those who had never heard the name of the Lord Jesus and did something about it were led by strong senior pastors with a vision. That resonated in Bill's heart, and he became increasingly burdened to see more churches involved in world evangelization. Bill made this a matter of prayer for two years. Perhaps he was to expand upon the seminars he was already teaching, trying to interest more and more church leaders for this important task. It was not only Jesus' explicit command to go into the world and reach the lost, but also Scripture teaches us, from Genesis to Revelation, that God's love is for all nations.

Finally, after agonizing before the Lord for two years about whether or not he should start a new ministry, Bill received a clear mandate from the Lord that he was to proceed. He resigned from CNEC, and on August 1, 1984, World Thrust was born and incorporated. The ministry grew for the next thirteen years. Thousands of churches all over the Southeast and in other areas caught the vision and sent out missionaries. The faith promise offering caught on after Bill and his team taught this method of giving. Multiple millions of dollars were given by people who trusted God to use them to pass funds on to missionaries to take the Gospel to the regions beyond.

Our good friend, the late Dr. Paul Smith of The People's Church in Toronto, Canada, invited us to come year after year to hold pastors' seminars in conjunction with the missions conference of his church. Dr. Paul and the church paid the expenses of every pastor who attended the seminar, putting them up in a nice hotel and topping the last day off with a free trip to the Canadian side of Niagara Falls.

Requests from overseas, which had begun when Bill worked with Christian Nationals Evangelism Commission, increased. Churches in Latin America, Asia, and Africa wanted to know how to be more effectively involved with putting their arms around the world. They were eager to learn.

As a rising senior, Arlita went with a group from the language department of Taylor University to the Dominican Republic. Their Spanish professor was eager to help the students practice and perfect their knowledge of the Spanish language. Arlita came home very burdened for the local people, who lived in abject poverty and misery.

Arlita graduated from Taylor University on May 18, 1985, with a bachelor's degree in communications. Ten days later, she was employed as a flight attendant by Republic Airlines, which later became a part of Northwest Airlines. Arlita loved flying and worked in that field for a number of years.

Doug, Gloria, and our first grandchild moved to Atlanta the first part of 1986. That summer Bill was invited to attend Amsterdam '86, another congress for itinerant evangelists put on by the Billy Graham Organization. That same year he also ministered to pastors in various countries of South America.

In May of 1987, Bill and I went to China. It was a great thrill to be able to show him some of the areas where I grew up. The children's home and my school were still standing when we visited Shanghai, but our former church was still closed and used as a warehouse. We only visited Chongren in the interior, but I did not recognize anything in the town I knew so well as a little girl. Locals did not know anything about foreigners ever having lived there. As Bill and I walked across the bridge of the river where we had often swum with Daddy, we stopped and recommitted our lives and our service to the Lord. Mom and Dad had served the Lord Jesus faithfully for many years with few apparent results. We could do no less!

Our next stop was Indonesia. Our ministry at the Evangelical Theological Seminary in Yogyakarta and in churches in Jakarata was well received. From there we traveled to Singapore for pastors' training seminars and missions conferences. It was a blessing to meet up with Dr. Paul Smith and to serve and minister with him.

Upon returning home, I busied myself preparing for Arlita's wedding. She had met her handsome fiancé, who was from the Detroit, Michigan, area, at Taylor University. Since Arlita's base with the airlines was Detroit, we managed to plan her wedding from a distance.

It was great to spend time alone with my younger daughter when she invited me to a mother/daughter trip to the Cayman Islands. It was wonderful to relax, enjoy the beach and ocean, talk and pray about her future, and have a wonderful Bible study on relationships and the family. Arlita asked me what book I used for the study. I just held up my Bible and told her that all we studied and discussed was written in the Word of God.

Arlita's commitment in marriage to Darrell Albert Ibach, Jr. took place on September 12, 1987, at First Baptist Church of Atlanta. After a honeymoon in Hawaii, the young couple moved into their own home in the Detroit area. Butch, as we call Darrell, worked for State Farm Insurance Company. Although he had been working in an auto parts recycling business his father owned, we were proud that he wanted to gain experience in the business world on his own.

Bill's father went to be with the Lord on April 8, 1989, at the age of eighty-four, a reminder that some day life will be over and we will stand before our Maker. It was wonderful that the Lord gave him an additional twenty-two years after his heart attack in 1967, when he was at the point of death.

December 1989 brought devastating news for me. During my yearly physical, the doctor discovered a lump, which he thought was suspicious. A biopsy proved that he was right. I will never forget the look on the surgeon's face after he came back into the room twenty minutes after he had completed the procedure. It was abundantly clear that the news was not good. Although he had been a surgeon for more than thirty years and had done this procedure thousands of times, he had tears in his eyes when he looked at me and said, "Sorry, but you have cancer." It was evident how much he cared.

"*Cancer*" is a horrible word, and there had been so much of it in my family. The outlook did not seem good. In my heavenly Father's foresight, He had put it in the hearts of the Board Members of World Thrust to give Bill and me a few days at the Grove Park Inn in North Carolina as a Christmas present. It was truly a precious gift from God when we needed it most. Not before or since has the Board given such a gift.

Those days after Christmas were meant to be special days with beautiful surroundings in a wonderful hotel. However, my whole world came crashing down. Questions engulfed my thoughts: What were we to do? How could we make a decision? Which option should we choose? It was good to be away from the hustle and bustle of life at home and to calm down and look to the Lord. Bill and I prayed and trusted Him to lead and guide us to the right decision. This process actually came naturally, as we had done it all our lives together. We felt the Lord gave us the answer.

On January 2, 1990, I had surgery, followed by six months of bi-weekly chemo and daily oral medication. In March of 1990, I wrote our prayer letter to friends and supporters:

Dear *SPECIAL* Friend:
As the result of my yearly physical, a mammogram, and subsequent biopsy I entered a *special* phase on December 29, 1989. Part of the *special* phase was a new vocabulary—malignancy; mastectomy; bone, liver and spleen scans; blood count; oncology; surgery; chemotherapy; side effects; and of course, the dreaded word—CANCER. Along the

way I met people that became *special*. My radiology technician who took the mammogram, my surgeon, my oncologist, several nurses and aids at the hospital, all know the Lord.

A total of more than 200 cards and letters, a hospital room filled with plants and flowers, many visits at the hospital as well as at home, phone calls assuring us of prayer. All this a proof of how *special* you, our friends, are.

God has given me a *special* family. Our girls—two daughters and three granddaughters—rallied around and with their husbands showed much loving concern. Bill has been a rock, standing with me every step of the way. How *special* when he is right beside me holding my hand every time I get the dreaded chemotherapy.

Above all God has surrounded us with His *special* love and held us up with His everlasting arms. I knew very little about breast cancer and that scared me. From what I was told by the oncologist I understand that if I live for five years after my diagnosis, I have a good chance of survival. The Lord Jesus allows me to find out whether or not what I have taught and believed for so many years is real. What a *special* friend He is!

Now I'm in the middle of my treatment. If all goes well I could be done by June or July. It may be the end of the summer. How *special* that every time I go in for chemotherapy, I cannot help but read Psalm 118:24 posted right over the treatment chair. "This is the day the Lord has made, let us rejoice and be glad in it." What a *special* reminder to take one day at a time in His *special* care. Please keep on praying that we may continue to honor the Lord in everything. No matter *what*!!

How *special* it was to be present at the third annual banquet of our ministry in February. The Lord Jesus gave us a *special*, evening with many of our friends. These last few weeks have been *special*, as I was able to attend a few of the meetings of the ever-increasing number of missions conferences Bill and his World Thrust team have been able to put together.

Keep on praying for wisdom, strength, and God's *special* enabling power for the ever-increasing growth of the ministry.

We thank the Lord Jesus for you, our *special* co-laborers!

Joyfully in His *special* love,

Joy K. Boerop

After the chemo treatments and because of some adverse conditions of my case, I had to see the doctor every six weeks for two years. These visits were gradually spaced further and further apart. At present, I have been cancer free for twenty years and see the oncologist once a year. My experience was not easy. There were weeks and even months when I could not pray, but I am immensely thankful that people around the world stood in the gap for me, praying when I could not.

In July of 1990, Bill and I traveled to Africa. The oncologist had concerns that the inoculations I received for tropical diseases would not be effective due to my chemotherapy, but the Lord undertook. We visited South Africa, where a ministry-changing experience occurred for us and World Thrust. Bill met a pastor whose heartbeat for the world was like his. The pastor showed interest in knowing about our ministry and later became one of the leaders of the World Thrust South Africa ministry. We spent some wonderful days with dear friends in Swaziland and then visited Bill's sister and her family in Nairobi, Kenya. Our trip concluded with our attendance at the Youth for Christ World Congress in Nairobi. Bill and I returned home well and fit.

Additional overseas ministries opened up for us in the coming years. In 1991, a long-time dream of mine came true. Bill and I ministered in New Zealand and Australia. We had accumulated enough frequent flyer miles to enable us to fly free to the land "Down Under." In both countries, we met old friends from Bill's days in Belgium and from my youth group and school days in Shanghai. Shortly after our return home, we celebrated Bill's 40th anniversary in ministry with a wonderful banquet in the Atlanta area. As a young man in 1951, Bill had started his career as a missionary. In the fall of 1991, Bill was thrilled to be back where he had started to help the Belgian Evangelical Mission with one of their efforts. He celebrated his forty years of serving the Lord by going house-to-house distributing literature as he had done so many years ago.

In the coming years, we received many calls from overseas requesting the aid of World Thrust in teaching pastors and church leaders. We traveled to Holland, France, Italy, India, Singapore, Brazil, and frequently to South Africa. Churches in some countries invited me to join Bill and conduct women's conferences in addition to helping teach the seminar.

While at home, I was involved in selling real estate so that we could expand the ministry and to help financially.

In the spring of 1995, I wrote to our friends and supporters in our prayer letter:

> As we look back over 1994, our hearts are filled with gratitude and praise! Five years ago the Lord gave me the verse: "When you pass through the waters, I will be with you; and when you pass through the rivers, they will not sweep over you. When you walk through the fire, you will not be burned; the flames will not set you ablaze" (Isaiah 43:2). At that time, going through chemotherapy with all of its side effects, there were rivers, water, fire, and flames, not knowing if I would reach the end of the first year cancer free.
>
> Now I have reached, by the grace of God, the milestone of five years without cancer recurrence. Our next goal is ten years. I still see the oncologist every six months. So please keep on praying.

For many years it was our tradition every summer to meet with our two daughters and their families and vacation together for a week at a lake house one of our friends lets us use. It was great fun as a family to enjoy activities together like boating, water skiing, playing games, picnicking, and exploring the area and its antique shops. In 1995, we deviated and all went to Germany and spent one week in the home my mother's father built in the "Reiherbach." One of my cousins and his wife had transformed the large home into several small apartments that they rented out to vacationers from Germany and Holland.

It was great fun to enjoy the nearby lake, "Edersee"; to go sightseeing; and to take long walks in the valley and forests nearby and search for family roots. We were also able to minister to the fellowship of believers where my mother was nurtured in the Lord when she first found the Savior before going to China. Some of the folks still remembered Mother and were glad to meet the family. They were especially thrilled to hear our grandchildren sing choruses.

Bill and I went on to minister in Belgium and Holland. In Belgium, we were excited to find there were some small evangelical churches in the very cities and towns where we had tried to preach the Gospel and had met with staunch opposition in the late 50s and early 60s. In

Holland, the pastor of a large evangelical church gave Bill the following introduction, "In every Christian's life God has used someone to lead them to the Lord. Today you are going to meet and hear the man whom God used in my life when I was a fifteen-year-old teenager thirty-six years ago. His name is Bill Boerop." We had thought our labor was in vain! It was a great encouragement from the Lord Jesus to let us see fruit from our ministry of long ago. He promises that His Word will not return void (Isaiah 55:11).

As a result of Bill' s meeting with one of the South African pastors during our first trip to that country in 1990 and in consequent meetings, the ministry of World Thrust South Africa (WTSA) was born in 1993. It was amazing how the Lord blessed with abundant growth. In the span of two to three years, over 1,000 churches had been impacted by the ministry of World Thrust. There were over 6,000 attendees in the South African seminars.

Our South African director shared with us that more than four million rand had been generated for world evangelization. Even greater than that was the flood of missionary recruits who responded to the call of God upon their lives. Church leaders from many other African countries asked World Thrust South Africa to come help mobilize their churches. As a result, the Board of Directors of WTSA invited us to come and help train pastors and lay leaders to teach the World Thrust Winning Strategies Seminar and World Thrust Focus on the World Weekends.

With its tremendous overseas opportunities, the Board of Directors of World Thrust, Inc., voted to formalize our overseas ministries by establishing a new coordinating entity called World Thrust International. On January 1, 1997, World Thrust, Inc., became World Thrust North America under the leadership of one of the staff members, and Bill became President and Founder of World Thrust International.

In the spring of 1997, in preparation for our move to South Africa, we sold our home in Stone Mountain and all of our furniture except a few pieces. We put our personal belongings in storage. It was not easy to leave our home of twenty-four years, where we had raised our girls and made special memories with our grandchildren. The Lord had allowed us to entertain innumerable friends, family, and strangers during those years.

Before we moved to South Africa, we ministered in Canada and Guyana, South America. In His wonderful timing, the Lord provided new office space in Lawrenceville, a suburb of Atlanta, Georgia, for the international office. We also prayed fervently for the right person, capable of managing the office while we were ministering in South Africa and other parts of the world.

While speaking in one of the Sunday school classes in our home church, Bill mentioned the need for an administrative assistant. On the day of our departure for Canada, six days later, God provided Cathy Holbrook. She was a tremendous godsend then, and continues to be twelve years afterward, at the time of this writing. Bill had only a few days to prepare her for the job, but she ministered with diligence and professionalism.

We left for South Africa on June 13, 1997. Stopping over in Frankfurt for almost six hours made it a 24-hour flight. Several friends met us at the airport in Johannesburg and escorted us to a nice brick ranch home where we would be house sitters for the next three months. Someone made coffee, and we all had a good time visiting. I soon learned why no one took off his or her winter coats, wool caps, or gloves.

In the Southern Hemisphere, the seasons are the opposite of those in the United States. June through August is the middle of winter in South Africa, where homes did not have central heat in the winter or air conditioning in the summer. Most homes had only one radiator filled with oil, which was rolled around from room to room as needed. Once plugged into the electrical outlet, the contraption would somewhat warm the immediate area. Our home also had only one heater, but thoughtful friends loaned us one of theirs and an electric blanket.

The nights and mornings were so cold until about noon that my laundry would freeze on the clothesline. Most days we had our lunch outside on the patio after the day warmed up to about fifty or sixty degrees. It was warmer outside during the day than in the house, so we spent a lot of time in the yard preparing our messages, getting ready for ministry, and reading and writing. The weather in Johannesburg is some of the best, with beautiful sunshine most days.

The South African team immediately presented us with a host of ministry opportunities. Bill and I served together at the "Love

Southern Africa" Congress held in Kimberley in June of 1997. Then we spoke and ministered in churches in six different denominations. God allowed us to proclaim His love for the world in a number of missions conferences and conventions, and we taught and trained a great number of associates.

Friends invited us to the famous Kruger Park in the eastern part of South Africa. This vast expanse of territory, about the size of Maryland, allows giraffes, elephants, lions, leopards, hippos, rhinos, kudus, springboks, and a multitude of other wild animals to roam freely. On a night drive, we saw a male lion about forty feet away from us. Another one showed up, and we listened as their mighty roars pierced the stillness of the night. It was quite an experience to watch the second lion shake his large mane and strut around marking his territory.

Our experience in Kruger Park reminded us that Satan also prowls around like a roaring lion. He is marking his territory. In a prayer letter, I wrote:

Crime is rampant. Hardly a day goes by that we don't hear of someone's friend, relative, or coworker who has been robbed, mugged, killed, or whose car was car-jacked (they call it hijacked here). A pastor friend lamented to us that never before did he have to bury five of his church members in just a few months' time. All were killed in separate carjackings.

There is much unrest in this so-called "Rainbow Nation." Corrupt music, movies, and pornographic materials are now allowed. Much strife exists in the various ethnic groups. We notice the increased influence of religions foreign to South Africa. The largest Buddhist temple in the Southern Hemisphere has been built not too far from us. We are also aware of a growing presence of Islam.

Yet, there is also much to rejoice and thank the Lord for....The next few weeks are fully booked. Satan doesn't like it. We are invading his territory—but all his roaring and strutting around doesn't scare us. God is with us, and He will lead us on. We are resisting him and standing firm in the faith!

Christmas of 1997 in South Africa was a lonely time. Since it is summer in December in South Africa, most of our friends had left for the beaches in the Cape area or the coast near Durban. We missed

Christmas parties and gatherings in friends' homes, carols being played in the stores, and concerts and special choir performances. We even had a hard time finding a church that had Christmas services, although the country was about forty-five percent Christian.

We moved four times in six months, but finally, in January, we found a furnished brick ranch. Again, I was able to exercise my gift of hospitality. Scores of friends came at different times for tea in the afternoon (a reminder that England once ruled this country) or dinner in the evening. We really felt at home.

During our year in South Africa, we ministered extensively throughout that beautiful country. We were able to see much of the land. Bill also had several cousins there. His father's eldest brother immigrated to South Africa in the 1920s and had several children who were still living. It was good also to be able to visit family.

In March of 1998, after ministry in Namibia, a country just northwest of South Africa, we took a much-needed week of vacation touring the country. This was a wonderful experience. Namibia includes the largest desert area and a 1,200-foot sand dune, the largest in the world. We visited a town that was once a thriving community during the heyday of the diamond mining era, but was now almost completely swallowed up by sand. We thrilled to wild horses frolicking in the desert replete with a gorgeous sunset glowing in the sky. The restricted diamond mining area had posted signs, warning people not to stop or leave their cars. We were told that workers are x-rayed every day as they are leaving their work shift in the mine to make sure no diamonds are hidden in their intestines.

Many of the Namibian towns have German names and reveal definite European architecture, proof that this corner of the world was colonized by Germany before World War II. When I asked for directions in English, a black gentleman answered me in perfect German. Apparently, German is still taught in some of the schools, as was evident when we heard young folks playing in a school yard shouting at each other in German.

The culmination of our trip to Namibia was a hot air balloon ride over the desert. I gasped when I saw the beauty of the sunrise over the sand dunes below with their flowing colors of light brown, yellow, magenta, and red. Various wild animals ran and played catch with the shadow of the balloon and basket as we slowly glided over the landscape.

It was a once-in-a-lifetime experience and a tremendous way to celebrate our upcoming 40th wedding anniversary in June.

Bill and I planned our departure from South Africa on June 13, 1998, exactly one year after we had arrived. The Lord had allowed us to schedule several meetings in Germany that June and July. We did not realize beforehand how the trip to Germany and the meetings there were ordained by God. Our friends in the Johannesburg area had a wonderful farewell party for us. We were grateful for all the Lord had accomplished, and we were a little sad to leave.

Bill's prayer letter in September of 1998 read:

> "But I trust in you, O Lord, I say: You are my God. My times are in your hands" (Psalm 31:14–15a). These words are very much on our hearts and minds. We have experienced in a new way that "our times are in His hands."

While in Germany for our series of meetings on our way home, we were notified that Bill's mom had passed away. Bill's sister and husband, missionaries in Nairobi, Kenya, were also in Europe at this time. The funeral was scheduled for July 4, the only day we did not have meetings. God's Word is indeed true that our times are in the Lord's hands.

It was a special blessing to meet some friends at the memorial service whom Mom and Dad had discipled years before. Mom's simple trust in the Lord to provide her every need is a legacy that will stay with us. The Lord answered prayers and sustained Bill as he conducted the funeral. Although his Dutch was getting a little rusty, he did fine with the Lord's help.

It was wonderful to be back home in the good old US of A again! We had another great family vacation with our children and grandchildren at our friends' lake house, with all twelve of us together again. It was another memorable week of fun and lots of sharing.

In September of 1998, we were able to sign for another home not far from the World Thrust International office. However, we did not rest long. In October and November, we had a busy schedule traveling to and/or ministering in Taiwan, Manila, Hong Kong, Singapore, Malaysia, Chennai and Delhi in India, and Jamaica. It was amazing how the Lord opened doors for the ministry of World Thrust International.

For many years, Bill had complained of chest pain periodically, but the pain increased so much that he finally had a catheterization on April 7, 1999. Immediately after the procedure, the doctor greeted me and said, "Mrs. Boerop, you can thank your family physician. He saved your husband's life. We will keep him here for open-heart surgery tomorrow. There is major blockage in three arteries, perhaps even more."

Bill's surgery involved a five-artery by-pass. Although several of the arteries were ninety to ninety-five percent blocked, Bill did not have a heart attack. The doctors agreed that this was indeed a miracle. The Lord Jesus was good to give us an alert family physician who was also a heart specialist. We know it was God who spared Bill's life. As someone said, the Lord still had work for him to do. We praised our heavenly Father that Bill did not have a heart attack on one of our many travels overseas.

The vision statement of World Thrust International is, "To see every local church in the world become a sending base for the Gospel of Christ so that a clear presentation and demonstration of that Gospel is available to all people." That statement has always spurred us on. It certainly was a motivation as we moved into the next century in the year 2000. Doomsayers predicted all sorts of disasters and collapses in technology and the financial world, but life continued normally in the new century, as did our ministry over the next few years.

The year 2000 brought several special times for our family. That summer Gloria and Arlita organized our one and only Burklin reunion since my parents had passed away. My brothers' families and ours, with all our children and grandchildren, totaled fifty-six members. We had a wonderful two days together in the North Georgia mountains, staying in rustic cabins. Getting to know each other, playing games, eating good food, and laughing and having fun together helped us all realize what a special family our heavenly Father had given us. There was also time for interaction, prayer, talks, and fellowship. The wonderful time ended with a worship service and communion. My parents would have been deeply blessed had they been present. To know that each and every one of their offspring had trusted Jesus Christ as Savior would have brought them great joy.

Bill had the privilege of baptizing three of our grandchildren, Kristin, Lindsay, and Kara Darr. The Psalmist talks about revealing God's truths to our children and to their children: "I will reveal these truths to you so that you can describe these glorious deeds of Jehovah to your children...and commanded our fathers to teach them to their children, so that they in turn could teach their children too" (Psalm 78:4–6a, TLB). We also read: "Then we...will thank you forever and forever, praising your greatness from generation to generation" (Psalm 79:13 TLB). There is no greater joy than to hear the testimonies of those who have been redeemed. Kristin shared how she was led to the Lord by her mom. She then led her sister Lindsay to the Lord, who then led her sister Kara to the Lord!

In the fall of 2000, Bill and I were thrilled to return to China. This time, Gloria, Doug, Arlita, and Butch joined us. It was wonderful to show them the numerous sights in Peking and then in Shanghai where I grew up. The church where I was nurtured in spiritual understanding as a teenager was now open again, and we attended a Sunday service. We had the privilege to teach in the Provincial Bible School in Jiangxi, the province where my parents served the Lord. It was my privilege to introduce our children to the pastor of the church in Ningdu, the last mission station where Mom and Dad served before leaving China. Pastor Liu's father had been discipled by my dad in the late 1940s, and he became the pastor when the missionaries were forced to leave. He passed the baton on to his son, Pastor Liu, who was now the minister of the church.

It was deeply rewarding to see many churches where my folks had served open once again. We reveled in the fellowship with Christians, and one of the ladies thanked us for our visit. She said it reminded her and the other believers that my parents had willingly given up their comfort and material wealth to come to China. She gave us a note she had written that said, "It was because of their obedience to God and willingness to endure difficult circumstances for the sake of sharing the gospel, that many in China now have eternal life through Jesus Christ."

The year 2000 also launched our yearly teaching ministry in India. Bill had ministered in India a few years before, but now God brought a wonderful brother into our lives who faithfully made all the arrangements for our teaching ministry. We traveled extensively throughout India with him. In many parts of the country, we found that our seminars were the first missions-related conferences the pastors had ever attended in their areas. It was a thrill to help multiple hundreds of pastors and church leaders. It was a great blessing to see them look beyond their own area and people groups to share the Gospel, not only with the lost in their own state, but also around the world.

A pastor came to us and shared that his church was now sending and supporting eleven missionaries in Nepal. The Lord burdened others for distant parts of India, as well as Pakistan, Bangladesh, and other countries. The Secretary of the World Evangelical Fellowship of India told us, "Because you and Joy came to teach the Winning Strategies Seminar in India, more and more churches have started to send missionaries to unreached people groups in our own country." It certainly is worth it to serve the Lord!

The year 2001 marked another milestone for my dear husband, Bill's 50th anniversary serving the Lord. On September 29, 2001, we celebrated with a "Focus on the World" dinner in his honor. Scores of friends from seven states joined us for a wonderful meal and program. Our grandchildren put on a comical skit for their "Pappy." There was also a visual presentation of Bill's life over his fifty years of ministry. Several pastors shared how God used the World Thrust ministry here in America to impact their churches. It was a wonderful evening, and our hearts were stirred as we all sang the hymn "Great Is Thy Faithfulness."

We have personally witnessed and experienced that God's faithfulness is indeed new every morning. In the next few years, the World Thrust International ministry reached out to many more countries, especially in Africa. Bill was extremely grateful that our friend Dr. Nicholas Osameyan and his dear wife, Moji, from Nigeria agreed to become the Africa director after they moved their family to South Africa. Nicholas is a wonderful coworker and helped ease the teaching load when I could not go. The work in South Africa kept on expanding. It is still going strong under the leadership of Reverend Richard Verreynne. Thousands of churches have been impacted by our seminars.

Whereas there were only about 280 missionaries going out from South Africa in the late 1980s, there were about 7,000 in 2008. Our materials have been translated into more than twelve languages, and we have taught our seminar in over thirty countries.

The late Reverend Willie Cuke of Barbados started the ministry of WTI in his home country and the Caribbean islands. Paul Hynam continues as an associate, having been a great help in shouldering the teaching load in the Caribbean islands. Paul joined us on assignments to India, Guyana, Trinidad, the Philippines, and Italy. The yearly seminars in India continued and were well received. There is much for which to praise the Lord!

A few lines from our "Boerop Bulletin," which was sent to our prayer partners, share this moving experience:

> One of the organizers of the seminar in Lonavala, India, gave a speech at the end of the conference. He shared that he had prayed for two years for a seminar that would show "How to put our arms around the world and how to become sending churches." Then he broke down, and with tears streaming down his face, he shared his disappointment. Fifty pastors promised him they would attend the Winning Strategies Seminar, but only thirty-six came. He ended with the big question: "Why only thirty-six, where are the other fourteen who had promised to be here?" To hear this from an Indian brother and to see his tears was very touching. He then turned to us and thanked us for coming…"This seminar was exactly what the pastors in my region needed!"

We continued:

> The schedule was hectic. While in India we co-taught eighteen sessions in ten days and Bill was privileged to preach on two Sundays. What a blessing to serve the Lord in this huge sub-continent where millions have never yet had the chance to hear the gospel.

The fall of 2004 brought an invitation to conduct a seminar in the Ukraine. We marveled that churches in the former Soviet Union could and would start sending out missionaries. Leadership in this once Communist-dominated country wanted to know how local churches could get involved in the evangelization of the world. This trip was very special to Bill.

Before 2004 ended, we ministered in Korea and went back to China. The Chinese Christians of Jiangxi invited us to the dedication of a church and a Bible school in the province where my parents started their missionary career. My parents had once wondered if their ministry was in vain as they lived through the Communist takeover and later learned about churches being closed; Bibles being burned; and religious people, including Christians, being imprisoned. Yet, God overruled! We were allowed the privilege of celebrating the dedication of a church with 3,000 to 4,000 in attendance and an overflow crowd in the yard. The Bible school in the capital of Nanchang is also going strong, and services are being held regularly in the chapel, with a huge crowd coming to hear the good news about the Lord Jesus Christ. How Bill and I wished my parents could have been there!

The summer of 2005 brought a life-changing experience for me. A Chinese pastor from Singapore had attended one of our Winning Strategies Seminars in Toronto with one of his deacons in the late 80s. Since that time, this pastor had implemented what they had learned. As a result, the Lord blessed the church, not only with local growth, but also with being able to put their arms around the world. They now had thirty-five missionaries whom they supported, and one of them was our Africa Director of World Thrust International.

We ministered in this church many times over the years. Bill and I were invited to attend their missions conference in June. Sunday, June 19, 2005, we enjoyed the last day of the conference, had lunch with one of our friends from the church, and then took a flight to Yogyakarta, Indonesia. The President of the Indonesia Theological Seminary, where we had ministered many years before, had invited us to conduct our seminar once again, as well as to attend a special year-end conference. I was to speak at special ladies' meetings as well as co-teach with Bill. However, that was not to be.

When we arrived the evening of June 19, it was dark and rainy. The lighting was scarce and dim, but I could see a huge crowd of people gathered to welcome friends and family as they exited the airport. In the Orient, there are always huge crowds at the airport when a plane arrives, especially if there are not frequent flights into some of the lesser airports. So it was here. The people pushed and shoved, crowding around a narrow ramp leading to the parking lot. I stepped off the side of that ramp, which I could not see, and fell on my left side. I fell hard! Sharp pain immediately shot through my left hip. As kind people around me helped pull me up out of the puddles and dirt while holding umbrellas over me, I turned to Bill and said, "I am sure I broke something."

It took a long time before someone came with a wheelchair. The pain was excruciating, especially when someone tried to put me in a car. I simply could not get in. Someone brought a van, but the pain was too great. I could not get in the van either. After two hours, the airport finally sent an ambulance to take me to the hospital. While Bill took care of things at the admissions office, the kind wife of the seminary president sat with me to comfort me until a doctor arrived.

In our many travels overseas, we had never taken out insurance for possible accidents. Two days before this trip, however, our heavenly Father had impressed upon Bill and me, separately at first, but then together, that we should pay for travel insurance. What a kind and merciful God is He! We could not have imagined what this experience would entail physically, emotionally, and financially.

The doctor immediately ordered x-rays. As I twisted and turned for the different views, I could not help but be amused to see the outdated equipment. I was sure it had been left by the Japanese in 1945 when they surrendered at the end of World War II and no longer occupied Indonesia. I am so grateful that the Lord let me see the funny side of things even though I was in excruciating pain. It helps to have a good sense of humor, especially when serving the Lord in strange and foreign lands. The x-rays revealed that my left hip was broken.

It was a comfort to me that my hospital room was large enough for a second bed in a special niche. My dear husband was able to occupy that large bed during the night. In some Asian countries, families move in with the patient and help with the care. They also cook in the patient's room, which can be a somewhat smelly affair at times. That was not so in my case.

The next morning a doctor showed up who gave me morphine for the unbelievable pain. I don't know if he gave me too much or if I was allergic to the morphine, but I started to throw up every twenty to thirty minutes. I became terribly weak. Finally, after two days, which seemed like an eternity, another doctor gave me an injection of some kind that helped.

Of course, there was also a language barrier. The doctors spoke broken English, but the nurses knew none. Our friend from the Theological Seminary arranged for some ladies from the school to come every day and sit by my bed to translate for me. This became comical at times, since these ladies did not know much about medical terminology, especially in English. To be honest, neither did I, especially when words were pronounced differently than in America.

Security was another issue. Indonesia is the largest Muslim country in the world. Many Christians are of Chinese descent and have suffered under the wrath of fanatic Muslims. Their businesses, churches, and homes were torched, and many lost their lives. So, every night the director of the seminary kindly posted guards outside of my hospital room. This showed the danger in which the Lord's workers often find themselves. Whenever Bill or friends from the seminary came to visit, security at the main gate asked for their identification and used mirrors to check for explosives under the car.

I was sorry that the planned seminar and ladies' meetings had to be canceled and postponed for another year because of my accident. It was a great blessing to me when the leadership of the women's ministry came and brought me a large, beautiful card signed by all the ladies who came to the conference. They assured me of their prayers and sent some Scripture verses with their love. I was immensely thankful for the care and concern of the local believers. I do not know what I would have done without the female students who gave time from their personal lives to sit by my bed and interpret for me. The young men who faithfully watched over me as they stood guard outside of my room were truly God-sent. It proved to me once again that there are no boundaries to the ties that bind true believers in the Lord Jesus Christ.

We finally received word from the insurance company that we could leave. Late Thursday morning, June 23, 2005, a wonderful Muslim nurse and a Chinese doctor cared for me in the medical plane that was to take us to Singapore. It was a little scary to be lifted on a stretcher into the small plane at a seventy-five-degree angle. I prayed that these small Indonesians would not drop me.

When we began to land after a short flight, we knew that something was wrong. Bill looked out the window and realized that we were not in Singapore but in Jakarta, the capital of Indonesia. We had to land because the small plane was having engine problems. The seats next to my stretcher were taken out by some mechanics who worked but appeared extremely frustrated. Finally, I was taken off the plane at the dreaded angle again and lifted into an ambulance that was sitting on the tarmac. After some time we learned the engine problem could not be fixed. Another solution had to be found.

Soon the Canadian owner of the Medical Transport Company in Jakarta came by with a huge bouquet of roses for me. I chuckled inside. My Chinese doctor and I were in an ambulance with no air-conditioning, sweating profusely in the terrible, 100-plus-degree heat, but I was treated to a bouquet of flowers! The roses did not like the heat either, since we were confined in the sweltering ambulance for an hour and a half.

Fortunately, the vice president of Indonesia had just landed, and his plane was close by and available for rent. My heavenly Father again took over. It took quite some doing to adjust the vice president's plane so it could accommodate my stretcher, but once again, I was finally lifted into the plane. Since the aisle was too narrow for the stretcher, several men had to climb over seats to pass me to get to the back of the plane. This procedure was not the most comfortable for me with a broken hip, but we made it and were finally on our way. We reached Singapore eight hours after we left Yogyakarta. Normally this flight only takes three hours.

Bill was absolutely shocked, and yet amused, at how the Singaporeans got me off the plane. My stretcher and I were lifted up and placed on the bent-over back of a man who carried me out between the rows of seats. Since I couldn't see what was going on, I had no idea what was happening. All I remember is that I wondered why my stretcher tilted from side to side.

The Medical Transport Company in Indonesia had notified the hospital in Singapore that we were coming. Because the flight took so much longer than originally planned, however, we were told at Mount Elizabeth Hospital, "We have no bed for her in the orthopedic ward. By now they are all taken." My heart sank. After the experiences of the past eight hours, I was totally exhausted and did not have much of a Christian attitude left. However, my heavenly Father came through for me. After about fifteen minutes and some anxious moments, Bill told me, "They are making room for you in the Ward for Overnight Patients."

Although it was 11 P.M., the Singaporean orthopedic surgeon came to see me. He said, "Mrs. Boerop, don't worry about a thing. Put all your burdens on my shoulders. I will take care of you." When he learned that my hip had not been put in traction at the Indonesian hospital, he was quite surprised. He acted immediately and put the traction device on my leg himself. It brought much relief!

The next day, after a battery of tests, checkups, and x-rays with some of the most modern equipment I have ever seen, I was ready for surgery. The doctor did not want to postpone the surgery even one day and operated on Friday evening, June 24, 2005. I was blessed by the efficient and tender care of the technicians in the various labs. Several of them were believers in the Lord Jesus Christ, as was my surgeon. We had some wonderful talks about the love of God and His concern and desire for us, His creatures, to become His children through faith in His beloved Son, the Lord Jesus. The surgery went well, and a day later, I was introduced to physical therapy.

It was a blessing to learn that about forty to forty-five percent of the medical professionals in Singapore are believers in Christ. When China was taken over by the Communists in 1949 and the missionaries had to leave, Overseas Missionary Fellowship concentrated on witnessing and winning the educated Chinese in Singapore to Christ. They worked with a lot of the medical students, telling them of God's love and His concern for them. As a result, many of them became strong believers. It was also comforting to know that my doctor had worked at the Mayo Clinic for two years.

Being in the Overnight Patient Ward, I had nine different roommates in eleven days. The nurses and care personnel came from many different countries. Some of them were Chinese, and I was amazed that some of my knowledge of Mandarin came back. At times, I had folks from six or seven countries around my bed trying to learn what a hip replacement was all about. Many of the nurses did not know what to do with a patient like me, but the doctor was kind enough to let them know how to treat me. He gave me the best care possible and came to see me every day. I will never forget when he told me that I needed to be spoiled a little. He personally made an appointment for me to get my nails done right there in my hospital room!

Many friends from our Singaporean church came to visit. The hospital personnel were amazed that I, a stranger, had so many local visitors. Bill was the only Caucasian who entered my room. I made progress slowly with a walker. My therapist was a cheerful and encouraging lady who was delighted that I had been to her country of India many times.

It was a joyous day when on Sunday, July 3, a tall, young American paramedic walked into my room. I knew I was going home! He was a firefighter/paramedic from Pennsylvania who flew all over the world and escorted patients back to the United States. He was certainly a godsend.

With great excitement, we left Singapore on the evening of Independence Day, July 4, 2005. The doctor and nurses got me ready for the trip, and some even hugged me goodbye, which is not a very Chinese thing to do. One of my fondest nurses, a Muslim lady, came to thank me for having been her patient. She then flung her arms around me, and we hugged warmly. She was leaving at the end of her shift, and I almost did not recognize her with her Muslim cover-up. Only her sweet face showed, although it was extremely hot. To thank the personnel for their care, Bill and I ordered a giant bouquet of flowers that was placed at the nurses' station.

In many ways, Singaporeans, who are mostly Chinese, are more advanced than we Americans are. When I left my hospital room, the ambulance service came with a wheelchair with a very high back. Just before placing me in the ambulance for the ride to the airport, one man electronically lowered the back of my wheelchair so that it became a stretcher. I was gently placed into the ambulance. Having experienced more trips on stretchers since then, I have never seen another one like it nor heard of anyone who has.

The flight home was a long, thirty-hour trip, which included a layover of six hours in Korea. We were glad to have a medical escort with us. He was fantastic and took care of the many details regarding passport and customs control, arrangements for wheelchairs, and dealing with airline personnel. He also administered shots and medication during that long flight back to Atlanta. It was a blessing to fly first-class since I was considered handicapped. Again, we marveled at the goodness of God that prompted us to take out travel insurance before leaving for this trip.

When we arrived in Atlanta, an ambulance was ready to take me to the rehab hospital in our area. After ten days at the rehab center, many months of therapy followed, until I was able to walk normally again. Looking back over those weeks in June and July of 2005, I always joke that not many can say that they experienced being a patient in three different hospitals in three countries in three weeks! That would be difficult to top!

I thank the Lord Jesus for having been by my side to see me through every step of the way. It was tough, and there was unspeakable pain, discomfort, and fear. There were times of great frustration and disappointment, but there was also laughter, sunshine, and even songs. My heavenly Father answered many prayers and sent me some wonderful people along the way to lift my spirits, cheer me on, support me, and pray for me. Without the prayers of family and friends, even strangers, I would not have made it. I will never forget my anesthesiologist coming to remove my epidural on Sunday morning. As he walked out the door, he said, "Mrs. Boerop, I am going to church now. I am going to ask my church family to pray for a speedy recovery for you." I continue to give God the glory as I go on serving Him.

In 2006, we had wonderful opportunities to minister in many different parts of the world. We were blessed to be invited by a pastor friend of ours from California to go with him and his church group to Israel. It had been a lifelong dream of mine to visit the Holy Land, and what a blessing it was! Bill was able to help with devotions. We were thrilled to walk where Jesus walked and to see so many of the places we have studied and read about in Scripture. The Bible really came alive. A trip to Greece and some of the islands ended this once-in-a-lifetime experience.

In June and July, we were back in Singapore and Indonesia. This time we were able to teach our seminar at the Theological Seminary, and I was able to have a wonderful session with the ladies. Many of the pastors and students came to thank me for having dared to come back after my fall at the airport the previous year.

After a short time home, we left for ministry in the Czech Republic, Germany, England, and Scotland. In the fall we taught the Winning Strategies Seminar in the southern part of India, in Hyderabad and Bangalore, and then in Chochin in the province Karala. This was our seventh year of teaching pastors and church leaders in India. I came home, and Bill went on to minister in Italy, Belgium, and Holland. We concluded the year by attending missions conferences and ministering in New Jersey, Maryland, and Connecticut. The Lord gave me the strength to handle a heavy travel schedule only one year after my hip replacement.

When I was young, I had fallen in a grocery store and hurt my right knee. An arthroscopic procedure helped clean out the knee, but the doctor told me then that I would develop arthritis in that knee as I got older. He was right. Although for twenty-four years I had faithfully walked five miles around Stone Mountain three or four times a week, my knee started to bother me. I finally had to have a knee replacement on February 26, 2007. I lost an enormous amount of blood and had to have four units of blood transfusions. Over the last twenty-five years, I have suffered tremendously with three kinds of edema. To overcome two major surgeries in two years took a great toll on my system, but with therapy, I kept moving.

I was able to co-teach with Bill at a seminar we held in Ontario, Canada, but 2007 was mostly a year filled with doctors' visits and therapy. We also had the joy of entertaining a number of local friends, as well as some from Canada, Europe, and Barbados. Some were school friends in Shanghai and the children's home.

In 2008, we again ministered in Barbados. It was good to see how the seminar attendees seriously worked to reach not only their own island but also other parts of the Caribbean. Bill continues to help our Caribbean Coordinator and friends to train teachers and further develop the ministry of World Thrust International.

Bill and I celebrated our golden wedding anniversary on June 21, 2008. It is amazing to look back over 50 years and see how quickly years seem to go by. There have been hard times, difficult circumstances, and sad times. Some days looked dark, and it seemed as if God had forsaken us. There were long hours of hard work, many frustrations, and even misunderstandings. Sometimes we felt alone as we weathered many disappointments. We often experienced a shortage of funds, first as a young missionary couple, then as students, and then as parents of two little girls.

There have been innumerable illnesses, migraines, cancer, a broken hip, and extreme edema. At times, I wondered if it was more than I could bear. I had once told the Lord that I would never become a missionary. I knew too much about the sacrifices and hardships in God's work. Then I volunteered. Whenever I complained to the Lord Jesus about how difficult the task was and that I could not take it any longer, He just kindly reminded me, "Remember, Joy, I never called you. You volunteered!"

With all the hardships, there were also unspeakable joys and wonderful days full of sunshine and light. To experience the smiles of a newborn baby and a glorious sunset and to meet precious people in a foreign land are wonderful privileges. To revel in God's beauty and creation in many parts of the world is indescribable. The blessings of our heavenly Father's surprises have uplifted us many times spiritually, physically, and emotionally. Bill and I can truly say that the Lord led us all the way.

The year 2009 was not different from other years, with ministry overseas as well as here at home. We taught pastors in seminars and trained students in theological institutions. We prepared lectures; translated materials for ministry in Europe; and entertained, discipled, and helped family. It is our great joy and fulfillment to be a part of God's eternal plan and purposes to declare His glory among the nations. In August of 2009, we celebrated twenty-five years of helping churches worldwide fulfill the Great Commission through World Thrust International.

One of our greatest blessings is our family. Our merciful heavenly Father gave us two beautiful daughters to teach and train as unto Him. They, in turn, married two handsome men, whom we prayed for and watched grow into spiritual leaders of their families. They all are burdened for the lost. Over the years, both couples have been involved with various hands-on ministries: doing construction; repairing, painting and cleaning homes for Christian workers; feeding and clothing the poor in several countries of the world, as well as here at home. Although they have busy lives with their families and their vocations, they are actively involved in their churches and various ministries.

I thank the Lord again and again that He gave Gloria and Doug four healthy daughters and Arlita and Butch two wonderful boys. We had the honor of praying for their parents. Now we have the privilege of praying for our grandchildren, Kristin, Lindsay, Kara, Shayna, Chad, and Drew. We have enjoyed watching them grow; have helped in any way we could; and have celebrated birthdays, special occasions, and graduations from high school and some from college. Several of them have been involved with ministry overseas. As they completely commit their lives to the Lord and continue to follow Him, they, in turn, will be used and blessed by our heavenly Father as their great-grandparents, grandparents, and parents have been. We could not ask for a greater legacy and heritage!

LaVergne, TN USA
02 May 2010
181180LV00003B/1/P